THE GREAT EXCEPTION

A WPA Employee Receives His Paycheck, 1939.
Courtesy National Archives.

THE GREAT EXCEPTION

THE NEW DEAL & THE LIMITS OF AMERICAN POLITICS

JEFFERSON COWIE

PRINCETON UNIVERSITY PRESS
Princeton and Oxford

Requests for permission to reproduce material from this work should be
sent to Permissions, Princeton University Press
Published by Princeton University Press,
41 William Street, Princeton, New Jersey 08540
In the United Kingdom: Princeton University Press,
6 Oxford Street, Woodstock, Oxfordshire OX20 1TR

press.princeton.edu

Second printing, and first paperback printing, 2017
Paperback ISBN: 978-0-691-17573-7

The Library of Congress has cataloged the cloth edition as follows

Cowie, Jefferson.
The great exception : the New Deal and the limits of American politics /
Jefferson Cowie.
pages cm — Politics and society in twentieth-century America
Includes bibliographical references and index.
ISBN 978-0-691-14380-4 (hardcover : alk. paper) 1. United
States—Politics and government—1933–1945.   2. New
Deal, 1933–1939.   3. United States—Politics and
government—1945–1989.   4. Liberalism—United States—
History—20th century.   5. Social conflict—United States—History—
20th century.   6. Political culture—United States—History—
20th century.   7. United States—Social conditions—20th century.
E806.C68 2016
973.917—dc23
2015024474

British Library Cataloging-in-Publication Data is available

This book has been composed in DIN 1451 Std & Sabon LT Std

Printed on acid-free paper. ∞

Printed in the United States of America

3 5 7 9 10 8 6 4 2

FOR NICK,

who taught me history,
voice, and friendship

CONTENTS

PROLOGUE
Philadelphia, 1936
1

INTRODUCTION
Rethinking the New Deal in
American History
9

CHAPTER ONE
The Question of Democracy in
the Age of Incorporation
35

CHAPTER TWO
Kaleidoscope of Reform
63

CHAPTER THREE
Working-Class Interregnum
91

CHAPTER FOUR
Constraints and Fractures in the New Liberalism
123

CHAPTER FIVE
The Great Exception in Action
153

CHAPTER SIX
Toward a New Gilded Age
179

CHAPTER SEVEN
The Era of Big Government Is Not Over
(But the New Deal Probably Is)
209

ACKNOWLEDGMENTS
231

NOTES
235

INDEX
263

THE GREAT EXCEPTION

"—To cast out them that sold and bought—"
—St. Mark 11:15

To Cast Out Them That Sold and Bought, 1934. "The money changers have fled from their high seats in the temple of our civilization," Roosevelt declared when he took office in 1933. "We may now restore that temple to the ancient truths."
Gregory Duncan for *Life* magazine.

PHILADELPHIA, 1936

As Franklin Delano Roosevelt made his way to the speaker's platform, he had to swing his steel-bound legs forward by thrusting one hip forward and then the other, forcing each, one at a time, between a cane on one side and the supporting arm of an advisor on the other. Even the shortest, most mundane walk involved pain. Simply standing caused grinding aches and exhaustion. On this day, as FDR advanced toward his specially modified podium, he stopped to shake hands, when suddenly the hinge that locked his steel braces at the knee sprang loose. His leg buckled. With his withered limbs unsupported on one side, the president collapsed helplessly to the ground.

An estimated crowd of 100,000 people packed the stadium before him, clamoring with anticipation for his appearance. Unaware of his fall, the boisterous crowd cheered, cajoled, gossiped, and debated with their neighbors while waiting for the most popular president in memory to accept the Democratic nomination for a second term as president.

The president's aides dove down to pick him up and dust him off. "Clean me up," Roosevelt quickly ordered as they relocked the support and propped his body upright. FDR's open secret was never in such evidence—a rare moment of public humiliation for a man who went to great lengths to keep his disability private. The mixture of power and vulnerability suggested much about the moment.

Composure regained, he headed into the lights, the crowd cheering his arrival. He gripped the podium for balance and proceeded to deliver one of the most extraordinary speeches in the history of presidential rhetoric. The crowd at Philadelphia's enormous Franklin Field stadium punctuated FDR's orations with thunderous approval as he accepted not just his party's nomination but also command of a war. It was not the foreign conflict to come that he sought to lead, but a battle cry to recover the lost territory of democracy from the monarchical powers of industry.

From the rostrum, FDR connected his location in historic Philadelphia with his urgent political message. The enemy was not the aristocracy of old but a new breed of "economic royalists" who threatened the nation's political traditions. The government was no longer the people's, but had succumbed to the "privileged princes of these new economic dynasties, thirsty for power" who sought "control over Government itself." The "political equality we once had won," he boomed, had been rendered "meaningless in the face of economic inequality." He shamed those who argued that the New Deal would "overthrow the institutions of America." Quite the opposite, he emphasized: the very *preservation* of "American institutions requires the overthrow of this kind of power."

In rhetoric that might have been delivered by a turn of the century socialist, an agrarian populist, or a radical union organizer, FDR defamed the new monarchs who had "carved out new dynasties" and a "new despotism" and established an "economic tyranny" that was "cloaked in legal sanction." The new industrial order now dwarfed the once celebrated democratic power of the people. "The hours men and women worked, the wages they received, the conditions of their labor," he lamented, "had passed beyond the control of the people, and were imposed by this new industrial dictatorship."

The most profound dimensions of that speech struggled to reformulate the American preoccupation with liberty and individualism. Looking to a new understanding of that powerful creed, FDR sought, in both his platform and his speech, to create a new definition of individualism that rested upon economic security. "Liberty requires opportunity to make a living—a living decent according to the standard of the time, a living which gives man not only enough to live by, but something to live for." Under this new vision, this New Deal, the government could play a role that would overthrow, once and for all, the antiquated notion that the state existed simply to protect the citizenry from incursions on their individual freedoms. Instead, government would help provide the types of economic foundations that empowered the people to enjoy those freedoms. Quoting an eighteenth-century English judge, he declared, "Necessitous men are not free men."

Moving toward his formal acceptance of the nomination, he most famously declared, "This generation of Americans has a rendezvous with destiny." Battle lines drawn, he lifted his arm forward and upward, palm open, leaving himself precariously balanced with only one hand to prevent another fall. Seeming to defy, even taunt, the collapse that had nearly humiliated him minutes earlier, FDR boldly committed himself to "a war against want and destitution and economic demoralization" and for nothing short of the "survival of democracy." "I accept the commission you have tendered me," he exclaimed with his soaring, stiff-jawed, accent. "I join with you. I am enlisted for the duration of the war."

That moment in Philadelphia was as close as any president has ever come to calling directly for the overthrow of
economic interests—let alone declaring what sounded to
many like a declaration of class war. No president, before
or since, had spoken like this—including FDR himself. The
stark language of class disparity, the expansion of the idea
of democracy into corporate affairs, the idea that a new
aristocracy had hijacked the American project, and the reconsideration of the nature of individual rights all made for
a stunningly daring speech. Many at the time, and since,
regarded it as the ultimate triumph of decades of reform
struggles in the United States. Yet the Philadelphia acceptance speech was something different: the product of a very
specific moment—and a precarious one at that. In fact, it
was not long after the election that FDR's enemies put him
on the political defensive, his soaring rhetoric quickly
trimmed by the sharp realities of American politics.

In 1936, Roosevelt was in the middle of an extraordinary,
short, dense "big bang" of rhetoric and legislation, one that
marked a dramatic departure from both the past and the
future of American politics. That period shaped politics for
decades to come—but it fell far short of the permanent ref-
ormation of capitalism many believed it to be. Given his
New Deal commitments, Roosevelt knew his attack on the
business community cost him little. As he would state months
later in a speech on the eve of the election, the economic interests "are unanimous in their hate for me—and I welcome
their hatred." His own party, however, was a very different
matter. By the next year, 1937, his vulnerability quickly became exposed, and he quickly retreated from his offensive.

While his New Deal and new rhetoric were wildly popular with the voters, many Democratic regulars were not
ready to abandon the party's traditions so quickly or so dramatically. Once loyal advisors like Ray Moley, an original
member of the president's "Brain Trust," broke with FDR's

new brand of class warfare. He was disturbed by FDR's abandonment of his previous efforts to cooperate with business. Preferring that the president focus on matters of policy and government organization, Moley believed that the president had selected to indulge in wild rhetoric over an engagement with the specifics of governing. The speech marked the end of an important friendship—a rift that never healed as Moley drifted rightward for the rest of his life.

FDR's tenuous ally and fellow New Yorker Al Smith, the Catholic Democratic presidential candidate in 1928, also felt the traditions of the party were being destroyed. He believed FDR was crushing the type of individualism and business cooperation that had been at the center of the party for generations. In an era of rising dictatorships globally, he was not alone in his concerns. Smith went so far as to compare, acidly, the New Dealers with Marx and Lenin. Not long afterward, Smith, who staked his life on the Democratic Party, told those gathered at a banquet of the anti–New Deal group known as the Liberty League that he would simply have to "take a walk" during the 1936 election. The progressive politician whom FDR had called the "happy warrior" when he nominated him at the 1928 convention now chose to desert his party at the apex of its power.

A member of the 1936 audience only had to glance over at FDR's side during his speech to be reminded just how radical a departure this was for the Democratic Party. There sat the vice president, John "Cactus Jack" Garner, who served as a constant reminder of the conservative constraints on the Democratic Party—as well as an assurance that with a segregationist on the ticket Roosevelt would not mess with the Southern racial order. A former Texas congressman and speaker of the House, Garner loathed most of the moves FDR made. Like many who grew to oppose Roosevelt, he detested everything from his deficit spending to his legislation allowing for the organization of labor unions.

FDR's attempt to rid his party of its Southern conservative base would come soon enough, but the resulting failure would merely prove the entrenched power of the Solid South to the Democratic Party. Garner's growing hostility to the New Deal became such that he ran against Roosevelt for the Democratic nomination four years later.

Perhaps someone in that enormous crowd who liked to toy with counterfactual speculation might have nudged the person next to them, pointing out that had that bullet hit the president-elect in the 1933 assassination attempt in Miami in which the mayor of Chicago was killed, history might have been shockingly, horrifically, different. In place of the ever-sunny FDR would have been the crusty, powerful, old anti-statist wing of the Democratic Party, which already controlled most of Congress and its many procedural mechanisms. Had Garner ended up taking the oath in 1933, perhaps there would have been nothing like the New Deal at all.

Some in the audience had surely heard that five days earlier the senator from South Carolina, "Cotton Ed" Smith, had stormed out of the convention. Having seen that his party, the party of the white South, had invited a black minister to deliver the invocation, he bolted. "By God, he's as black as melted midnight!" Smith exclaimed. "Get outa my way. This mongrel meeting ain't no place for a white man!" As Cotton Ed recalled, the black minister "started praying," and "I started walking." In a well-rehearsed version of the story he perfected for the South Carolina campaign trail, he recounted, "it seemed to me that old John Calhoun leaned down from his mansion in the sky and whispered in my ear—'You did right, Ed.' " Like Garner, Ed Smith began as a New Deal supporter but quickly became more concerned about Northernization of the South, anything that remotely smacked of challenging the racial status quo, and skepticism about rising federal authority. Racism fused with economic conservatism, creating a problem for the Democratic Party that would never go away.

FDR risked alienating some of his own intellectuals, the Solid South, and even Northeastern urban progressives like Smith, but the voters loved the speech, the New Deal, and the president. His political read of the moment had been close to perfect, and he won reelection by taking every state but two in that November, consolidating a political coalition—albeit a fragile one—that would last for generations.

Few, if any, in the thunderous crowd that evening might have been able to see that a series of extraordinary political currents, mostly unrelated to Roosevelt, had changed direction in the country, helping to propel that moment in Philadelphia forward. It would certainly require FDR's cheery disposition, one that masked both an iron will and an almost ruthless sense of the possible, to unite the nation. For FDR to have any traction at all, however, the voters had to put aside their deep-seated individualism and their many antipathies and hatreds that historically had divided them in so many ways. Out of the historic fault lines of American political culture—individualism, anti-statism, cultural conflicts, and racial and ethnic divisions—emerged the sociological foundation for a rare period of political unity that contrasted with much of American history.

Trends culminating in the mid-1930s set the foundation for what appeared to be a permanent set of transformations in the political and economic system. The forces that helped create the New Deal would prove bold and determined but simultaneously as vulnerable as the president himself. That moment in Philadelphia in 1936 marked something less than a complete victory in the war FDR declared on the monarchs of industry, and something more like the beginning of a "great exception" in American political culture.[1]

American Standoff, 1912. American ideals face off against
American authority in the "Bread and Roses" strike in Lawrence,
Massachusetts—one of the many dramatic labor conflicts that, prior to
the New Deal, resulted in only short-term gains.
Photo courtesy of Lawrence History Center.

RETHINKING THE NEW DEAL IN AMERICAN HISTORY

My argument can be stated boldly and succinctly: the political era between the 1930s and the 1970s marks what might be called a "great exception"—a sustained deviation, an extended detour—from some of the main contours of American political practice, economic structure, and cultural outlook. During this period, the central government used its considerable resources in a systematic, if hardly consistent, fashion on behalf of the economic interest of nonelite Americans in ways that it had not done before or since. The depth of the Depression and the crisis of World War II forced clear realignments of American politics and class relations, but those changes were less the linear triumph of the welfare state than the product of very specific, and short-lived, historical circumstances. American liberalism has had many "protean" forms, but the version generated by the trauma of the Depression and World War II proved extraordinary because it was not about morality or individual rights or regulation alone, but about *collective economic rights*.[1]

The power of labor liberalism in this period proved distinct and commanding, but also truncated and brittle. The "fragile juggernaut," a phrase coined by the historian Robert Zieger to describe the industrial labor movement of the day, might be the best description of the combination of power and vulnerability inherent in the political alignments that burst upon the national stage during the 1930s and 1940s. The New Deal alliances seemed to come together in an all-powerful force capable of implementing progressive liberal policies with limited regard for conservative opposition. Yet when challenged, this same juggernaut crumbled, its internal contradictions pushed to the breaking point by the compromises it made with the very complexities of American history and politics.[2]

The great exception is strikingly clear in a series of graphs that chart its rise and fall. A variety of measures form an anomalous historical hump or trough that begins in the 1940s and returns back in the 1970s: economic equality improves and then tumbles, union density climbs and then falls, working people's income goes up before dwindling, and the percentage of wealth possessed by the most affluent dips before roaring back with a vengeance. There is even a unique and measurable pattern of bipartisanship—the "liberal consensus"—in the postwar era that appears neither before nor since. The minimum wage, created under the New Deal, follows the same pattern, rising to close to a living wage in the late 1960s before falling well behind the rate of inflation. Seen in statistical form, the New Deal order (roughly 1935 to 1978) appears sandwiched between eerily similar periods in terms of the relationship between the power of business and the role of the state. Paul Krugman called it an "interregnum between gilded ages."[3]

The New Deal gave the illusion of permanence—for many, the inevitable domestication of capitalism—yet marbled throughout its very creation were a series of social and political fissures that help to explain its ultimate fall four decades later. That list includes a number of themes to be

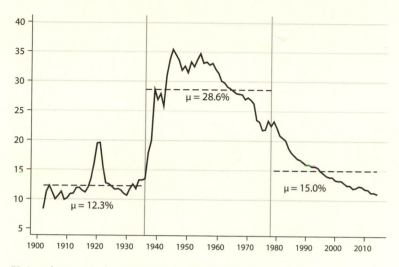

Union density in the United States (1902–2014).
Data: Leo Troy, "Introduction to Trade Union Membership, 1897–1962," *Trade Union Membership*, 1897–1962 (UMI, 1965; G. Mayer, 2004), n.p.; *Union Membership Trends in the United States* (Washington, DC: Congressional Research Service, 2004); Barry Hirsch and David Macphearson, "Union Membership, Coverage, Density, and Employment among Private Sector Workers, 1973–2013." Unionstats.com (accessed 5 June 2015).

developed throughout the rest of this book: the massive but temporary transformation of the role of the state; the historic fragility of organized labor even at the height of its power; the tensions between native-born and immigrant workers; the profound racial costs and complications of the New Deal; and the broader issues of culture and religious politics. Wrapping around all of these issues were the complex *ideologies* of a Jeffersonian individualism, which were muted but never resolved even as the New Dealers waded cautiously into collective waters.

Share of annual income earned by the top 1 percent (1913–2012).
Data: Emmanuel Saez, "Income Inequality in the United States." http://
eml.berkeley.edu/~saez/ - income (accessed 5 June 2015).

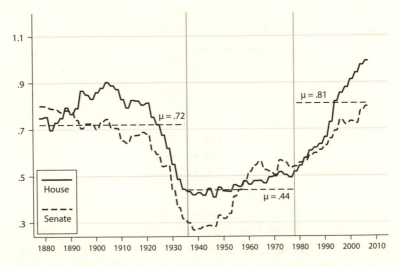

Political party polarization in the U.S. Congress (1878–2008).
Data: Keith Poole, "The Polarization of the Congressional Parties." Vote
view.com (accessed 5 June 2015).

Grappling with these core themes requires keeping two seemingly contradictory ideas continually in mind: the Depression caused a key rupture in American politics, and simultaneously, the rupture of the 1930s was never permanent but always connected to and permeated by earlier historical problems. These core issues, long central to understanding American history, underwent an incomplete suspension, a mitigation, during the period of the great exception. But they never fully went away.

Historians have long argued about how best to think about the bundle of legislative achievements and political alliances that we call "the New Deal." As early as 1968, the noted historian Richard Kirkendall found himself in a quagmire of confusing questions about the New Deal and its interpretive complexity. "Was the New Deal a radical innovation or a continuation of earlier themes in American life?" he asked. "Was it a revolution or part of a long-term evolutionary development? Was it a watershed in American history or a deepening and widening of a stream that had its sources in earlier periods? Should historical interpretations of the New Deal stress change or emphasize continuity?" Out of Kirkendall's snarl of questions, three broad interpretive approaches have emerged. By connecting the New Deal's founding to its decline, the circumstances of its birth to the causes of its death, this book advances an argument that challenges existing frameworks.[4]

From the perspective of liberal historians, perhaps the most dominant view in the field, the post–World War II decades constituted the new mainstream of the nation's politics: the final product of a long struggle for American reform. Postwar liberals might differ on whether FDR had led the "third American Revolution" or a "halfway revolution," but there was a sense that a version of the industrial democracy, called for since the nineteenth century, had finally arrived. The new "liberal consensus" recognized that state involvement in social and economic policy was now a proven benefit in redistributing wealth, propping up consumption, and bolstering the foundation for the future expansion of the liberal project. Its permanence at the time seemed obvious to many. As the literary critic Lionel Trilling famously and prematurely noted in 1950, "In the United States at this time liberalism is not only the dominant but even the sole intellectual tradition. For it is the plain fact that nowadays there are no conservative or reactionary ideas in general circulation."[5]

A sharply different view emerged from the turmoil and heightened political expectations of the New Left of the 1960s. For scholars influenced by the new social movements, New Deal liberalism was simply a form of "corporate liberalism" that sought not to transform society but merely to prop up capitalism in its time of need and, more importantly, to contain and control a deeper, more popular, and more radical threat to the system. Despite the changes the New Deal did bring, as the argument is developed by one of its leading proponents, Barton J. Bernstein, the New Deal "failed to solve the problem of depression, it failed to raise the impoverished, it failed to redistribute income, it failed to extend equality and generally countenanced racial discrimination and segregation." Rather than a transformative moment, Bernstein argues that New Deal policy "was profoundly conservative and continuous with the 1920s."[6]

From the resurgent political right has come a third interpretive stream, one quite critical of the New Deal. Those gathered around the person and the ideas of Fredrick von

Hayek, William F. Buckley's *National Review*, and a grass-roots conservative movement shared a core belief: Franklin Roosevelt and his New Deal policies undermined traditional American values of individualism and the free-market economy, a view that received its intellectual validation with the 1963 publication of Milton Friedman and Anna Schwartz's analysis of the New Deal and Great Depression, *A Monetary History of the United States*. This school of thought argues that government intervention—in regulating monetary policy, intervening in financial markets, meddling in industry, governing labor relations, and intruding in ever-broader swaths of daily life—actually deepened rather than solved the economic crisis. Pundit Amity Shlaes updated this view to widespread applause from conservative commentators by arguing that the "deepest problem" of the Depression Era was government intervention due to "the lack of faith in the marketplace."[7]

In contrast to all three of these approaches, I argue that the New Deal can more accurately be understood as a positive but unstable experiment. The New Deal was a triumph of redistributive policy, not the failure that the New Left would have it. It was hardly the unnecessary intervention that the conservative right claims, since it fostered what many still see as a model for our own time. Yet the New Deal was also far from being a revolution that permanently vanquished the savageries of the labor market, as old-school liberals would have it. The New Deal reforms played a transformative role in working people's lives, fostering what many call the "golden age" of American capitalism for the white, male industrial working class.

One might readily argue that this extraordinary period was simply a by-product of the unique structure of global capitalism at the time, but I find this perspective far too reductive. A crisis hit, the argument goes, reforms were implemented, and then the glory days of an American economy facing little international competition afforded high-paying jobs in geographically sticky industries that served as the foundation for a Fordist bonanza. Yet on close examination, this falls apart. First, most economic crises do not end in empowering workers—quite the opposite, as business more typically gains the upper hand in an economic downturn. Second, those much vaunted "good manufacturing jobs" used to be terrible manufacturing jobs prior to the 1930s. The labor uprisings of the Great Depression and World War II made bad jobs into good jobs. Third, even though the New Deal order was created in a period of "deglobalization," one merely has to think of the days of the McKinley protectionism of the 1890s, when tariffs on manufactured goods averaged 49.5 percent, to realize that insulation from foreign competition does not necessarily equate with employers being receptive to workers' demands.

In short, the economic structure may have been a *necessary* component of the postwar order, but it was in no way a *sufficient* one. The relationship of labor and capital is not one of simple exchange. As the old axiom goes, it is a relationship of political power. As Thomas Piketty has shown so clearly, capitalism naturally tends toward inequality—unless there are forces and mechanisms that encourage the distribution of wealth. Those forces are a political, not an economic, question. The presence of a set of countervailing powers to that of business was crucial to the postwar paradigm. And if the politics matters then political culture must be foundational to that story. This book is about the social foundations of that political culture.[8]

One final interpretive note: *The Great Exception* ought to be clearly distinguished from the "consensus" school of

American history. One of the most rightfully maligned sets of beliefs about the American past, best illustrated by Louis Hartz's *The Liberal Tradition in America* (1955), claims that a deeply ingrained commitment to individualism, limited government, and property rights prevented the development of class consciousness and political conflict in American history. While acknowledging the presence of those values in American culture, this book flips that interpretation by arguing that a strong Hamiltonian state actively intervened on behalf of capital, suppressing the demands of an often-contentious working class. The profound hostility of the state (through the laws, courts, and troops) to workers' collective voice, and, in marked contrast, the power of business to pursue its own collective interests through the power of incorporation, proved a remarkable mismatch. Solidarity often failed not because of workers' abstract devotion to some Lockean social contract but because of deep divisions in the polity by party, skill, ethnicity, race, gender, and immigrant status. American political culture is not one of consensus of values as much as a contest over them—and an often bloody one at that.

The main body of this book proceeds as a narrative reinterpretation, a broad historical sketch, of the place of the New Deal in American history. I would like to clarify each of the themes that will be embedded in that story as a sort of road map through the arc of this story from Reconstruction to Obama. I briefly develop all six touchpoints of the argument here:

First, consider the radically transformed role of the state. The dire need of the Depression years catalyzed many im-

portant social and political trends in such a way as to overcome the nation's historical ambivalence about using the
state as a champion for the interests of working people.
While many historians stress the continuity of the New Deal
reforms with earlier reform traditions—from the populists
of the nineteenth century through the progressives of the
early twentieth—most are unaware of just how drastic the
moment of departure was. Harry Hopkins, one of FDR's
closest advisors, suggested this when he described the unprecedented process of creating national relief as being "almost as if the Aztecs had been asked suddenly to build an
aeroplane." As partisan a champion of the New Deal as
Arthur Schlesinger, Jr., described its dawning as a "unique
episode" in the nation's history "which grew out of a unique
crisis"; historian Richard Hofstadter echoed this tone when
he noted that it marked a "drastic departure" from the anti-
statist, anti-monopoly traditions of American reform. The
contemporary political scientist Ira Katznelson argues that
the policies of the 1930s had previously been "outside the
scope of imagined possibilities" for Washington insiders.[9]

Nothing emerges out of nowhere, of course, and the New
Dealers built upon a number of historical trends: the Progressive Era labor struggles, Theodore Roosevelt's demand
for the regulation of big corporations, and, above all, the
massive federal mobilization during World War I. The new
corporate paternalism of the 1920s, known as "welfare
capitalism," raised expectations of what the employment
relationship could and should offer—just before it all collapsed following the economic crash of 1929. All that said,
and it is admittedly not a short list, the New Deal made as
clear a break with policy tradition as any in American history. Herbert Croly had already declared as early as 1920
"the eclipse of liberalism or progressivism as a force in

American politics," and much of that politics had been more moral than economic. There is no doubt that many aspects of the New Deal had been worked out prior to 1933, but, as one historian put it, "a significant emancipation from past inhibitions" remained the necessary ingredient to establish the new order. Earlier reform trends, it can be imagined, never would have found traction within American politics without the massive structural crisis of the Great Depression or the subsequent wartime emergency.[10]

Yet as much as Roosevelt famously "betrayed his class" by wagging his presidential finger at the "economic royalists" at mid-decade, he did so only briefly. The window for substantive collective economic policies opened late in FDR's first administration and closed less than three years later, making 1935–1938 the *anni mirabiles* in U.S. public policy. The subsequent 1938–1939 period made up the forgotten years of the Roosevelt administration: the years of defeat and retreat; then the return of hard times; then the possibility that the 1936–1937 industrial organizing and strike wave, which had opened up a generation of working-class affluence to come, would be just another noble failure like so many that pockmark the labor history of the United States.

Still, it took the state's role in the total mobilization for World War II to consolidate these achievements, especially then-vulnerable union strength, while simultaneously marking an end to the most vibrant era of experimentation and reform. As the war ended, macroeconomic planning for mass consumption and full employment began to overtake the chaotic inventiveness of the Progressives and the New Dealers. Though New Deal reforms continued to play a transformative role in working people's lives, the nation ended up with a much tamer postwar politics that Alan

Brinkley calls "more coherent, less diverse, and on the whole less challenging to the existing structure of corporate capitalism than some of the ideas it supplanted."[11]

The second major theme flips the scholarly preoccupation with immigration to suggest the importance of the relative *absence* of immigration. Political and social tensions around nativism span American history from before the birth of the republic to our own time. One prominent American leader, for example, complained about disorderly droves of the "most ignorant and stupid" immigrants who "beat their mothers" and were prone to "abusing and insulting their teachers." "Few of their children in the country learn English," he continued, and "unless the stream of their importation could be turned they will soon so outnumber us that all the advantages we have will not be able to preserve our language, and even our government will become precarious." Those were the 1753 lamentations of Benjamin Franklin, who was complaining about Germans coming to America. After more than a century and a half of open immigration (with important Asian exclusions), the 1924 suspension of immigration from anywhere other than Northern Europe and the Americas meant that tensions between native born and immigrant, long and deeply embedded in American politics, had been temporarily relieved.[12]

Historian Matthew Frye Jacobsen's description of the period between immigration reforms of 1924 and 1965 as "the ascent of monolithic whiteness" suggests the homogeneity, however problematic, of the period. As a result, when the 1929 crash hit, nativism was largely at bay and the workers living in this country were presumed to be here to stay. This in itself was enough to engender more of a sense of unity among working people than before. By effectively neutralizing one of the most common reasons why a sense of unity or shared economic destiny had fallen apart in the past, the mitigation of the nativist impulse helped shape an age of greater equality.[13]

When immigration resurfaced slowly in the generation after the 1965 immigration reforms, so did neo–Know Nothings and the militant nativism of an earlier age, returning "the" working class to historical patterns of internecine hostilities and political divisions reminiscent of the pre–New Deal Era. As throughout much of the twentieth century, few issues generate more visceral and divisive political reactions among native-born citizens than immigration—be it the immigrant cauldron of Five Points in New York in the 1830s or tensions along the militarized Arizona border today. To put it plainly, for most of American history, battle lines have been drawn around the social reality and policy issues of immigration—except during the period of the New Deal order.

The dip in centrality of the third theme, the divisiveness of religion, revivalism, and cultural values, also played a central role in making space for New Deal politics. As so many historians are aware, American religious identity "has not merely been epiphenomenal, simply an analytical category separable from the *real* class identity at the core of all social life, but has instead been a central, constitutive component of American culture from the seventeenth century to the present." Salience and centrality has also meant conflict. The term "culture wars" may be a contemporary one, but it defined the nineteenth and early twentieth centuries as well as post-1960s America. Populist "culture war" challenges to the rise of the New Deal were evident, but even the most devoted Christian believers and moralists embraced the new role of the state in the midst of the economic crisis. Religious moralism, a powerful, central, theme in American political history, declined so dramatically during the New Deal period as to make it, as James A. Morone put it in *Hellfire*

Nation, "the great American alternative" to the long-conflicted political history of Puritan morality. A vague Judeo-Christian faith, even at a time of very high church attendance and declared religiosity, was enough to define Cold War Americanism. The great exception maps onto what the historian of religion Garry Wills calls the "Great Religious Truce" of the postwar era.[14]

During the 1930s, religious frictions within the American community subsided, making way for broader understandings of the worldly needs of the broadest version of congregation. Although evangelicals, Catholics, and even Jews would chip away at that consensus in the postwar era, it would finally fall apart in the 1970s as cultural issues like abortion, busing, prayer in school, pornography, and birth control began to repoliticize religion's place in American life and undermine the coherence of the New Deal coalition. The death rattle of economic liberalism arrived hand-in-glove with the return of Protestant revivalism of the Moral Majority and other Christian groups as echoes of earlier crusades against secularism and evolution in the early twentieth century reverberated into the new millennium.

The fourth central problem is that of black-and-white race relations. Historically, U.S. politics rested on a consensus based on the systematic exclusion of African Americans (Jim Crow) or roiling divisions over inclusion (Reconstruction, Civil Rights Era). The central role of the Solid South in shaping politics meant that the New Deal did not mean some minor set of accommodations to segregation, but that race was central to the politics of the New Deal. The Democratic Party's political success required the support of the Solid South, which meant that the New Deal limited African Americans' right to participate in most of its programs by the explicit exclusion of domestic and agricultural labor as a sop to the very powerful Southern bloc. Several familiar issues account for the South's power: Southern political apportionment was inflated by African Americans who were counted as citizens but could not vote; the extraordinary longevity of Southern congressmen in a one-party system allowed the region to control the all-important congressional committee structure; and, finally, a militant commitment to racial hierarchy that ran deeper than their opponents' commitment to most anything else. The tragedy and the irony of the New Deal was how such an advance in economic democracy required compromise with "the most violent and illiberal part of the political system."[15]

Yet the story of race was not just about the exclusion of African American occupations from much of the New Deal, as the more interesting dimension is how the 1930s and 1940s marked a tenuous moment of transition in Democratic politics with regard to race. The power of the Roosevelt coalition depended not just on the white Solid South but also on African American voters who began to switch their historic allegiance from the party of Abraham Lincoln to that of FDR in the 1930s. And while the Congress of Industrial Organizations (CIO) devoted itself to a massive organizing drive in the North, boldly challenging workers to move forward together without regard to race, its project at times was hamstrung on the racism of the white rank and file—not to mention the continued segregation of much of the older American Federation of Labor (AFL). Once the civil rights questions moved more centrally into the Democratic Party, the once Solid South proved a tenuous ally to the New Deal coalition and often an obstacle to its further advancement. In short, the 1930s and 1940s marked a very rare moment of racial politics when Democrats could have it both ways—simultaneously embracing segregation and gaining the allegiance of African American voters. It was not a balance that could long endure.

The burden of America's racial history, in sum, forms one of the most fatal cracks built into the New Deal juggernaut. When pressure was applied to this fracture—as when the Democrats introduced a civil rights plank in 1948 or when African Americans rose up across the South and the urban North in the postwar era—the entire Democratic edifice cracked, as Southern whites bolted from the party and politics in the urban North cleaved along racial lines. The fragile unity crumbled, and many whites abandoned the politics of their class for those of their race. Left behind in the process was the hope of a shared economic identity. Simply put, the New Deal would not have happened without the white South, but, at the same time, the white South would not remain in the coalition when racial justice moved to the center of the party's agenda. Most problematically, the weakening of the South's support for the Democratic Party crippled the party's ability to sustain a viable political coalition after the 1960s.

This collection of historical circumstances—changes in the state, immigration, culture, and race—made possible the fifth theme: a limited but powerful sense of working-class unity. The white, male, industrial working class gained, for the first time, a sense of economic citizenship under the New Deal. As much as it was a great leap forward, it was also based on a blinkered sense of solidarity, grounded as it was in white, male, industrial privilege. Nonetheless, the working-class successes of the New Deal Era stand in bright contrast to the rest of American history. For most of the U.S. past, the courts and state, local, and federal governments have been largely anti-labor, often militantly so. From 1877 through 1934, in almost every instance from the Knights of Labor through the great Southern textile strikes of 1934, the government made it its job to keep employment rights an individual, not a collective, matter.

Yet the 1935 National Labor Relations Act (or Wagner Act) suddenly burst through the fog, despite FDR's own ambivalence about organized labor, and made it federal law to "encourage" the act of collective bargaining. The subsequent rise of industrial unionism created the most powerful change in American political and economic organizations since the industrial revolution itself. For three years between the passage of the Wagner Act and the conclusion of the CIO's heroic period of industrial organizing, labor won, and won big, bringing steel, auto, electrical, rubber, and numerous other core industries into the union fold. Yet, this "culture of unity" rested on some unstable alliances—not the least of which was federal policy that recognized labor rights primarily as a means of boosting consumption.[16]

"Labor did it!" Harry Truman famously exclaimed to the press about the secret behind his improbable 1948 victory. Indeed, the unions seemed capable of most anything in the late 1940s. Yet organized labor, one of the great redistributive agents in the postwar era, was less empowered than contained by the state; capital proved less committed to embracing workers' rights than engaging in a tactical and temporary recognition of them. While the new industrial unions formed the political backbone of the New Deal coalition and transformed the distribution of wealth in the country for decades to come, the real story is labor's legislative game of defense for most of the postwar era, relying almost exclusively on its one-time massive breakthrough during the Depression and war.

By the end of the twentieth century, the once vaunted
Wagner Act had become worse than null and void—it had
become, as David Brody put it, a "tool of management."
Attempts to revitalize labor law failed under every Democratic administration from Harry Truman in the 1940s to
Barack Obama in 2009. Union density, and thus the redistributive role unions played, slipped back to levels comparable to the bad old days before the New Deal. Radically
confiscatory marginal tax rates of the 1950s, once over 90
percent, dropped. After decades of restricted success, labor
drifted into the dark night of a declining and dysfunctional
industrial relations system, trapped in old and dying industries as capitalism moved on to new projects. The ferment
that did take place was often outside of the old New Deal
mechanisms—much of it unsuccessful.[17]

The sixth and final theme is the ideology, though hardly
the reality, of an American individualism that served as a
key foil to the entire New Deal story. For centuries, Americans embraced a reflexive, complicated, and ongoing commitment to various incarnations of Jeffersonian individualism even in the face of a bureaucratized, corporate world.
This preindustrial ideology has proven as archaic as it has
enduring. The collective dimensions of the New Deal, however limited they may have been to begin with, were never
able to take root in the uniquely challenging ideological
soils of the United States where "individualism for the
masses" remained one its most powerful contradictions.[18]

Even Roosevelt never offered a clear alternative to the
individualist ethos so deeply embedded in himself and
America's public culture. In fact, so persuasive were FDR's
evocations of that American ideology that Brain Truster
Rexford Tugwell thought that even when Roosevelt tried to
construct a new vision of individualism suitable for modern

society, those efforts "too had not been immune to our national myths." Bristling at the limits on policy and politics, Tugwell "learned that there would be no quick change from an individualist to a more collectivized society, that the New Deal would comprise measures that, from his standpoint, were essentially superficial." Still, the scale of the revival of "Jefferson and Jesus" in the postwar era would have astounded even those who struggled to make sense of the durability of the ideas of individualism even in the midst of the collective crisis of the 1930s.[19]

The success of the new social movements of the 1960s and 1970s expanded the individual rights tradition, gaining long-denied individual rights and opportunities for uplift to excluded peoples. Less about redistributing the economic pie, post-1960s liberalism ended up more about providing people with the skills to compete for a decent slice—even as the competition grew more desperate in the new millennium. While demands for "diversity" would eventually mesh easily with corporate-driven ideas about "meritocracy," leaders from Richard Nixon to George W. Bush would continue to call upon the same stark gods of nineteenth-century individualism as they avidly sought to steer and enlarge a mammoth governmental entity that, partnered with massive corporations, overtly betrayed the quaint picture of individual uplift they so often campaigned upon. In many ways, the 1960s celebration of the social individual made the 1980s celebration of the economic individual possible.

In the long arc of the twentieth century, the 1970s stand as a sort of "anti-1930s" bookend to the New Deal order. Labor declined, the ideology of individualism became central to all things, race divided politics, tensions over immigration returned, and the state flipped back to being hostile to workers' rights. Inequality of the type many believed long since vanquished returned with a vengeance. After 1978, economic gains became concentrated at the top in a sustained way, limited benefits and raises accrued to the nonrich, income flat-lined for working people, and the promise of upward mobility stagnated. Workers turned to two-income households, then borrowing on credit, to fill the void. The efforts of New Deal liberals descended into defensive battles, trying to shield and protect Social Security from attack, while the National Labor Relations Act withered further in relevance. Democrats have since surrendered issues of collective economic justice in order to focus on their commitment to progressive pushes for social issues and the expansion and democratization of individual rights. The dual movement of the 1970s—the rise of the new social movements and the decline of labor—meant that those left out of the original New Deal package, women and minorities, sought their citizenship outside of the realm of collective economic rights.

Many historians and political scientists point to a host of variables to understand the "fall" of the New Deal order in the late postwar period, including racial backlash, the attack on labor unions, stagflation, identity politics, the Southern strategy, deindustrialization, family values, and globalization, to name but a handful. Each of these forces has much explanatory power, depending on the framing of the question, but each ignores the extent to which understandings of the New Deal's decline may be evident already in the historical circumstances of the New Deal's creation. Liberal breakthroughs of the 1930s and 1940s remained so deeply conflicted in their original articulation—grounded as they inevitably were in the contours of the American past—that their public rupture decades later appears, on reflection, to be quite understandable, perhaps even axiomatic.[20]

Liberals of the 1970s and 1980s hoped, often presumed, there would be a return to what they regarded as the normality of the New Deal order, but the nation was drifting back to a contemporary version of Grover Cleveland's America, not FDR's. Framed in this light, conservative achievements seem all the more inevitable and postwar liberal economic victories seem all the more extraordinary. Given the intense brevity of the New Deal's "fragile juggernaut," it might therefore be more accurate to think of the ensuing "Reagan revolution" as the "Reagan restoration"— a return to a more sharply conservative, individualistic reading of constitutional rights and liberties; a return to economic policies in which the state looks after the corporation; and a return to a working class fragmented by race, religion, immigration, and culture. It is very important to note that this "restoration" was in no sense a return to small government as Reagan and others had so forcefully advertised. The issue never really was—and rarely ever is— whether that ever-expanding government was large or small, as political rhetoric might have us believe. The real issue is toward what ends and whose interest those massive institutions are to be driven.[21]

An understanding of the New Deal order as an exceptional period returns us to one of the thorniest and notoriously complex issues in U.S. historiography: the weakness of social democratic traditions in the United States, or what some more awkwardly called "American exceptionalism." Within the diverse spectrum of comparative national political cultures (all of which could be regarded as "exceptional" in different ways), the United States' distinction is the lack of a labor-based or social democratic party tradition, the absence of a complete national health care system, and the historical weakness of working-class mobilization or representation. As Daniel Rodgers has noted, the United States has no major modern party with the word "labor" or "socialist" in it. Many, but not all, commentators on this puzzle point to the challenges to collective mobilization fostered by this country's cultural, racial, and ethnic heterogeneity, by its deep tradition of individualism, and by the diffuse nature of U.S. working-class identity.[22]

The irony of American history (with apologies to Reinhold Niebuhr) may be that its most successful economic era for the nation's working people came concurrently with the suspension of some of the most defining aspects of U.S. history. The cultural homogeneity of the postwar era—while deeply flawed, problematic, and forced—made the United States just a bit closer to Northern European–style politics, providing, in Richard Hofstadter's terms, a "social-democratic tinge" where it existed neither before nor after. This is not to say that all of American politics can be defined by any one thing or set of things. But in the vigorous, sometimes violent, contest of ideas in American politics, the values of collective economic security tended to lose rather consistently to other forces. Except once. For just one period, Americans found sources of unity, however distasteful elements of them were. Finding another source, hopefully one not based on exclusion, is necessary if we are to once again challenge the problem of economic inequality.[23]

The New Deal's emphasis on collective economic rights also makes it unique even as compared with the list of other major American political achievements. The most important democratic advances of U.S. history—for instance, the

Emancipation Proclamation and the Civil Rights and Voting Rights Acts—stand as milestones in a continuing struggle to expand individual rights. Although collective economic rights were part of the debate that led to those achievements, they were ultimately absent from the policies that passed the U.S. Congress. Eric Foner titled his short book on emancipation and Reconstruction after the remarks of a contemporary observer that slaves had received "nothing but freedom." This tradition of liberty, one defined by freedom from restraint, has long overshadowed another definition of freedom in the United States: that derived from freedom and capacity to act based on a position of economic security—"freedom from want" and "freedom from fear." Liberty without work, good pay, and occupational rights is an empty promise.[24]

For readers in search of a "usable past," the idea that there was only a one-time mitigation of a long history of U.S. inequality presents a problem. Many pundits, strategists, and scholars point to a return to New Deal politics as the route out of present difficulties. As political linguists explain, people tend to think in metaphor, and there has been no bigger metaphor in progressive politics than the singular success of the New Deal. Yet that metaphor looms too large, like a great and crumbling edifice that obstructs the view of other useful elements of the past, blinding us to the possibility of what Barrington Moore once called "suppressed historical alternatives." If a way out of the decades of inequality is to be charted, and this is the most urgent of projects, we must begin by stripping away stale political analogies—however seductive they may be. If economic democracy is to be part of our future, we must try to understand the core problem: that Americans seem to like to fight with each other more than they do with the economic powers that rule them. Simultaneously, what can happen once can perhaps happen yet again in some other, as of yet unconsidered, form.[25]

———————

This extended historical essay—more theory and sketch—tends toward the interpretative rather than the exhaustive. It is designed to be brief and provocative, skimming above much of the fray to make a set of old-fashioned, broad claims about American politics. By imprinting a broad argument over the drama and turmoil of U.S. history since the end of Reconstruction, I necessarily condense the richness and detail of American history. I can only hope that it does so in a useful way.

By my values, the thesis of this book is an American tragedy. I am a historian, not a political cheerleader, however, so I am compelled to call it like I see it—not how I would prefer it to be. The themes of this book connect with a rich tradition of American letters that struggles with the distance between the promise and the disappointments of American democracy. The ideas here come from wading into the muddy tributaries of skepticism fed by Melville rather than walking the sunny fields of Whitman; its sentiments are more allied with the sparks in the twilight of Eugene O'Neill rather than intense fires of brotherhood of Clifford Odets; its kinship is with the burdens of the past carved into Lincoln's visage rather than the indefatigable smile of FDR. The United States is a complex and conservative place. As much as I would wish to lighten the load of the American past for those looking to map ways toward a better future, it cannot be easily done. There is no "magic door," leading to a "lost Kingdom of peace" as O'Neill told us. We can only struggle forth, feeling our way, charting anew, with a clearer map of where we have been.[26]

It is my hope that *The Great Exception* places the reader in a struggle with the American past. It is my desire that this work not be taken as any kind of final word, but a spur to further exploration, deeper thinking, and point of reflection for the future of American politics.

The Bosses of the Senate, 1889. The new power of the corporation challenged democratic ideals in the final decades of the nineteenth century. Here, plutocrats swagger into the Senate through the "Entrance for Monopolists" while the "People's Entrance" remains locked.

Joseph Keppler, lithograph for *Puck*, 1889. Courtesy of Office of the Senate Curator.

CHAPTER ONE

THE QUESTION OF DEMOCRACY IN THE AGE OF INCORPORATION

"The old relation has been completely destroyed," declared the *Commercial and Financial Chronicle* in 1885, "and that which has taken its place is something far different and much less satisfactory." The businessman's journal laid out its list of concerns for democracy and capitalism in the Gilded Age with remarkable candor. In a quick threefold summary of some of the most profound transformations in American work and business culture, the journal listed: "first, the magnitude of modern industrial undertakings, which has led to a minute subdivision of labor; second, the substitution of corporate for individual employers; third, the growth and adoption of the spirit of modern political economy, which logically inculcates the treatment of labor with the same consideration, and no more, that is accorded to any other of the raw materials or tools of manufacture."[1]

The once tight social, geographic, and economic relations of many small towns and cities were quickly reshaped by the economic levers wielded by distant forces. Large-scale centralization and command of the economy overthrew the traditions during the last quarter of the nineteenth century, as the United States made the final passages into an age of permanent wage dependency, massive accumulations of capital, a deeply class-conscious elite, and an array of radical new ideas poised to challenge the system. The rapidly rising new order, acknowledged the *Commercial and Financial Chronicle*, undermined democracy, bred discontent, and required aggressive efforts to quell labor unrest.

Changes wrought by the massive leap in corporate power in the last decades of the nineteenth century were evident almost everywhere. Before 1880, few industrial enterprises employed more than 400 workers, and the majority of those few firms were capitalized at less than $1 million. By the 1890s, large-scale enterprises had grown common. Individual firms in steel, oil, and especially several of the larger railroads, employed over or near 100,000 workers. By 1900, John D. Rockefeller's Standard Oil reported its capitalization at $122 million, and the United States Steel Trust, formed from an amalgamation of the holdings of Andrew Carnegie and J. P. Morgan in 1901, reached the previously unimaginable figure of $1.4 billion. By 1880, a contemporary observer noted that artisanal work was vanishing, as at least four-fifths of the nearly three million people working in "mechanical industries" were now in the factory system, the pace of their labors pressed forward by the power of steam and water. The corporations soon outweighed the government, in size, bankroll, and, increasingly, power.[2]

Although corporations had existed and been a subject for debate since the dawn of the republic, it was in the last third of the nineteenth century that they gained in size and power. At one time, the right to incorporate was granted just to those fulfilling some sort of public need—a bridge, a road, a canal—but had evolved into a standard way of pooling capital. By 1886, the corporation had its legal status affirmed by the fiat of Chief Justice Waite in *Santa Clara County v. Southern Pacific Railroad*, in which the court acquiesced to a presumption: that corporations were fictitious

people worthy of equal protection under the Fourteenth
Amendment. "The court does not wish to hear argument on
the question whether the provision in the Fourteenth
Amendment to the Constitution, which forbids a State to
deny to any person within its jurisdiction the equal protection of the laws, applies to these corporations. We are all of
opinion that it does." Corporations, as one wag noted, may
have been legal persons, but they had "no soul to be damned
and no body to be kicked." Yet the Fourteenth Amendment
was written to protect freed slaves, not corporations. In
1937, Justice Hugo Black would note that only one half of
one percent of the Fourteenth Amendment cases that came
before the court had anything to with African Americans or
former slaves, while over half of the cases were about protecting the rights of corporations.[3]

The other side of the equation, the collective right of
labor to bargain with employers, was rarely so endorsed,
celebrated, or protected. Workers acting collectively in pursuit of their interests tended to be regarded as a conspiracy
against the public good, a violation of property rights, or an
infringement upon the rights of other workers. When workers did act together, the employer could readily pursue an
injunction against them, any violation of which by anxious
workers could deliver the militia. Only rarely, as one Nebraska judge suggested in an 1894 case against the Northern Pacific Railroad, were the organization of capital and
labor seen as equally important. "A corporation is organized capital; it is capital consisting of money and property.
Organized labor is organized capital; it is capital consisting
of brains and muscle," the judge argued in a performance of
rare legal reasoning of the day. "What is lawful for one to
do is lawful for the other to do." Both, he concluded, act
from "enlightened selfishness." Perhaps one of the most fascinating things about American history is that precious few

judges saw it in the same way as that Nebraska judge. Most saw in combinations of working men a threat to the states' own power, a threat to the ability of capital to expand as necessary or, more fundamentally, a threat to American liberty itself. In short, capital combined under the right of incorporation and the protection of the Fourteenth Amendment. Workers combined under the threat of injunctions and militias. Yet both were regarded as expressions of individual liberty.[4]

The days when Abraham Lincoln could boast "there is no permanent class of hired laborers among us" had long ended. More people had more money, but more were losing it, too; jobs were for the taking, but workers lacked power and control; the economy grew, but democracy suffered; the unrestrained capacity of the corporation expanded, but the rights of workers did not. Material improvements for everyone in the cycle of boom and bust were rampant, as power and technology were brought together with previously unimaginable amounts of humanity toiling anonymously in large cities. The new rising bourgeois and social Darwinist paeans to individualism must have sounded absurd to the new immigrant working class, which clung to family, mutual aid societies, ethnic and religious communities, and a broader culture of reciprocity to make their way in a new land.[5]

The centralization of economic power in what had, not too long ago, been a small producers' democracy, led many to see the era in dramatic terms. Reflecting the period's reputation for corruption, speculation, greed, and scandal, as early as 1873, Mark Twain prophetically referred to his own time as the "Gilded Age"—an age in which superficial ornamentation hid a rotten core of scheming patronage and political profiteering. Twain's story captured individuals adrift in greed, ambition, and lost hope for the American project. His moniker stuck among historians as the dominant description for the period. Half a century later, the great historian Vernon Parrington described the politics of the late nineteenth century as the "Great Barbecue," an era in which corpulent plutocrats and the politicians they hired to do their bidding fed off the state at the expense of the people. More than a half century after Parrington, Nell Irvin Painter captured the feeling of the era from the streets with the title *Standing at Armageddon*.[6]

The problem with such richly evocative metaphors is that they allow us to distance ourselves from the era more than we should—to think of it as something other than what we are now, other than what the nation "really" is or believes itself to be. Yet another historian argued for a label more literal than metaphorical to describe the culture of late nineteenth-century America. Alan Trachtenberg suggested that the period was really something more straightforward and more profound: it was, simply, *The Incorporation of America*. This name, less separate, less alien, and less dramatic, points directly and exactly to the roots of our present dilemmas in the alleged extremes of the past, when the power of the corporation first became a permanent and inescapable dimension of American economic and social life. Condemning our own time to the otherness of a "new" Gilded Age is supposed to serve as an indictment of the United States' descent into the most heinous period of capitalist buccaneering and political servility in American history. But maybe the issue of that era and our own is something more simple and more constant and more ever-present: the culture, politics, and economics of an ever-evolving large-scale capitalism.[7]

———

The core question of the rough-hewn world of grassroots political philosophy was: what was the role of the traditional freeholder's sense of individualism in this new age?

The market revolution and the rise of the corporation upset the tradition of republican practice and ideology, a set of ideas that depended upon the close relationships between land and citizenship, between hireling and boss, and between people and commerce. For Jefferson, Madison, and other founding thinkers, the republican intellectual worldview was not just one of opposition to the monarchy and aristocracy of the old world. Freedom and individual rights were firmly grounded in a type of independence secured by ownership of productive property. This kind of ownership provided a means of production, a means of citizenship, and a means of distributing wealth. Most importantly, it provided a foundation for liberty against power and corruption. Fears of corruption, especially those corruptions produced by the state, were part and parcel of what it was to be a native-born white American.[8]

Questions about democracy in this era of "ransomed individualism," in the words of social gospel minister George Herron, were thus profound. What of the people's interest, and what of the civic virtue and republican traditions once promised by a smallholder society? What did it mean to champion the tradition of individual rights in a society ever more dominated by corporations? What was democracy when corporate influence over politicians and lawmakers gave the lie to the republican myth that any individual citizen's vote could carry deciding power? What did citizenship mean when corporate directors, hundreds if not thousands of miles distant, made decisions that might devastate one community even as they bestowed temporary blessings on another?[9]

While protection from corruption and declension could only come from a strong, independent, republican citizenry, the decades had not been good to that ideal. By 1896, noted the *Atlantic*, the very backbone of the republican vision, the "sturdy yeoman" with his passion for civic virtue stand-ing in opposition to tyranny and monarchy, had in elite opinion tumbled to little more than a "hayseed," grasping at backward-facing populist panaceas and cheap credit to sus-tain him in the new industrial age. As for the "yeomen of the city," as Jefferson called skilled craftsmen, they too had en-visioned their artisanal capacity as a bulwark against sub-servience much the way property owners thought of their land. And, like the land, the symbolic power of the work-place as a source of political identity slowly weakened under the strain of mass production, deskilling, and scientific man-agement. Unmoored from earlier associations with indepen-dence, control, and political will, work drifted increasingly toward a means to a goal rather than an end in itself, its purpose squarely anchored in the emerging consumer soci-ety. This loss of control—or, conversely, the increasing con-centration of control in the hands of a few—echoed through-out social and political life.[10]

Adapting the ideals of individual independence and pro-ducerist values to a new mass industrial age became a cen-tral problem in the Age of Incorporation. In 1878, the Knights of Labor, one of the early and most effective and pluralistic organizations to redirect the old ideas against the new aggregates of capital, declared, "the alarming develop-ment and aggressiveness of great capitalists and corpora-tions, unless checked, will inevitably lead to the pauperiza-tion and hopeless degradation of the toiling masses." Traditions of individual self-worth and self-reliance were at stake in this conflict: "It is imperative, if we desire to enjoy the full blessings of life, that a check be placed upon unjust accumulation, and the power for evil of aggregated wealth." As the Knights' leader, Grandmaster Workman Terrence Powderly, explained the connection, "One hundred years ago we had one king of limited powers. . . . Now we have a hundred kings, uncrowned ones, it is true, but monarchs of unlimited power, for they rule through the wealth they possess." Although the Knights' ideas were often fuzzy and naïve, they struggled valiantly to preserve republican traditions, civic virtue, and individual rights—even through collective organization and political action—in the face of the republic's new aristocracy.[11]

In short, the idiom of republican independence and individualism hardly died along with the old order; instead, republican values steadily weakened in power and practice but remained strong in ideology. Historically, the state had long been the target for common people's anxieties about aristocracy, power, and corruption. The transition to seeing the corporation as the new threat to democracy, which the Knights alone handled with reasonable clarity, remained incomplete for large swaths of the American population. Republican values may have been attractive on a visceral level, but it was ultimately a weak weapon in battles against the thickening partnership of capital and the state by century's end. "Under the guise of republican freedom," social reformer Florence Kelley feared in 1889 about the hollowed out values of American history, "we have degenerated into a nation of mock citizens."[12]

The problem of republican individualism connects directly to the questions of the uniquely American cry for "free labor"—neither of which can be understood apart from both slavery and racial ideology in the United States. Few terms mobilized antebellum working class voters, or infused the rise of the new Republican Party, more than the promotion of "free labor" through the expansion of "free soil" into Western lands. The idea of free labor typically contrasted a Southern society of stagnation and degradation with the mighty forces of individual uplift and commerce in the North. The expansion of slavery westward not only reduced the amount of land available for independent white settlement but also violated and degraded values of independence and property ownership that received an endless stream of rapturous praise among northern workers and the party politicians seeking to mobilize them. "It is the energizing power of free labor," Congressman and future Illinois governor Richard Yates explained to Congress in 1854, "which has built our railroads, set the wheels of machinery in motion, added new wings to commerce, and laid the solid foundation for our permanent prosperity and renown." By contrasting free wage labor in the North with slave labor in the South, the standard for white American working class identity was set low: not enslaved.[13]

While free labor ideas could provide a powerful critique of the expansion of slavery, they proved inadequate to mounting a cohesive attack on the new corporate order— and perhaps even helped to usher it in. Lincoln's own ideal of American independence was one in which "a large majority are neither hirers nor hired," he explained in 1859. In their toils, free laborers sought "no favors of capital on the one hand, nor of hirelings or slaves on the other," creating the formula for a "just and generous, and prosperous system." What may have proved ideologically potent at midcentury for defending the North's labor system against the slave South would prove problematic ideological material for an offensive position against the rise of corporate capitalism.[14]

After the Civil War, as parties sought simultaneously to mobilize votes and restrict workers' demands, free labor ideology evolved from the idea of workers who were unchained to those who were merely unconstrained. The partisan logics might have been different, but the end results were the same. A Democratic newspaper in Chicago, for instance, argued that workers' collective demands for shorter hours

would result in the enslavement of capital. If collective demands were honored, the paper claimed, "the workingman
would be at liberty to seize the capitalist's money, and the
capitalist would have the corresponding liberty to seize the
other's labor by reducing him to the condition of slavery."
Meanwhile, Republicans could simultaneously discredit
working-class appeals for state support—whether for bread,
work, or protection—as a return to the type of state-
sanctioned servitude they had just vanquished. A Republican paper, responding to the same demand for the eight-
hour day as the Democratic paper, argued it was "An effort
to prevent men from selling their own property (their labor)
on such terms as were agreeable to both seller and purchaser.
It was the voice of the slave power crying out—You shall
work only when, where and on such terms as we dictate."
Associating unions and collective bargaining with slavery,
argues Cedric de Leon, "Chicago's elites moved to crush labor's uprising just as the North had crushed the southern
rebellion."[15]

Free labor proved as much a lubricant for the coming of
corporate capitalism as it was an adhesive for working-class
action. As mobilized by political elites, free labor ideology
drifted into simple individualism, free-market principles,
freedom of contract, Horatio Alger mythology, and even
social Darwinism. The things that stood in the way of an
individual's right to make his own individual contract with
his own employer were trade unionism, collective bargaining, and, above all, state regulation of employment. As the
historian Leon Fink explains, when our nineteenth-century
forbearers—"ranging from industrialists and conservative
jurists to trade unionists and socialist agitators—declared
the system of 'free labor' to be at risk from the hands of one
antagonist or another, they were engaging in a peculiarly
American intellectual and political argument." While it

might offer ideological grounds for protection against abuse, it had limited backbone as an alternative to the emerging corporate order.[16]

As for freed slaves themselves, no land and very little assistance was forthcoming for the four million newly emancipated workers after the Civil War. Without the land, there was no freedom. Tossed mercilessly onto a coercive labor system, they were expected to work hard, accumulate property, and enjoy the bounty of their freedom. As one freed slave said after the war, "Gib us our own land and we take care of ourselves, but without land, de ole masses can hire us or starve us, as dey please." Under an aggressive program of Reconstruction with Northern military and financial support, the inklings of a biracial democracy had begun to take hold in the South. Then, abandoned by the North in the 1870s, former slaves found themselves fighting off a return to new forms of bondage. Without the land, however, freed people quickly regressed back to the near-slavery of the sharecropping system. As W.E.B. Dubois put it, "the slave went free; stood a moment in the sun; and then moved back again toward slavery."[17]

A war and Reconstruction once based on a free labor ideal had, by century's end, succumbed to lynching, violence, disenfranchisement, and finally Jim Crow laws to "redeem" the South from Northern aggression. New forms of servitude like sharecropping and gang labor delivered labor power back to land still possessed by Southern elites in such a way as to make a mockery of the free labor principles under which the war was fought. Scores of hate strikes, as white workers walked off the job upon hearing of the hiring of black workers, took place in the last two decades of the nineteenth century. In the North, racism blocked black workers from unions, from skilled trades, from most anything but the most menial work in the new corporate economy.

Reconstruction exposed an enormous flaw in Civil War Era thinking: that the nation's new commitment to free labor would lead simply, naturally, to upward mobility and class harmony for all races. With class conflict simultaneously raising questions in the North, the level of state intervention necessary to make the free labor dreams of Reconstruction actually work merged with fears of the need for federal intervention in the labor market, not just in the South, but nationally. Both regions' need for government intervention belied the hope that a free labor system was a perpetual motion machine that would run smoothly on its own. Rather, it became clear that these objectives would require broad federal intervention, and even seizure of property in the South, to make things right. As a result, Northern Republicans forfeited their optimistic free labor framework back to the subjugation of Southern white rule and its ideology of racial supremacy. As Heather Cox Richardson explains, "Northerners turned against freedpeople after the Civil War because African-Americans came to represent a concept of society and government that would destroy the free labor world." The interests of white elites converged in opposition to blacks, economic regulation, and labor rights. Federal intervention in the labor market and the question of race thus grew up hand-in-hand—a unity that lasted through to the twenty-first century.[18]

Race was not simply a question of black and white, as a massive influx of immigration transformed the sounds, the complexion, the gods, and the community identities of the

United States in less than a generation. Following on the waves of German and Irish immigrations of midcentury, masses of new immigrants—now from new ancestral communities in Southern and Eastern Europe and Asia—flooded to American shores to do the semi-skilled work of the new corporate economy. For many "white" Americans (a category that included only Anglo-Saxons at the time), working people as well as corporate executives, the post-1880 surge of immigrants from Eastern and Southern Europe caused great concern. Perceiving these newcomers through America's racial prism, many considered them to be intrinsically different from the mainly Northern Europeans who had comprised earlier immigrations. They were held to a lower rank in the taxonomy of racial hierarchy—on a par for some with people of African descent, who were relegated to the lowest rung. Resistance to these immigrants on racial grounds encouraged many nonelite whites into political alliances with those whom, in a different moment, they might very well strike against. With rhetoric that would also echo well into the twenty-first century, native-born Protestants argued that immigrants lowered wages, diluted the culture, could not be assimilated, and were unfit to be Americans.[19]

The result of racial and ethnic divisions was a staggeringly complicated political jigsaw puzzle that trumped hope for anything more than a temporary multi-ethnic working-class solidarity. Skilled, native stock, Protestant workers tended to be Republican and often carried cards in the craft unions of the old American Federation of Labor. Old Irish and German Catholics might also be in the skilled trades but were most likely in the Democratic Party. The new immigrants from Southern and Eastern Europe were often unskilled workers; they not only joined different political parties from their skilled brethren but also invoked their sharp opposition to craft unionism with sporadic attempts to build broad-based industrial unions. Black workers in the North tended to be Republicans, which placed them at political odds with those Northern workers who were closest to them economically. At the same time, they encountered systematic exclusion by working-class whites who often favored uncontested whiteness over interracial solidarity. If there was one thing uniting the working people of both parties, it was their mutual distaste—and demand for exclusion—of yet another segment of the working class, Chinese immigrant laborers brought to the United States in near-slave-like conditions to build the infrastructures of the West. Continue to tally up American workers' responses to the host of other political, racial, regional, ideological, and ethnic differences that characterized the United States at the start of the industrial age, and you find something that resembles less a coherent working-class political force and far more a splintered series of votes based on ethno-political antagonisms.[20]

These ethno-racial tensions were defined—and compounded—by attitudes about religious faith. Catholicism, in particular, challenged the idea of a Protestant nation. Republicans attacked Democrats for "Rum, Romanism, and Rebellion," striking at the core of the Democrats' coalition that was as improbable as it was awkward: Southern Protestants (rebellion), Catholic immigrants (Romanism), and those against prohibition (rum)—all of which were seen in different capacities to be a threat to upright Nordic moral character. Protestant Northern Republicans, in contrast, emphasized the government's role in reforming and removing sin from the nation, stressing their piety, their temperance, and their interest in moral reform. The Women's Christian Temperance Union, for instance, fusing social activism and Christianity, sought to free the land from alcohol and vice in order to deliver the nation to a "sober and pure" state. With Catholic churches and Jewish synagogues sprouting up in Northern cities, questions of assimilation often peaked around parochial educational programs that provided "foreign" religious education in different languages; such attempts by immigrant communities to maintain contact with their cultural roots proved politically motivating for Republicans in often visceral ways.

At the same time, massive urban religious revivals swept through the nation beginning in the 1870s and lasted throughout the Gilded Age. Led most famously by figures such as former Chicago shoe salesman D. L. Moody, revivalism demanded a return to "old-fashioned" religious faith, as *The Nation* put it, and moral uplift in response to society's interest in both secular political reform and scientific reasoning. One's personal relationship with God was all that was necessary in a rapidly changing world; the sacred ought not be cluttered up with worldly concerns. Presaging the fundamentalism of the early twentieth century that would culminate in William Jennings Bryan at the Scopes trial, Moody argued that faith trumped science: "What can a geologist tell you of the Rock of Ages?"[21]

Undoubtedly, religious revivalism helped ease the way into the new order. While preaching small-town values of days gone by, they did so in an almost industrial fashion, helping to ease the transition to the age of incorporation with an evocative call for individual salvation on a mass scale. With revivals popping up all over the country, organizers like Moody built a massive network of preachers and revivals with meetings in huge stadiums, organized by large bureaucracies, involving huge amounts of money. In Richard Hofstadter's comparison of the differences between the revivalism of the Second Great Awakening earlier in the nineteenth century and that of the Gilded Age, he noted how the small-scale world of "Andrew Jackson and Lyman

Beecher" had been replaced by the corporate scale of "Andrew Carnegie and P. T. Barnum." When Moody died at the end of the century, mourners claimed he had spoken to 100 million people and had single-handedly reduced the population of hell by a million. Yet there was an irony of mass audiences demanding individual uplift and purity of others, harkening back to small-town values, individual relationships with Jesus, all the while smoothing the way for, and using the tools of, the corporation. By the early twentieth century, fundamentalists, drawn from old-stock native-born whites, would express their feelings of displacement in the face of the tides of Catholics and Jews swelling the U.S. population in very explicitly nativist ways.[22]

The era's liveliest dissenting movements also often cleaved along religious lines, deepening the divisions of cultural conflict even as they argued for a unified political critique. The agrarian populists alienated many urban workers and immigrants with their fiery brand of Protestant revivalism. The emergent social gospel advocates gathered inspiration not from the threat of hellfires but from the morality of good works and collective salvation to build their godly kingdom on earth. Eugene Debs invoked a manly Christian virtue and morality to tame capital, while Yiddish socialists looked to vibrant cultures of resistance from the old country. Catholics, in turn, could draw on the corporate social good advocated by Pope Leo XIII in *Rerum Novarum* (1891), his encyclical on the Rights and Duties of Capital and Labor, which advocated both unionization and the protection of private property. While the critiques were lively, they often spoke in distinctly separate voices.

———

Politics, argued the descendant of presidents and statesmen Henry Adams, has "always been the systematic organization of hatreds." Political parties proved successful in rallying working people, but just as significant in driving the era's social fragmentation. Astounding levels of party attachment and activity defined the Gilded Age: extraordinarily high election turnouts (often 85 percent or more), local mobilizations, vibrant electioneering parades, extended speechifying, and visceral party affiliations shaped the lives of working people profoundly. Yet here, too, these affiliations and activities were often organized around ethnic and racial animosity. Although recent scholarship on political behavior has shown that politics did often hinge on actual policy issues, not far below the surface were deep issues of ethnic hostility.[23]

The Republicans sought to retain the power of the native-born Protestants, support industry, and bolster the protective tariff against a raft of "intruders." Democrats, in contrast, funneled Catholic and Jewish immigrants into urban machines, fought the tariff as a conspiracy against the interests of the common man, stood up for those left out of the Anglo-Saxon mythology of American politics—and believed a body ought to be able to have a drink now and then. The Southern racial order compounded the complexities of political allegiance tremendously. The Solid South maintained its militant devotion to the Democratic Party, partially out of the politics of waving the "bloody shirt" of wartime sacrifice and loyalties, but mostly as a way of defending against fears of "black Republicanism." The Democrats in the North had similar fears, as immigrants often faced those just below them in the racial and economic pecking order with racial fear and contempt rather than any form of political solidarity.[24]

As the father of industrial relations studies, John R. Commons, put it, there was no shortage of opportunity for "playing one race against the other"—race then defined to include a variety of immigrants, cultures, religions, and lan-

guage groups. Like religious affiliation, political party affiliation and union affiliation were often at such cross-purposes
as to make unions politically impotent. As the secretary of
the Bricklayers Union expressed the complexity, "We have
excellent trades' unionists, who are warm democrats and
zealous republicans . . . and who are ready to point with
suspicion to every movement on our part toward the formation of political organizations. . . . The only way we can be
successful with our local and national trades unions is by
excluding politics from them."[25]

The salience of religious faith in dividing American politics might seem superficial at first glance, yet in Robin Archer's *Why Is There No Labor Party in the United States?*,
he determines that the ways that religion functioned in
party politics and union structure are central factors in the
creation of the distinctive path of American political development. Labor leaders, he argues, feared that the formation
of a labor party would prove less uniting than alienating to
workers, as religious conflict would engulf class solidarity.
"Unions needed to maintain the support of workers who
were Republicans and Democrats, Protestants and Catholics, Evangelicals and Liturgicals," he shows. "Labor leaders
feared that if workers were forced to choose between union
solidarity and their partisan and religious loyalties, they
would choose the latter, and the unions themselves would
be destroyed." Religious freedom and diversity therefore
played a central if surprising role in limiting the politics of
class consciousness in the United States.[26]

Policy issues further fueled the ethno-regional divisions.
The most significant policy question of the day was the tariff—a seemingly technical issue but one that had the capacity to make partisan blood boil. Republicans were industrial
protectionists who saw in growing industry more demand
for labor; Democrats were populist free traders who saw
higher prices for the people inside of industry's policy de-

sires. Rudyard Kipling satirized some of the absurd loyalties of the tariff and the party system after his visit to the United States. Republicans and Democrats, he wrote,

> are both agreed in thinking that the other party is run-
> ning creation (which is American) into red flame. Also
> the Democrat as a party drinks more than the Repub-
> lican, and when drunk may be heard to talk about a
> thing called the Tariff, which he does not understand,
> but which he conceives to be the bulwark of the coun-
> try or else the surest power of its destruction. Some-
> times he says one thing and sometimes another, in
> order to contradict the Republican, who is always
> contradicting himself.[27]

With its near infinite ability to absorb political energies and anger, both major parties used the tariff as a tool of unifica-tion and differentiation, as it had the capacity to deflect any discussion of more substantive political questions in the Gilded Age. The Sherman Anti-Trust Act of 1890 initially had a similar, perhaps more pernicious, function. Created in this same political climate and designed to placate public fears of corporate contracts, combinations, trusts, and con-spiracies to restrain trade, Sherman was only rarely wielded against corporations in any successful way—even in a case against the American Sugar Refining Company, which con-trolled 98 percent of the industry. Sherman was, however, used mercilessly to bludgeon organized labor for allegedly creating monopolies in the labor market.[28]

Economist Simon Patten put the pieces together in an 1896 essay, explaining how one person's freedom in the Gilded Age seemed to depend on another's subjugation:

> Each class or section of the nation is becoming con-
> scious of an opposition between its standards and the
> activities and tendencies of some less developed class.

The South has its negro, the city has its slums. . . . The friends of American institutions fear the ignorant immigrant, and the workingman dislikes the Chinese. Every one is beginning to differentiate those with proper qualifications for citizenship from some other class or classes which he wishes to restrain or exclude from society.

When Robber Baron Jay Gould boasted that he could "Pay one half the working class to kill the other," he might have added that he didn't really have to do so.[29]

Despite the fragmented working-class identity, class conflict was not just alive in the streets of Gilded Age America—it often raged. Combinations of nostalgic and forward-looking populists, tough-minded trade unionists, threatening anarchists, Debsian socialists, believers in the social gospel, and committed party organizers all sought to resolve the fraught question of democracy in the age of incorporation. For some, this meant restoring the democratic system to its rightful glory, for others it meant trying to advance the nation into a new transcendent democratic order, and still others were resigned to the emerging system but bent on strategizing ways to get the most out of it. Approaches differed, but in the streets, the taverns, the workshops, and the party headquarters, many acknowledged the "labor question" and set themselves to the task of sorting it out.

Resistance by collectivities of working people, small farmers, and a smattering of foremen and lower-level managers remained persistent and dramatic, if episodic. National strikes in the railroad industry in 1877, 1886, and

1894; major strikes in steel, coal, textile, and other industries throughout the last decades of the nineteenth century;
the protest of small farmer-owners prone to the power of
the bank and railroad monopolies—all were spurred by
technological innovation, pressed by wage reductions,
pushed by management's desire to more completely control
the work process, and complicated by the endlessly vicious
cycles of boom and bust that structured the Gilded Age.
Whenever it came to head-to-head conflict, the legal and
marshal power of business typically outgunned the fragile
solidarity of the working class.

Following on the national railroad strike of 1877, the
movement for the eight-hour day and the Haymarket tragedy of 1886, and the building of the farmers' alliances in the
Southwest, movements for democracy appeared to be culminating in something greater than the individual protests
by the 1890s. Yet that decade—one of financial panic, bitter
depression, and mass unemployment—ended in defeat for
the various people's movements that had emerged in the
Gilded Age. In 1892, the Amalgamated Steel Workers struck
and were locked out of the Homestead works. In response,
Andrew Carnegie's man Henry Clay Frick triggered injunctions and troops, breaking the strike and along with it a
tentative solidarity that had formed across lines of skill and
immigration. Despite other national steel strikes, the industry would not be organized until the New Deal. The miners'
strike in Coeur d'Alene ended with the descent of federal
troops and the destruction of the union. Even in New Or-
leans, where a phenomenal interracial struggle produced a
general strike in the city, workers' demands were ultimately
met, but lasting union recognition was not. The Bituminous
Coal Miners Strike of 1894 nearly destroyed the United
Mine Workers, which would also not revive until the New
Deal. The list could go on.

Two different tactical approaches to worker organizing illustrate the key themes of government hostility toward their collective action and the social fragmentation of the working class itself in the late nineteenth century. The first is Sam Gompers and the American Federation of Labor (AFL), and the second is Eugene Debs and the American Railway Union (ARU). Both understood the problem of state repression, but each came to radically different conclusions about what to do about it.

The militant but blinkered craft unionism of the American Federation of Labor, founded in 1886, has been a scholarly puzzle for generations. Many have tried to account for the "conservatism" of the federation and its unions, which did not seek to change the system but simply to bargain for "more" for its own members—specifically skilled, white, male, native-born tradesmen. Rather than *only* defending a subgroup of American workers, however, the AFL's "pure and simple" ideology can also be seen as a tactical, survivalist response to a repressive state. Founding AFL president Samuel Gompers began his career believing in the class struggle, but drew back his ambitions dramatically as the years went by, ultimately giving up the fight to change the system in favor of bargaining through narrow, craft-based trade unions with a form of anti-statism known as "voluntarism."

The economic system as a whole remained relatively untouched in this approach—and the new armies of relatively unskilled labor pouring into the new factories ignored—but the AFL unions survived and its members enjoyed the fruits of collective bargaining. Lower hours and higher wages meant more leisure and more consumption—a bridge from the moral fortitudes of republicanism to the palliatives of the consumer's republic.[30]

"Voluntarism is labor's version of laissez-faire," explains legal scholar William Forbath. It is "an anti-statist philosophy" that, as Sam Gompers put it, argues that the "best thing the State can do for Labor is to leave labor alone." As a tactical approach to bargaining in an age of "government by injunction," it worked for the limited numbers of skilled workers; as a vision for the entire American working class, the idea fell dramatically short and seemed like a system of protection just for the aristocracy of labor. The AFL's anti-injunction struggle may have been limited, but the unions felt they were still struggling against industrial feudalism—anything more was a long way off. No surprise that at the 1894 convention of the American Federation of Labor, the members overwhelmingly approved a "Political Programme" that declared that "party politics whether democratic, republican, socialistic, prohibition, or any other should have no place in the convention of the A.F. of L."[31]

Eugene Debs offered a much bolder position: if the state was hostile to workers, as Gompers understood, then workers must not cower from federal power but take it over—peacefully and electorally. For Debs, the preservation—really the advancement—of republican values lay in widespread working-class power that could challenge the rise of corporate power through the ballot box. Once a skilled member of the Brotherhood of Locomotive Firemen, an exclusive, native-born, skilled trade union, he launched the American Railway Union as a broadly inclusive industrial union. Of the many strikes of the nineteenth century, his reluctant leadership of the Pullman Strike of 1894 delivered the largest and most symbolic conflict of the era. Thousands of workers involved in making Pullman railroad cars outside of Chicago walked off the job in response to wage cuts—cuts made without corresponding price cuts in the cost of living in Pullman's model company town. The union launched a massive national boycott against Pullman, which drew hundreds of thousands of railway workers of a variety of skills, ethnicities, and immigrant status into the conflict. The American Railway Union quickly rivaled in size the combined membership of the various unions federated in the AFL.

The federal government issued a court injunction against the union and its leadership, however, ordering them not to interfere with the mail, which the combined forces of the employers, the General Managers Association, had specifically placed on Pullman cars. President Grover Cleveland then dispatched 12,000 troops to suppress the strike. In response, Debs called for a general strike in Chicago, but ran afoul of the skilled brotherhoods of the AFL, which refused to support his call. Successful up to that point, the ARU stoppage broke on the failure of solidarity between skilled and unskilled workers. Hostile to both Debs personally and to the strike as a cause, Gompers called the strike action "impulsive" and declared, in words that would both end the strike and burn in Debs's mind, "A general strike at this time is inexpedient, unwise and contrary to the best interests of the working people."[32]

Both Debs and Gompers were responding to the state's hostility to their interests—one through tactical retreat, the other through a bold attempt to redefine the workings of American democracy. While Gompers played the statesman, Debs was arrested and jailed, his case sent to the Supreme Court, where the federal government's interest in breaking the strike was upheld. With his case lost, and his union destroyed, Debs was sent to prison. Upon his release, in order to keep his long-standing democratic vision alive, to span the gap between the republican ethos of old and the new mass production era, Debs declared himself a socialist and ran in every presidential election between 1900 and 1920—the last time from Atlanta Penitentiary. His popularity, as biographer Nick Salvatore explains, "rested upon his ability to articulate and symbolize something of the severe disloca-tion experiences by all Americans in the transformation to industrial capitalism."[33]

American farmers struggled mightily with the same prob-lems of corporate dominance as did Debs and Gompers. In 1896, the agrarian Populists united in a fusion ticket with the Democrats. The pivotal election came at the end of a vibrant agrarian movement seeking to challenge the power of the railroads and the banks. The "Great Commoner" William Jennings Bryan became the standard-bearer for the fusion ticket. He followed his rousing "Cross of Gold" speech at the Chicago Democratic Convention with an en-ergetic campaign of six hundred speeches in twenty-nine states to rally the people.

Yet Bryan's agrarian, free silver politics failed to inspire industrial workers—at least partially because his revivalist rhetorical style proved so very foreign to the urban immi-grant working class. The inflationary demand of "free sil-ver" overshadowed all other aspects of the populist pro-gram, whittling a vibrant movement culture with a number of significant reforms of the corporate order down to what appeared to be a one-plank platform. "Few political or so-cial movements," the historian Charles Postel writes about the populists at their best, "brought so many men and women into lecture halls, classrooms, camp meetings and seminars or produced such an array of inexpensive litera-ture." Yet as all eyes focused on the national election, Mc-Kinley's front-porch campaign ended in a victory not just for one election but as a triumph in "an intense, generation-long struggle for control of industrializing America." The in-

corporation of America had been safely delivered through
the upheavals of the Gilded Age to the other side, making
the United States into what the historian Sven Beckert described as "the most bourgeois of all countries."[34]

Gilded Age political leaders, especially in the executive
branch, tended to be bland, gray, and weak executives lost
between the power of Lincoln and the dynamism of the
twentieth-century Progressive Era figures to come. Neither
party offered direct relief to American workers. A laissez
faire Democratic Party claimed to work "for the people"
but held no tools to do so besides less government and less
tariff. A pro-industrial Republican Party, running on the
prosperity of the "full dinner pail," enjoyed the support of
an activist government freely exercising trade protectionism and the suppression of labor. The people, in turn, often
looked for commitment and identity in community, ethnic
or religious separatism, and individual upward mobility.
It was, argues one political scientist, "probably true that
more workers sought to overcome the difficulties they faced
through individual endeavors than by joining in a collective
effort to improve their lives"—whether this meant tramp-
ing in bad times or finding ways to access the extraordinary
mobility the nation promised in good times.[35]

American workers were hardly liberal individualists—
even though they could not find a way, even in the most
dramatic circumstances, to join together to overcome the
challenges of the new order in effective ways. Whatever the
many horrors of working-class life, hard work could still
pay off, and mobility and growth were both dynamic and
real in the United States to a much greater extent than they
were in other countries. A combined ethos of individual ef-

fort and collective action continued to define working-class experience. Though they were in no position to build a more humane social order on the national scale, these efforts provided a backdrop and quiet counterpoint to a climate in which, as David Montgomery put it succinctly, "American workers in the nineteenth century engaged in economic conflicts with their employers as fierce as any known in the industrial world; yet in their political behavior they consistently failed to exhibit a class consciousness."[36]

The main challenge American workers faced in the age of incorporation—of rising to a sustainable level of commonality and mutualism that branched beyond the immediate space of community, the immediate place of employment, or the immediate power of ethnic ties—proved elusive. The main political parties offered little compelling alternative to the rise of oligopoly, while the state proved its hostility—and the workforce its fragmentation—time and again. In sum, "Rhetoric about what all 'producers' had in common could not sustain tenuous bonds between people who had long mistrusted one another on racial, occupational, or religious grounds," as Michael Kazin argues. " 'Workingmen's democracy' lasted only as long as skilled and unskilled, black and white, native and immigrant, Protestant and Catholic, were able to submerge their defensive loyalties."[37]

Submerging those defensive loyalties proved difficult and elusive. Those same dividing lines among the working class, seen from a different perspective, were actually the social foundations for communities of workers in a time of profound uncertainty. At the very time that the promises of a once-potent republican idyll came into the shadow of the powerful new form of individualism in the land, that of the corporation, appeals to ethnicity, race, skill, and community were as much handicaps as sources of power in the age of incorporation.

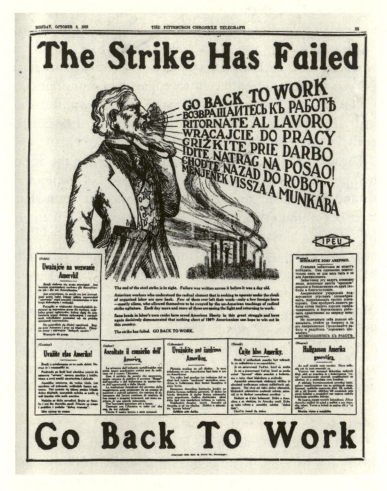

The Strike Has Failed, 1919. When state support for unionization evaporated after World War I, workers in the Great Steel Strike of 1919 proved vulnerable to their own internal divisions.
Pittsburgh Chronicle-Telegraph, 6 October 1919, reproduced from William Z. Foster, *The Great Steel Strike and Its Lessons* (New York, 1920).

CHAPTER TWO

KALEIDOSCOPE OF REFORM

As compared to the dramatic political standoff of 1896, in which the agrarian uprising led by the fiery oratory of Democratic challenger William Jennings Bryan appeared to threaten the corporate order, the election of 1900 was a wholly perfunctory affair. Voters easily reelected William McKinley in a rematch with the deflated Bryan, affirming the corporate order, the new overseas empire, the industry-protecting tariff, and the full dinner pail. In 1901, however, an anarchist named Leon Czolgosz, frustrated by the repression of workers' demands in the 1890s and possessed with the fantasy of igniting a revolution, shot the president during a visit to Buffalo, New York. With a bullet lost in his abdomen, McKinley succumbed to gangrene two weeks later. The death of the stalwart of business and protectionism hardly brought the nation closer to revolution, but it did leave the White House to McKinley's pugnacious wild-card of a vice president, Theodore Roosevelt.

TR represented a new kind of elite, exhausted with short-sighted and obstinate capitalists who would not recognize that creating the social basis for a secure and functional capitalist democracy was in their own best interests. He had equal impatience for the strikes, disruptions, and radicals who threatened to overthrow the system. Roosevelt became the national leader of a rising middle class that felt squeezed between the upheavals from below and the power of corporations from above. Restless, impatient, and independent, he delivered the modern activist executive from the managerial presidents that had dominated the Gilded Age.

That feeling of being trapped between irrational extremes of the age of incorporation fueled the political fires of the Progressive Era (1901–1919). While the dichotomy between Gilded Age and Progressive Era is typically overdrawn, the new century delivered middle-class men and women, often with significant religious commitments in their youth, to an engagement with the crisis as their calling, their vocation. This generation, often with college training, belief in progress, and confidence in a scientific approach, felt compelled to solve the complex problems of corporate power and its attendant social, cultural, and political consequences. They flooded into the tenement districts of the poor in cities across the nation, established settlement houses to train and assimilate new immigrants, and worked for legislation to reform working conditions, education, sanitation, and health care. Equally important for some was their support for the trade union movement, an essential player in the burning issue of the day, "the labor question."[1]

The activists and politicians known as "progressives" were many and varied and conflicting, but, in general, they sought a place between the rise of the plutocrats and the demands of a restless working class. Their vision included a desire to control class conflict, to deliver enlightenment and uplift to the immigrants, to make sense of new questions of gender relations, to democratize politics and industry, and toward the end, bring democracy to the world. As the historian Paul Boyer puts it, middle-class progressives possessed "infinite capacity for moral indignation." Less committed to ending economic and social inequality than one might readily expect, as the historian Michael McGerr put it, progressives were a meddlesome bunch, "radical in their conviction that other social classes must be transformed."[2]

But beyond its vague, forward-looking outlook, this "movement" was not unified in much of anything. Widely heralded for its promotion of democratic reforms such as the direct election of U.S. senators, progressivism also embraced within its fold a contradictory impulse toward an "expert" city-manager form of urban governance to curtail the growing influence of immigrant-driven political machines. Believing in a kind of industrial rationalism, many progressives seized on efficiency as the answer to America's cultural, political, and economic problems. They admired Frederick Winslow Taylor's efforts to apply his principles of scientific management to the industrial factory, including supervisory and clerical staffs, and perceived in Taylor's methods the central reforms necessary to advance the goal of American progress. Some progressives, often motivated by religious convictions rooted in a fading Calvinist tradition, stressed that their engagement with social issues was central to a meaningful faith.

This commingling of sacred and secular, between the expert executive and the democratic spirit, the anti-monopoly and the regulatory, provided bridges between social gospel advocates and the emerging new social scientific professionals in government and the academy. Their shared vision of a scientific path to material progress simultaneously united them against a common enemy in the then-nascent Fundamentalist and Pentecostal religious movements. The historian James Kloppenberg's evocative description of progressive thought as having "all the neatness of a shattered kaleidoscope, and some of the same chaotic brilliance" perhaps captures the rich confusion better than any other.[3]

Yet when historians stare at the Progressive Era long enough, it tends to disappear. Every few years comes an intellectual survey that claims to pin it down, dismiss it, reclaim it, or bury it. Criticized and scrutinized for its limits as a "movement," its tendency to "banish the language of class from the vocabulary of reform," its tendency toward "making the world safe for inequality," its strong undercurrent of white supremacism, and, above all, its individualism, the Progressive Era has, in turns, been disassembled, scrutinized, celebrated, and written off. Some still cannot draw a distinction between the Progressive Era and the Gilded Age, while others cannot find enough coherence in the period to even declare much of anything. Perhaps this is all because, as Richard Hofstadter put it, reformers were trying to "institutionalize a mood."[4]

Given the truncated parameters of American reform, perhaps one of progressivism's greatest strengths lay in what many have seen as its weaknesses: its ill-defined nature, its shifting allegiances, its cross-class alliances, its orientation toward a local scale of action. The very fluidity of its movements allowed many elements of reform to surface, yet none to become definitive. In a polity that historically places tremendous obstacles to substantive social change and economic regulation, getting carried away with explaining what did not happen during the Progressive Era can be a dangerous analytical game. The richness of the period is that it eludes a reductive, causal analysis. The apparent muddle of progressive thought masks the enduring tactical potential of its decentered political action and the complexity with which reformers grappled, albeit imperfectly, with issues at the heart of American democratic philosophy. The end result did not make much headway against the class structure itself, and the philanthropic dimensions often made matters worse rather than better, but the overall *struc-*

ture of mobilization, the "shattered kaleidoscope" effect, may offer a better, if much messier, historical analogy for the future than the more successful but more static breakthrough of the New Deal bloc.[5]

The famous legislative achievements of the Progressive Era are truly remarkable, even if they tended as they did toward regulation (in contrast to redistribution) to balance the power between society and the corporation. The list includes the Pure Food and Drug Act (1906), the Meat Inspection Act (1906), the Hepburn Act (railroad rates, 1906), and the Federal Reserve Act (1913), to name some of the highlights. There were also key Progressive Era constitutional amendments: democratic demand for direct election of senators, religiously infused success of prohibition, and the moral power of women's suffrage. These complemented state reforms that included direct primaries, referendums, recalls, and initiatives.

Of the many acts and amendments of the first two decades of the twentieth century, a few stand out as being especially significant for the future development of the New Deal. One is the Clayton Anti-Trust Act (1914), which purported to exempt unions from anti-trust legislation—a feature that did not last long after the courts finished with it. The Clayton Act did, however, make a very important philosophical point, one that had proved elusive in the Age of Incorporation: "the labor of a human being is not a commodity or article of commerce"—an important philosophical first step toward regulating the labor market. Another was the Sixteenth Amendment, which established the power of the federal government to levy tax on income, a new source of federal revenue that, after World War II, would also become a key instrument for regulating income and distribution of capital.

This rush of progressive legislation slammed headlong into the court's historic hostility to regulating the labor market. The "law in spirit is individualistic" triumphantly proclaimed an economist in 1923, but that individualism was highly selective. While incorporated capital enjoyed uncontested status as an individual and, as such, enjoyed equal protection under the Fourteenth Amendment, workers did not. Prior to the 1930s, the U.S. and state governments' hostility to the collective interests of working people was unremitting and often violent. Justifications for state involvement were grounded in broad, often counterintuitive interpretations of law.

During the first half of the nineteenth century, the "conspiracy doctrine," an import from British common law, held that workers in pursuit of their collective interests constituted a conspiracy against the common good. Later, it became common to find that workers seeking collective representation violated "liberty of contract"—that is, an individual worker's right to make his own independent deal. Many pathways led employers to the courts when labor disputes emerged, but prior to the New Deal many of those paths ended in the same place: the injunction. Once an injunction was issued, then organizing workers were in violation of the courts. Sending in the state militia to break up unions was often the next step. As one contemporary put it in the *Harvard Law Review*, "In these days of huge and powerful corporations, which form in the eyes of the law single persons . . . why should the law be such that if two steel workers plan a certain act which the law regards as tortuous, they should be subject to fine and imprisonment; but if, let us say, the United States Steel Corporation plans and executes the self-same act, the criminal law should be unable to touch it." It was a question that haunted labor relations for decades.[6]

The example of the New York State Bakeshop Act is illustrative. The act was passed in order to regulate the number of hours that bakers could work—partially because baking was a dangerous occupation, but also because skilled craft union bakers were trying to thwart immigrant workers who were willing to work more than 10 hours per day and 60 hours per week. In *Lochner v. New York* (1905), the Supreme Court ruled that New York's regulation of hours was a violation of the Fourteenth Amendment, an "unreasonable, unnecessary and arbitrary interference with the right and liberty of the individual to contract." This decision launched what is often called the "*Lochner* era"—a period of sustained, ideologically rigid, court opposition to regulation of hours and wages that lasted into the second half of the 1930s.

In contrast to the United States, most Western industrializing democracies had made significant strides in creating a variety of public benefits, regulations, and labor protections by the early twentieth century, which the United States proved uniquely slow in doing. Pensions for Civil War soldiers had been the only experiment of any size in federal public benefits prior to the twentieth century. Veterans and their dependents, the logic went, constituted a uniquely meritorious group deserving of state largesse because of their participation in the Union cause. Despite the best efforts of some reformers, Civil War pensions could not be transformed into a broader welfare system comparable to those of other advanced industrial countries. In progressives' demand for "good government," pensions were more typically seen as a source of patronage and corruption rather than the type of advancement in economic security upon which reformers could build. "From Mugwumps to progressive reformers," argues sociologist Theda Skocpol, "many elite and middle-class Americans viewed Civil War pensions as a prime example of governmental profligacy and electorally rooted political corruptions." Indeed, outside of veteran pensions, there were few protections that could prevent male breadwinners facing unemployment or disability from descending into poverty.[7]

Comparative history suggests that strong welfare states tended to be the product of vigorous labor movements and densely woven civil societies that could make direct claims for social citizenship—key elements missing in U.S. federal politics. The varieties of capitalism and the varieties of welfare states globally have been heterogeneous, but the United States, especially compared with other advanced industrial powers, such as Germany and Great Britain, lagged behind in both legislative achievements and concerted working-class demands that would lead toward the development of strong welfare states.

In a world in which even the major labor federation, the AFL, opposed social insurance, women played the most significant role in carving progressive paths around the American tradition of anti-statism. The hostility toward a broader political agenda for all workers created some traction for regulating work for women. In the absence of protections for even male breadwinners (what might be called "paternalist" reforms), an emerging *maternalist* welfare state partially filled the void. In lieu of European-style state development, gender-specific tactics for solving labor market problems functioned as "surrogates" that, in the absence of robust and successful class-based strategies, sought to solve the particular problems of women. Put another way, the lack of strong class cohesion resulted in "more space left for maternalism in the shaping of fledgling modern social politics." Women, like veterans, could be seen as a specific group

worthy of protection—an exemption to the otherwise unregulated general labor market. As a result, women as advocates, recipients, and often administrators of the incipient
welfare state played a unique role in shaping the benefits for
a particularly "worthy" group.[8]

The courts' insistence on the unconstitutionality of wages
and hours legislation stymied reformers until well into the
New Deal Era. Three years after its rejection of hours regulation in *Lochner*, the court upheld hours legislation specifically for women in *Muller v. Oregon* (1908). "The physical
well-being of woman becomes an object of public interest
and care in order to preserve the strength and vigor of the
race," argued the court, "she is properly placed in a class by
herself, and legislation designed for her protection may be
sustained, even when like legislation is not necessary for
men and could not be sustained." There were even minimum wage laws for women in many states prior to the decision in *Adkins v. Children's Hospital* (1923), in which the
Supreme Court found minimum wages—even for women—
to be in violation of liberty of contract. The regulation of
women's work therefore formed a possitive exception, if a
checkered one, to pre–New Deal history.

Paralleling the idea of veterans as a special class worthy
of pensions, many states passed Mothers' Aid or Mothers'
Pensions laws. Pioneered by Illinois and Missouri in 1911,
by 1930 Mothers' Pensions had been enabled in forty-six of
the forty-eight states. The state laws merely allowed counties to enact a pension system and carried no state funding
or administration. Such pensions provided public funds to
keep families together and out of poverty in the absence of
a male breadwinner. Even though many states passed enabling legislation for such pensions, funding and implementation was typically left to cities and counties. Payments
were tiny, legislation was weak and vulnerable to attack, eli-

gibility restrictions were tough, and recipients were few in number. When the Depression hit, however, much of the local patchwork of funding for the pension system was quickly drained in the crisis, leaving mothers in the lurch when it mattered most.[9]

Mothers' Pensions would later become the foundation for Aid to Dependent Children (ADC) of the Social Security Act (1935). Often criticized for its punitive and selective implementation, ADC's target was also narrow: keeping poor white women in the home raising children when male workers had died, disappeared, or become disabled. ADC remained connected to a problematic stigma for recipients. As Linda Gordon points to the irony of this history, ADC was designed not in backrooms by misogynist politicians but by moralistic Progressive reformers who wanted to keep women out of the labor market and in the care of children. Yet it was all a product of the stringent limits on the prospects of American reform. The gender exemption to the "great exception" was as real as it was limited.[10]

In the first decades of the twentieth century, just as it had for the last two decades of the nineteenth century, class conflict continued to rage—in New York City's garment trades; at the "Bread and Roses" strike in Lawrence, Massachusetts; among the silk workers in Paterson, New Jersey; in Colorado's Ludlow massacre; and many, many others. Theodore Roosevelt seemed to signal a new day by helping to set up arbitration for striking coal miners in 1902, as coal operators fumed at unprecedented federal intervention in business affairs. For the most part, women, African Americans, and immigrants had little contact with the unions of the American Federation of Labor, though they did get the attention of the radical Industrial Workers of the World.

Perhaps the most iconic labor conflict was the Uprising of the Twenty Thousand in New York City, in which young, female, mostly Jewish, shirtwaist makers braved almost three months of often freezing cold temperatures on the picket lines, at times with their middle-class women allies, to try to bring justice to a subcontracting system that made garment work into sweatshop labor. Facing down the manufacturers, the police, and the courts, the shirtwaist strikers won significant gains, all of which fell short of recognition of the closed shop. A year later, the Triangle Shirtwaist Factory caught fire, and 146 garment workers either died in the flames or jumped to their deaths from the eighth and ninth floors. While the tragedy resulted in changes in New York City politics and a new set of city fire, safety, and sanitary legislation, it also foreshadowed the future. A reformer named Frances Perkins had watched the fire in horror, and it became a turning point in a career that would eventually lead her to become secretary of labor under FDR. New York State senator Robert F. Wagner served as chairman of the Factory Investigating Committee; when he later became a U.S. senator and prominent New Dealer, he sponsored the central enabling legislation for the modern American labor movement, the National Labor Relations Act (1935), known more commonly as the Wagner Act.

While all of the strikes in the first part of the twentieth century often helped workers gain a decent settlement, they typically fell short of winning union recognition or collective bargaining agreements—especially for industrial workers. Middle-class progressives often sided with labor in the abstract but would prove suspicious of working-class independence in reality and quite fearful of radical intruders in industrial life in general. Middle-class progressive thought centered on an abiding faith that individualism and class harmony would flourish if more avenues were opened to hard work, education, initiative, and upward mobility—echoes of free labor ideology in a new political era. Placing an emphasis on the Deweyan community, social harmony, voluntary association, and, when necessary, the state, many middle-class progressives believed that the jungle of the market could be tamed without collective representation. To most, rationalization, regulation, and moral uplift appeared to be enough.

―――――――――――

Although progressivism typically had its richest and most radical expressions on the local level, the four-way presidential race in 1912 brought political conflicts about the crisis of the individual in the corporate state to the national stage. All candidates were nominally progressive, all were concerned about the fate of democracy in the age of economic concentration. And all of them had different answers.

The resurgent Theodore Roosevelt, running as a Bull Moose Progressive since his erstwhile protégé William Howard Taft had the Republican nomination sewn up, proclaimed the need for "more active governmental interference with social and economic conditions in this country than we have yet had." His ambitious agenda, influenced by Herbert Croly's *The Promise of American Life* (1909), included wide-ranging labor reforms, social insurance, and government regulations. His platform came close to a proto–New Deal vision, at times even exceeding the reforms that proved possible decades later. Woodrow Wilson campaigned to redouble the Democratic Party's allegiance to the Jeffersonian vision by using the state to open up new paths of entrepreneurial and individual initiative. He advocated "a body of laws which will look after the men who are on the make rather than the men who are already made," arguing that "Ours is a program of liberty, and theirs is a program of regulation." Eugene Debs attempted to preserve American democracy through a socialist republic, uniting themes of republicanism and independence through democratic socialism. Finally, despite the fact that his trust-busting efforts exceeded even TR's, William Howard Taft's tactless, rump effort to defend his technocratic and legalistic progressivism left him most closely aligned with the powers of big business.[11]

"In the election of 1912," the historian Jackson Lears summarized it, "TR stood at Armageddon, Taft stood pat, and Wilson easily defeated his divided opponents." Debs's 6 percent of the vote was "an indication of just how far the election had swung to the view that monopoly capitalism must somehow be tamed." Yet even when voters were united in their demand for change at the high-water mark of an era of reform, they remained politically fractious.[12]

Indirectly benefiting from the discord of so many progressive voices, Wilson won two terms from 1913 to 1921—one defined by keeping the nation out of war, and the other defined by sending the nation to war. Though occasionally pious and often nostalgic, Wilson was a genuine believer in reform. His dream of restoring small-town individualism was by definition a chimera, but one with broad appeal in American political culture. As the journalist Walter Lippman critiqued the politics of reviving that Lincoln-esque small-proprietor America in his famous *Drift or Mastery* (1914):

Those who cling to the village view of life may deflect the drift, may batter the trusts around a bit, but they will never dominate business, never humanize its machinery, and they will continue to be playthings of industrial change. At the bottom the issue is between those who are willing to enter upon effort for which there is no precedent, and those who aren't.[13]

As it turned out, Wilson lost track of his vision for a robust domestic agenda as he allowed World War I to seduce him into believing he could change not just his nation but the world. The outbreak of war in the fall of 1914 increasingly occupied Wilson's attention, and the administration's promise of strict oversight of trusts that were, or might become, full-scale monopolies turned more benign. The war caused the Progressive movement to lose direction, as long-held differences grew more intense—particularly in debates over America's role in the world. Reelected in 1916, the Progressive Wilson was ever more absent, as his administration embraced demands for "100% Americanism" and trammeled First Amendment liberties with the Espionage and Sedition Acts. The New Freedom ended ironically, in an enormous, if temporary, concentration of governmental power in a quixotic, tragic, effort to remake the world.

For labor, the war was the "event without precedent" that Lippman had mentioned as it found a new ally in the federal government. The *New Republic*, stunned by the sudden changes, announced, "We have already passed to a new era, the transition to a state in which labor will be the predominating element." Mobilization provided a model for how important the support of the federal government could be to the erstwhile "pure and simple" philosophy of the AFL. Woodrow Wilson and the AFL had formed a pragmatic political partnership prior to the outbreak of hostilities in Europe. The Wilson-initiated U.S Commission on Industrial Relations (USCIR), charged with investigating the reasons for massive labor unrest, declared in unambiguously bold terms, "Political freedom can exist only where there is industrial freedom; political democracy only where there is industrial democracy." When the United States entered the war, many of the ideas of the USCIR found expression in the National War Labor Board (NWLB) in a way that explicitly connected concern for labor to nationalist pride. Progressives began talking of the "de-Kaisering" of industry in favor of the USCIR's exciting, if nebulous, new term "industrial democracy." As a result of federal investment in this idea, by the end of the war, AFL membership had grown to 3.2 million—a million more than before the war. When FDR took office, the wartime mobilization was his political metaphor for how best to handle the crisis of the Great Depression.[14]

Yet as soon as the war ended, the federal interest in labor peace rapidly melted away. The NWLB lasted barely more than a year. After the allied victory, a pallor fell over the Progressive agenda—especially with regard to labor. As Wilson's labor mediator Felix Frankfurter wrote to friends, "Now the starch is out of the administration. Cold feet prevail on a wide area. . . . [Wilson's] subordinates are meek and timid. They have practically announced bankruptcy and invited the Republicans as receivers. God help us!" The emerging conservative coalition of the Democratic South and pro-business Republicans proved particularly anxious to end the government's "industrial democracy" experiment. Once the NWLB collapsed, Wilson distanced himself from labor, the Red Scare justified the elimination of radicals, immigrants, and subversives from society, and the AFL union membership once more dropped to prewar levels. The defeat of an industry-wide steel strike in 1919—along with drives in meatpacking, police, and the Seattle General Strike—demonstrated that without government support—or at least neutrality—corporate opposition could not be overcome. Labor won the war, but dramatically lost the peace. (See the dramatic rise and fall of union density after World War I on page 11.)[15]

Progressivism's ideals were never far from issues of ethnic and racial purity. Enforcement of racial boundaries was often seen as a Progressive achievement. The question of African American freedom never became part of the Progressive agenda in a significant way—they rarely challenged the existing racial order of Jim Crow in the South or de facto segregation in the North. Woodrow Wilson, a son of the Confederacy, resegregated parts of the federal government, believed that "segregation is not a humiliation but a benefit," and wrote of Reconstruction as a "dark chapter" in American history. Support for the decades-long struggle for a federal anti-lynching law was tepid, and only a minority of white Progressives supported the National Association for the Advancement of Colored People (NAACP) after its 1909 founding. Some even held that disfranchisement of African Americans, as of the new immigrants, actually preserved American ideals, in a reactionary sense of racialized nationalism. Between the different immigrant groups, sharp tensions existed over competition for jobs, control of neighborhoods, and education—and even sharper tensions existed between immigrant working people and African Americans. For former sharecroppers who came North during the war to work in defense production in the Great Migration, tensions, segregation, and race riots pockmarked the path to economic freedom.[16]

Fear that too many Jews, Catholics, and other immigrants were watering down the old stock of Protestant Americans continued to define American politics. Many elites advocated literacy tests as a mechanism for keeping foreigners out of the United States. Magazines like *The Menace*, which whipped up fears that Catholicism was a threat to Americanism, had a circulation of one million by 1914. Madison Grant's notorious *The Passing of the Great Race* (1916) was a popular and militant defense of Anglo-Saxonism in the face of race mixing. The arguments and fears that immigrants were responsible for the undoing of America ran the gamut: they were responsible for the declining intelligence of Americans, they possessed a genetic propensity for crime, they had a weakness for anarchism and political violence, they tended toward begging and general pauperism, and even their facial features were inferior to the native born.[17]

Joining the expansion of democracy as a key unifying element of middle-class progressivism, ironically, was an obsessive preoccupation with the vice, morality, and virtue of these newly arrived groups. Born from a combination of the social gospel, fear of immigrants, and class antipathy, the progressives' emphasis on character, cleanliness, Americanization, and prohibition played an enormous role in shaping the "moral community" of the day. In fact, the key element that would set apart the reform efforts of the 1930s from those of the previous fifty years, argues Gary Gerstle, was that in the 1930s the American people were divided less into moral and ethnic categories, and more into economic ones. In contrast to the shifting questions of values in the Progressive Era, in the 1930s, "Economic issues, metaphors, and antagonists" would dominate "the New Deals' language of political mobilization and conflict"—but would only do so until cultural values returned once again to dominate the political scene in the 1970s and beyond.[18]

The culmination of a series of restrictions and quotas following the wartime decline in immigration, the Johnson-

Reed Immigration Act was designed, in the words of the U.S. Department of State Office of the Historian, "to preserve the ideal of American homogeneity." Influenced by a wide array of arguments with regard to racial purity, eugenics, "mongrelization," and ethno-racial essentialisms of many kinds, the act closed down an open-border policy with regard to European immigration that had endured for nearly one hundred and fifty years. In a shockingly explicit statement of the Darwinist logic behind this decision, Congressman Fred S. Purnell, a Republican from Indiana, declared, "There is little or no similarity between the clear-thinking, self-governing stocks that sired the American people and this stream of irresponsible and broken wreckage that is pouring into the lifeblood of America the social and political diseases of the Old World."[19]

The act restricted immigration to 2 percent of the total national population as of the 1890 census, which radically favored Northern European peoples whose countrymen arrived before the "new immigration" from Southern and Eastern Europe. In addition, Johnson-Reed also all but eliminated nonwhite immigration from origins outside the Western Hemisphere—an important exemption demanded by Western agriculture, which depended on labor from Mexico. As the historian Mae Ngai puts it, "the national origins quota system proceeded from the conviction that the American nation was, and should remain, a white nation descended from [Northern] Europe."[20]

While fundamentally racist, the restriction of immigration in 1924 had the ironic effect of hastening the process of integration for many newer immigrants who had previously lived in ethnic enclaves, ultimately leading to a lessening of ethnic tensions and fragmentation among working people. The "breathing space" that immigration restrictionists discussed did help create stability of the older immi-

grants' residency and allowed once-racialized peoples from
Southern and Eastern Europe, Catholics and Jews, to become "white" in the eyes of native-born Americans and
"their" state. By the time FDR took office, there had been
precious little immigration to the United States since World
War I—a span of nearly two decades—and some of the
most divisive elements in American politics since the middle
of the nineteenth century had abated. This gave the U.S.
polity—at least those regarded as within the realm of citizenship—an illusion of homogeneity that surpassed any
seen in generations.[21]

The fundamental problem with Democratic reform politics in the Progressive Era may have been most directly attacked in John Chamberlain's *Farewell to Reform* (1932).
The New York literary critic ripped into the antiquated,
misty-eyed, idealistic forms of individualism that lay at the
heart of American politics during the Progressive Era—especially singling out Wilson's New Freedom. Eviscerating
his subject, he argued, "In the United States 'reform' has
always had a 'return' connotation," in which the historic
purpose of the Progressive movement in America had been
to restore the "methods and possibilities of a more primitive
capitalism." That nostalgic impulse had to be vanquished in
American life, Chamberlain believed, along with reformers'
paranoia about the existence of big corporations, their fight
against the trusts, and their search for a restoration of the
Jeffersonian ideal. It was the republican nostalgia holding
Americans back; the idyll of preindustrial individualism had
a conceptual stranglehold on an age in which it simply
no longer applied. The New Freedom "was looking both
backward and forward, hoping somehow to restore the age
of competition in an age whose technological discoveries
worked irresistibly toward mass action, mass marketing,
mass bargaining at the factory door." Yet spanning the ines-

capable individualist ideologies and the need for modes to distribute the largesse of corporate capitalism remains the most difficult task in American politics.[22]

The elasticity of individualism carried different meanings during this era, as Americans struggled to find a cohesive alternative language to express the role of the individual in the corporate era. Calls to transcend self-interest came from both Theodore Roosevelt and the socialist Eugene Debs, in contrast to Wilson's more familiar charge to preserve opportunity for the man on the make. But beyond the intellectual and political elite, American political rhetoric of individualism reflected the gravitational pull of earlier usage, even as the weight of corporate power continued its transformation of the society. Except during wartime, the progressives showed an equal inability to confront the American tradition of anti-statism, which Grant McConnell described accurately as "the pervasive and latent ambiguity in the movement."[23]

Further crippled by their inability to rise above the nation's legacies of racism and unable to deal with the problems of class as they emerged from events as disparate as the calls for "industrial democracy" or the Great Steel Strike of 1919, ultimately the progressives offered vital critiques of the new corporate order, made important efforts to regulate it, but stopped far short of finding ways to redistribute its bounty.

———

Various forms of moralism, typically religiously inflected, had been a core part of the history of American politics. Since the Civil War, social and economic upheavals fed a continuous stream of anti-modernist thought in American culture, and the period immediately after World War I saw a rising wave of Protestant fundamentalism. Scientism, secular reform, and the failed military crusade in Europe (aggressively opposed by the nation's leading evangelical, William Jennings Bryan) led many whose traditions had been turned upside down to seek a return to religious "fundamentals." William B. Riley organized the World's Christian Fundamentals Association in 1919, seeking to reestablish religious faith against the degeneration of the secular world order. At the founding convention, he railed against the ways in which Protestant denominations were "rapidly coming under the leadership of the new infidelity, known as 'modernism.' " In its fight against the teaching of the scientific theory of evolution, the new fundamentalism found a vocal ally in Bryan, who had been fighting the idea of evolution for two decades, insistently asking "What shall it profit a man if he shall gain all the learning of the schools and lose his faith in God?"[24]

William Jennings Bryan, the Great Commoner who carried the Democratic flag into three presidential contests as well as serving his term as secretary of state under Wilson, was in many ways the very embodiment of progressive Democratic reform. Yet it was this same Bryan whose faith led him into his anti-evolutionary stand in the Scopes "Monkey" Trial in 1925. Social conservatism and reform were not that far apart. His anti-evolutionary position was in sync with his progressivism, as it sprang forth from his confidence in the sentiments of the majority of the people, his belief in the reforming crusade, and, above all, his belief in the scriptures. Throughout his life, he delivered a uniquely American combination of independence, anti-statism, and the Holy Spirit—best summarized by his biographer as "Jefferson and Jesus"—all of which combined

with the promise of direct and democratic access to the
Lord, the Declaration of Independence, and equality before
God and man.[25]

Squaring off against Bryan at the Scopes "Monkey"
Trial was Clarence S. Darrow, defender of science, evolution, and the Enlightenment. The result was that religious
fundamentalism, mocked into irrelevance by H. L. Menck-
en's sardonic commentary on the trial, appeared to have
been vanquished as an important factor in modern America. Hardly finished, the fundamentalists turned toward
building a potent and widespread alternative culture that
nurtured their faith and would, in time, return in force to
the public square. The public scorn heaped upon the fundamentalists forced religious activists to turn away from
political engagement to focus on their communities of
faith. In so doing, Scopes helped launch modern liberalism
by separating reform from a preoccupation with the pious
and righteous. What appeared to be a clear-cut victory for
modernity would prove only a temporary triumph.[26]

Polyglot America often proved at war with itself, as religious conflict mapped almost directly onto immigration
conflict, making it among the most intractable set of problems in American politics. John Dewey, a philosopher of tremendous faith in humans' capacity to resolve their problems
in democratic fashion, despaired over the racial and ethnic
conflict he saw raging in the United States. "Individuals here
and there achieve freedom from prejudice and rational control of instinctive bias with comparative ease," he believed,
"but the mass cannot attain it." For the immediate future,
he saw "no great hope for alleviation. The simple fact of the
case is that at present the world is not sufficiently civilized
to permit close contact of peoples of widely different cultures without deplorable consequences." The Johnson-Reed
Immigration Act of 1924 proved Dewey's point.[27]

By the 1920s, with immigration restricted, the strike wave of 1919 crushed, radicalism routed, and a minimal structure of economic regulation in place, the locus of reform efforts moved toward enlightened capitalism. "Long-standing concerns" about capitalism "centered on the problematic relationship between economic concentration and democracy," writes Mark Hendrickson. With the rise of the "new capitalism" of the 1920s, this older view had been "replaced with a new vision of a highly productive and expanding consumer-driven economy," one in which the answers to the "labor question" could be found within the business enterprise itself. It began to seem possible to create a high-wage, high-consumption economy in which workers could be partners and consumers in the industrial enterprise, not simply raw and dispensable labor power. If the labor force could transcend its discontent, then a stable body of workers who were also consumers could absorb the dizzying new array of consumer goods produced by immense leaps in productivity. Most economic thought and business practice in the 1920s, however, focused almost exclusively on expansion of output rather than redistribution—the very problem that helped usher in the Great Depression.[28]

While the New Deal and the decades to follow would focus on the "countervailing powers" necessary to redistribute wealth and income, the new capitalism of the 1920s tried to present itself as a kinder, gentler, reformed incarnation of corporate capitalism. A set of programs developed in the 1900s to stave off both the unionization efforts and the progressive state became known as "welfare capitalism." Though perhaps overplayed as a precursor to New Deal reforms among historians, it did set a higher standard

for what workers might be able to expect from the employment relationship. Proponents advocated treating workers
in more humane and dignified ways through various forms
of corporate paternalism. Adopted mostly in the largest and
most generous corporations, welfare capitalism schemes
served only a limited number of workers. Still, the programs
won the allegiance of many employees through employee
stock ownership plans, recreation clubs, sports teams, loans,
education, and employee representation organizations—
that is to say, company unions. Effectively co-opting and
taming the idea of "industrial democracy" that had flour-
ished so strongly in the previous decade, corporations
brought demands for change into their own purview and
sponsored them in limited, self-serving, tightly controlled
ways. Yet welfare capitalist activities did raise a new sense
of possibility when it came to the employment relationship—suggesting that even industrial workers should expect their workplace to be more than just a place to sell
their labor power. When these programs collapsed, workers
slowly turned to the state and the labor movement to fill the
gap of economic security originally promised by welfare
capitalism.[29]

Historians have tended to see welfare capitalism as a
stopgap between progressivism and the New Deal, but had
it not been for the economic, and thus political, trauma of
the 1930s, the course of corporate paternalism might well
have continued uninterrupted as the main current of American industrial relations. As David Brody argues, "It is comforting to think that welfare capitalism never was a success,
never persuaded workingmen that they were best off as
wards of the employer, and never took deep roots in the
American industrial order. The facts, however, suggest otherwise." Furthermore, the boss's answer to "the labor question" hardly disappeared during the Great Depression.

Never fully bankrupted by the Depression nor defeated by New Deal policies, welfare capitalism went on hiatus but would return. The push for a moral capitalism from above in the 1920s helped feed the rise of the labor movement when capitalism failed. But that top-down approach to employment relations also returned to fill the void when the labor movement collapsed in the 1970s and beyond.[30]

Changes in business culture also had the ironic result of boosting social unity. With corporate-sponsored "Americanization" initiatives, the rise of national standards in branding, marketing, and communication, as well as a large number of national chains usurping the roles of small-proprietor ethnic capitalism, many urban workers found themselves swept up in a mass market. Similarly, the reorganization of production over the previous decades, engineered by Frederick Winslow Taylor, Henry Ford, and their associates, also restructured group identity, particularly by leveling the distinction between skilled and unskilled workers.[31]

Finally, the civic mythology of individualism in America still ran deep, that is, until the bottom dropped out of both the economy and the ideology as the Great Depression dragged on. Herbert Hoover, who had done tremendous things in the field of humanitarian service, closed his 1928 campaign with a speech of unintended irony titled "Rugged Individualism." "By adherence to the principles of decentralized self-government, ordered liberty, equal opportunity, and freedom to the individual," Hoover declared, "our American experiment in human welfare has yielded a degree of well-being unparalleled in the world. It has come nearer to the abolition of poverty, to the abolition of fear of want, than humanity has ever reached before. Progress of the past seven years is proof of it." The following year, the U.S. economy collapsed, and immediately reframed Hoover's certainty and declaration of "progress" as the naïve optimism of a bygone era. The ethos of individualism faded slowly, not immediately, even in the dark early years of the Depression. Hoover's ideas were eventually repudiated both economically and politically, as the United States launched the boldest set of domestic reforms in its history. By 1930, John Dewey dismissed Hoover's ideal as not rugged but "ragged" individualism. To the degree that following decades would overcome those antiquated ideas, however, it would do so only partially and only temporarily.[32]

———————

Perhaps one of the most common historical fallacies is to see the Progressive Era as a mere dress rehearsal for the "real" age of reform—the New Deal. The connection seems obvious enough. One can see premonitions of the New Deal in Roosevelt's "New Nationalism" speech of 1910 in Osawatomie, Kansas, and in the state's planning for World War I. One can see it in the progressive reform impulse to rebalance power relations between corporations and the people, and in the desire to tame the labor question. Yet to frame the New Deal as simply the next step forward in the development of the Progressive Era makes a risky historical leap. Not only does this logic suggest a Whiggish narrative of the welfare state's ascent to its natural modern form, it reduces the visibility of the Progressive Era's own complexities, which prove both damning and instructive for understanding the New Deal. Furthermore, it discounts the role of frankly extraordinary global economic circumstances in setting the stage for and solidifying the advances of the New Deal order.

There were elements of the Progressive Era that did prove to be dress rehearsals, but without the economic crisis, one might wonder if the reformers' ideas of that age would have found much political traction. Lacking an explicit ideology, formula, or definition of what was to be done besides promoting the ebullient radiance of the new president himself, the New Dealers exchanged and debated ideas, some of which turned into bold new legislation and others into terrible policy failures. Only mobilization for World War I and the unfulfilled promises of FDR's cousin Teddy had begun to approximate the active government role in economic planning that would unfurl in the 1930s and 1940s. Yet "planning" is still too bold a word for the New Dealers' lurching series of pragmatic, sometimes incoherent, attempts to control the greatest economic crisis in the nation's history. For a few charmed years, the president held sway with Congress in an unprecedented manner. Even the Supreme Court eventually followed suit. The New Deal broke with American political traditions more dramatically than any other period since the Civil War, ushering in an unprecedented age of rough and incomplete, but nonetheless real, economic justice.[33]

Despite the many changes and reforms of the first two decades of the twentieth century, it is folly to see a simple linear relationship between the advances of the Progressive Era and what was to come. The reforms prior to the stock market crash had been exhausted, even though strong precedents had been established. Even with the working-class and progressive triumphs, the New Deal, particularly in labor policy, remains very much a "big bang" in American political history.[34]

Chrysler Sit-Down Strike, 1937. Workers occupying an auto plant show their intention to defy the law by ceremonially shredding a court injunction. With the Wagner Act, workers found a new, if temporary, ally in the federal government.
Courtesy of Walter P. Reuther Library, Archives of Labor and Urban Affairs, Wayne State University.

CHAPTER THREE

WORKING-CLASS INTERREGNUM

In a presidential campaign appearance broadcast coast-to-coast in April 1932, Franklin Delano Roosevelt delivered one of his most revealing speeches, "The Forgotten Man," to his largest audience to date. As the Great Depression dragged through its third dismal year, Roosevelt's claim on the Democratic nomination laid out a vision for how a broad coalition of shopkeepers and professionals, farmers and working people, both employed and unemployed, could be mobilized by the state as if for war. "These unhappy times call for the building of plans that rest upon the forgotten, the unorganized but indispensable units of economic power, for plans like those of 1917, that build from the bottom up and not from the top down, that put their faith once more in the forgotten man at the bottom of the economic pyramid." He sought to unite "Main Street, Broadway, the mines, the mills," and farmers in a vision of shared sacrifice, accountability, and recovery all built around the sense of capacity and urgency shown during the extraordinary federal mobilization for World War I.[1]

FDR's speech laid out the tentative beginning of a new political vision that would—slowly and episodically, unevenly and incompletely—create modern liberalism. By the time of his reelection in 1936, he would head a political coalition based on the forgotten people that would grow to dominate the middle of the twentieth century. It was as great a rupture with political tradition as any peacetime president had ever made.

In its most favorable light, the New Deal and the postwar New Deal order appeared to be a permanent vision of economic security for the American people—an economic enfranchisement of the forgotten man that gave him a fighting chance with the power of the corporation. On closer examination, however, it seems a chaotic and tenuous legislative beast. Its policy initiatives were often dramatic but nonetheless compromised by some of the confounding issues in American political culture. The combination of inviolability and vulnerability, grand superstructure and shifting foundations, made the New Deal less a permanent revolution than a decades-long experiment in the economic enfranchisement of the American working class.

The roots of the phrase "forgotten man" are telling. Brain Truster Raymond Moley lifted the phrase from social Darwinist William Graham Sumner's 1883 address by the same name. Sumner's original incarnation was one of uncompromising independence, a figure wanting little more than freedom from the interventionist state and the nagging concerns of the undeserving poor. "What the Forgotten Man really wants," Sumner argued, "is true liberty"—from anything that held him down, be it the poor, the state, or the do-gooder who tried to mobilize both. Sumner's forgotten man had no responsibility for the "nasty, shiftless, criminal, whining, crawling, and good-for-nothing people." While few believed in Sumner's ruthless brand of social Darwinism, even in the Gilded Age, the historic brand of individual rights liberalism he espoused remained a central animating principle in American politics and law. Moley, responding to what he saw as the "despair, frustration, and privation" of the Depression, inverted Sumner's use of the phrase, and in so doing, overturned the entire premise of ruthless individualism on which it was based. FDR's forgotten man was an individual, to be sure, but one enmeshed in a shared national fate. His liberty would not be assured by insulating him from the pesky demands of those in need, but through a new kind of freedom grounded in economic security— rather than a freedom from barriers, this promised the foundation for freedom of action and the ability to direct one's own life.[2]

Even in the dark days of the Depression, with nearly one out of three workers unemployed, *Time* magazine dismissed FDR's appeal to the forgotten man as "rabble rousing." Many Democratic traditionalists—including Al Smith, previous Democratic presidential candidate and Roosevelt's touch-and-go ally—were nothing short of apoplectic. Fears of centralized federal power had cemented political links between urban machines like Smith's Tammany Hall and the Democrats of the South and West, forging an odd coalition that perceived the state as a force mostly likely to be used against them and for the industrialists and the WASP and Republican establishment. Even in the worst of economic times, Smith believed, the rhetoric of class antagonism, let alone the policy concerns that went along with it, had no place in American politics. "I will take off my coat and fight to the end against any candidate who persists in demagogic appeals to the masses of the working people of this country to destroy themselves by setting class against class, rich against poor," Smith fumed, in terms understood by many Democratic Party regulars.[3]

As Democratic campaigns progressed to the national convention at Chicago Stadium in July 1932, Roosevelt continued to struggle to define his new politics. He defeated Al Smith, winning the nomination by placating the powerful Southern and Western wings of the party (to which he largely owed the nomination) by promising "bread not booze" to those fearful of an urban, Catholic, anti-prohibitionist "wet" like Smith. In his campaign, FDR also promised to balance the budget and, ironically, chastised Hoover for his extravagant federal spending. FDR's concern about federal deficits was not mere campaign rhetoric, as he continued to fret the red ink throughout his presidency. But his cautious campaign concealed bigger plans. He took the unprecedented, and certainly theatrical, step of flying to the convention to accept his nomination in person. "Let it be from now on the task of our Party to break foolish traditions," he boomed. While offering the expected paeans to the terrible cost and burdens of government spending, he declared that the way out of the "days of crushing want" would be through a pledge to deliver what he called, in vague but confident terms, "a new deal for the American people."[4]

What was this "New Deal" that was about to unfold, and how did the "forgotten man" fit in the bargain? Roosevelt himself hardly knew at that point. The explicit campaign promise was that a future Roosevelt administration would try something. "The country needs and, unless I mistake its temper, the country demands bold, persistent experimentation," he intoned. "It is common sense to take a method and try it: If it fails, admit it frankly and try another. But above all, try something."[5]

In his famous 1932 Commonwealth speech, FDR laid out a history of the individual's relationship to democracy and the economy. While holding sacrosanct individual liberty and responsibility, he declared the moment right for a "reappraisal of values," a process that would unfold in the years to come. The New Deal's spirit of experimentation ultimately concluded as a general commitment to economic security, expressed through a hodgepodge of programs and policies. Roosevelt's method was chaotic, yes, but slowly over the course of the 1930s and 1940s a set of answers emerged to the question that had dominated American politics since the dawn of the industrial age: what was the role of the individual in the mass industrial era?

If there was one theme, it was final abandonment of the party's dominant anti-monopoly tradition. The Democrats' historic mission had been to restore the individual smallholder and his community to a place of economic prominence through dismantling the trusts—and, often, the state that did their bidding. This was not an easy legacy to overcome, and it was not without costs. As Moley put it, even the Washington New Dealers still had to overcome the antiquated notion that lay at the heart of much of American politics: "that if America could once more become a nation of small proprietors, of corner grocers and smithies under spreading chestnut trees, we should have solved the problems of American life." Industry of once unimaginable scope and scale now dominated the economic landscape, and the "Brain Trust" that Roosevelt gathered around him had come to believe that the future of the political economy lay in regulating monopoly—not eliminating it. It was Rexford Tugwell, whose mind seemed to race faster than anyone else's, who put forth the "underconsumptionist" thesis: that workers' wages, and therefore buying power, had failed to keep up with the great leaps in productivity.[6]

When FDR assumed power with his inaugural address in March 1933, he delivered a final piece to his vision for the common man in the form of increased federal power to compensate for the failures of the market. "Only a foolish optimist can deny the dark realities of the moment," he declared to the throngs gathered in front of the Capitol. "The rulers of the exchange of mankind's goods have failed through their own stubbornness and their own incompetence, have admitted their failures and abdicated," he explained in an unprecedented presidential critique of the financial elite. "The money changers have fled from their high seats in the temple of our civilization. We may now restore that temple to the ancient truths. The measure of the restoration lies in the extent to which we apply social values more noble than mere monetary profit." He redoubled his demand that the federal government mobilize with the urgency of war—the only available analogue for national economic coordination—but did so in terms far more explicit than in his earlier campaign. "I shall ask the Congress for the one remaining instrument to meet the crisis—broad Executive power to wage a war against the emergency, as great as the power that would be given to me if we were in fact invaded by a foreign foe." After three years of desperate depression, the crowds gathered before the Capitol gave Roosevelt's demand for war powers the loudest applause of the speech.[7] It was a dramatic moment for a people known for their historic fear of centralized government authority.

The New Deal began with a bold call for a reconsideration of the individual's relationship to the state and the corporation, but the legislative path forward was long and confused. In retrospect, the New Deal can be divided into four phases—a device more intellectually useful than historically accurate—that help make sense of the lurching policy paths cut during FDR's extraordinary four elections to the presidency. The "first" New Deal, from 1933 to 1935, offered experimental policies but ended in a series of failures and significant changes in personnel. The "second" New Deal, from 1935 to 1938, followed, providing a more cohesive, proto-Keynesian, vision for reform and the most enduring policies—including Social Security, collective bargaining, and fair labor standards. This second New Deal consolidated Roosevelt's position as one of the most popular presidents in history—and one of the most visionary. By 1938, in what can be considered its third phase, the New Deal hit the ropes, entering an often-overlooked period of political retreat and retrenchment that threatened to stall, if not force into retreat, the rising welfare state. Finally, the task of winning another world war simultaneously consolidated existing policy achievements and curtailed further reforms. By the end of World War II, the experimentation with reform had ended in a new political order that embraced a regulatory regime of macro-economic planning for full employment that would finally transform the figure of the "forgotten man" into a mass of unforgotten consumers.

In sum, modern liberalism hardly emerged intact from FDR's First Hundred Days; rather, it took the better part of a decade, an unyielding economic crisis, a false start, and, finally, a world war, to achieve its high modern form. Perhaps the single best definition of what was about to unfold comes from Isaiah Berlin, who noted that the New Deal managed "to reconcile individual liberty . . . with the indispensable minimum of organizing and authority." That indispensable minimum, while transformative, was a relative newcomer to federal politics in the United States, and would prove vulnerable to some of the deeper impulses in American culture as the postwar order unfolded.[8]

———

Without the sense of dire urgency that built up between the stock market crash and the ascension of Roosevelt in 1933, it is possible to believe that there would have been no New Deal. The most extraordinary element in the creation of the new liberalism was arguably this sense of emergency itself. FDR took office over three years into the Depression, and

five months after an election that left his opponent Herbert
Hoover a lame duck bobbing helplessly in the crisis. Meanwhile, the economy continued to tumble without leadership
in the "interregnum of despair" between November and the
March inauguration. The savageries of the business cycle
and the many depressions in U.S. history had held working people hostage since the dawn of the republic, most of
which had ended in the empowering not of working people
but rather business. The misery of those years has become
almost too commonplace in popular lore—perhaps too
mythically familiar to elicit sympathies, too big to grasp,
too iconic to be real, and, most problematically, far too extraordinary to be a lasting framework for how American
politics might work in normal times. But there was a sense
in the 1930s that this economic crisis extended beyond "the
natural limit of personal imagination and sympathy," as
New Dealer Harry Hopkins put it. "You can pity six men,
but you can't keep stirred up over six million."[9]

Across the nation, 5,000 bank failures eliminated $7 bil-
lion in depositors' assets; hundreds of thousands of families
had lost their homes; farmers staggered under the burdens
of plummeting prices, drought, and debt; local and state
welfare agencies lay drained of resources; and the Gross
National Product (GNP) was cut in half. Farming, already
in depression for the better part of a decade, shriveled like
drought-stricken cotton. In Roosevelt's own New York, unemployment approached 30 percent, and between one-
quarter and one-third of the rest of the nation lay idle. The
people's deep and visceral loss of faith was evident in the
fact that even the birthrate declined during this period, and
the marriage rate slid by 22 percent. People who began to
wander the roads and the rails quickly found a new underground world of others in similar situations. *Fortune* magazine spoke of "the vast, homeless, horde" of young people,

which a twenty-year-old unemployed future broadcast journalist, Eric Sevareid, was forced to join. On the road, Sevareid entered

> a new social dimension, the great underground world,
> peopled by tens of thousands of American men,
> women, and children, white, black, brown, and yel-
> low, who inhabit the "jungle," eat from blackened tin
> cans, find warmth at night in the boxcars, take the sun
> by day on the flat cars, steal one day, beg with cap in
> hand the next, fight with fists and often razors, hold
> sexual intercourse under a blanket in a far corner of
> the crowded car, coagulate into pairs and gangs, then
> disintegrate again, wander from town to town, anx-
> ious for the next place, tire of it in a day, fretting to be
> gone again, happy only when the wheels are clicking
> under them, the telephone poles slipping by.[10]

The Great Depression was more than an economic description—it captured the national mood. Lorena Hickok,
a reporter whom Harry Hopkins had sent on a mission to
report on the condition of the nation's people, wrote back:
"I just can't describe to you some of the things I've seen and
heard down here these last few days. I shall never forget
them—never as long as I live," she wrote. "Southern farmer
workers, half-starved Whites and Blacks struggle in competition for less to eat than my dog gets at home, for the privilege of living in huts that are infinitely less comfortable than
his kennel."[11]

While the veterans known as the Bonus Marchers descended onto Washington by the tens of thousands to demand their bonus pay from World War I, and the Communists organized marches of the unemployed in Detroit, such
collective visions were not necessarily a unifying theme of
most responses to the early Great Depression. Rather, early

reactions were characterized by individuals personally shouldering the blame for their joblessness, and a deep burden of shame that went with it. The supposedly collectivist "red decade" actually featured a long line of individual declarations of self-blame, guilt, doubt, and despair. Given the massive economic failure, the ways in which working people internalized the blame for their situation bordered on the pathological. It is difficult not to be moved by the painful letters and memoirs of the 1930s that detailed neither strikes nor organizing meetings nor even direct political anger, but a painful sense of impotence and responsibility. "Can you be so kind as to advise me as to which would be the most human way to dispose of my self and family, as this is about the only thing that I see left to do," wrote a Pennsylvania man to the new president. "No home, no work, no money. We cannot go along this way." Robert McElvaine, having surveyed the letters of the unemployed to Roosevelt, summarized their widespread attitude succinctly: "There must be something wrong with a fellow who can't get a job."[12]

When Roosevelt took office, working people began to look to him personally as a beacon of hope—a political symbol that drew people out of the silence of their individual desperation, a figure who transformed the individual's relation to the state from something of an almost foreign distance to a sense of near intimacy. Almost half a million letters poured into the White House during FDR's first week of office alone. Like no previous president ever had, he served as a conduit for citizens' individual concerns, their personal connection with the government. As one person wrote to the new president,

Winter coming on, no coal in our coal bin, and the children needing warm clothes to go to school. . . . Is there some way or some person who I can go to that can help me through my difficulty[?]. I have never as yet begged, but must and will be very candid, that I would appreciate some kind of help for just a short period of time. . . . I have always put up a good fight, and worked many a day when I was almost unable to stand up; but all to no avail.

Even when appealing to the president, the epitome of public power, such requests were very much framed as an intimate, private affair. The preceding writer's one other request was that his name be kept confidential—his embarrassing plea was a personal matter between him and his president. Other letters asked for personal loans, gifts of old clothing, or intervention in the employment affairs in isolated hamlets across the nation. Some saw in him a class ally. As one South Carolina millhand put it, FDR was "the first man in the White House to understand that my boss is a son of a bitch."[13]

Between March and June of 1933, bewildered Americans rapidly found themselves enmeshed in a new world of federal programs, with an alphabet soup of abbreviations and symbols swirling about them in the "first" New Deal. Overnight—or at least over the course of one hundred days—business, workers, farmers, and bankers found their relationship to the state completely transformed, buoyed up by the hope of governmental action once the buoyantly optimistic president took office. Those hundred days saw a staggeringly large set of political and legislative accomplishments. "For a deceptive moment in 1933," explains Arthur Schlesinger, "clouds of inertia and selfishness seemed to lift." As FDR sensed, cultivating the *feeling* of action would be the government's most important contribution to recovery. In fact, much of this famous legislative wave would add up to a magnificent set of failures that lifted the spirits but only marginally helped the economy. But as Ray Moley explained, "It was enough to know that something was happening that had not happened before. The American People wanted their government to do something, anything, so long as it acted with assurance and vigor." There was more groping for solutions than there were obvious answers or unity of purpose. "It simply has to be admitted," explained Rexford Tugwell, "that Roosevelt was not yet certain what direction he ought to take and was, in fact, going both ways at once."[14]

Despite the emergency and his clear political mandate for action, FDR tended toward moderate legislative choices. The limits on the first New Deal could readily be seen in its first order of business: saving the banks. The new president immediately closed the banks for a "holiday" to give the administration a chance to figure out how to save the system. The legislative mood was such that the bank bill passed the Senate 73–7, with almost no debate or opportunity for amendment. There was not even enough time to print the bill—legislators voted on a copy read aloud. FDR could have ushered through most anything at that moment, but he cautiously chose one of the most conservative options available to him. Many believed that such a propitious moment was ripe for a more ambitious agenda: the creation of a truly national—even nationalized—banking system. Progressive senators Robert M. La Follette of Wisconsin and Edward P. Costigan of Colorado, for instance, called upon Roosevelt to rebuild the banking system as a unified national system. "That isn't necessary at all," Roosevelt explained in his irrepressibly exultant way. "I've just had every assurance of cooperation from the bankers." The same "money changers" Roosevelt had accused of fleeing the temple in the time of the people's need "were now swarming through the corridors of the Treasury."[15]

The bill turned out to be remarkably similar to what Hoover had hoped for late in his term but was unwilling to introduce without the new president's support. The Emergency Banking Act guaranteed the nation's banking system and got deposits flowing again, yet did so on the most conservative possible terms. Roosevelt then passed the Economy Bill, which, of all things, allowed him to cut government salaries and veterans' benefits. He then moved on to legalizing beer and wine in advance of the repeal of the Eighteenth Amendment. The *New Republic*, hoping for more progressive measures from the president and an anxiously compliant congress, feared that the first three elements of the New Deal meant they had helped to elect "the greatest President since Hoover."[16]

More visionary legislation quickly followed. The Civilian Conservation Corps put people to work developing natural areas and parks. The highly contested Agricultural Adjustment Act, a potpourri that included a little something for everyone in Congress who had a stake in agriculture, faced a two-month battle in Congress before finally passing. This legislation restricted agricultural output in order to drive up prices—an old economic remedy, but perhaps not the wisest in times of starvation and dire want. The Tennessee Valley Authority Act, one of the boldest and most radical departures for the federal government, promised regional development, hydroelectric power, soil conservation, and flood control using centralized federal planning that covered the seven states surrounding the Tennessee River—the single most aggressive regional planning endeavor ever in American history. In the financial sector, the Glass-Steagall Banking Act separated commercial banking from investment banking, and created the Federal Deposit Insurance Corporation (FDIC). The Securities and Exchange Commission (SEC), which provided oversight of the stock market, passed the following year. The abandonment of the gold standard sought to inflate the sagging currency, but also spoke to the continuity of the currency issue since the populist era. This line of legislation continued through federal relief, homeowner loans, farm credit, the railroads, and other areas.

━━━━━━━━━━

Rising above the legislative din in the first New Deal was the central effort at national economic planning, the famed National Industrial Recovery Act (NIRA) and its symbol of certified compliance, the blue eagle. If ever there was a piece of legislation that suggested the New Dealers' continued political confusion over democratizing the corporate economy, the NIRA was it. The legislation was a set of initiatives that once would have been Democratic anathema, including micromanagement of the industrial economy by suspending anti-trust rules and ceding the project of regulation to industry itself. The NIRA came as a bit of a legislative afterthought (and a counter to what were seen as more reckless measures—a thirty-hour work week bill or plans for currency inflation)—and it showed. Its official goal was "to promote the organization of industry for the purpose of cooperative action among trade groups" by allowing industrial cooperation to prevent cutthroat competition. Like much of the first New Deal, it was the product, as Jonathan Alter put it, of "no master plan, only an instinct to improvise."[17]

As a program for industrial cooperation, the NIRA freed industry from anti-trust laws and then created national codes that regulated prices, wages, hours, and working conditions for hundreds of industries. When it came to negotiating the terms of the codes, however, business won most of what it wanted. Nobody else—government or labor—knew the inside issues of the industries, so business essentially gained a program of self-regulation. The bill basically offered up the cartelization of the American economy: the exact opposite of everything the Democratic Party had stood for since the Civil War.

The NIRA quickly became a policy mess for all concerned. There were over 500 codes negotiated in the first year, which would climb to over 700 before it was over. In this ungainly system, a single employer could fall under dozens of different codes. Enforcement beyond the moral suasion of displaying the famous blue eagle proved nearly impossible. Though attacked from the left as a sop to monopoly capital and criticized on the right as anti–free enterprise, the NIRA was actually more ill-conceived and contradictory than conspiratorial. Before long, even enlightened corporations had reservations that evolved into outright hostility to the act. The NIRA, explains the historian Anthony Badger, "contained something for almost everybody—which is why such a stark reversal of traditional government policy could secure majority support in Congress." Neither the ticket out of the Great Depression nor even a reasonable platform for planning, the National Recovery Administration (NRA) established to implement the legislation quickly earned the moniker "the National Run Around."[18]

The most lasting impact of the NIRA, and the most dramatic reversal of decades of policy, was for organized labor. Roosevelt wanted the AFL's support for the bill, and so Section 7a of the bill granted an explicit if problematic "right" for workers to organize into unions. The United Mine Workers leader John L. Lewis compared the NIRA's Section 7a with Lincoln's Emancipation Proclamation. It seemed to open an entire new world of policy possibilities. Harold Ickes, the secretary of the interior, felt the NIRA had delivered the United States to the other side: "It's a new world," he proclaimed. "People feel free again. . . . It's like quitting the morgue for the open woods." The president concurred. "History probably will record the National Industrial Recovery Act as the most important and far-reaching legislation ever enacted by the American Congress," FDR speculated. Like the NIRA itself, Section 7a was more of a mess than a plan for recovery, promising rights without any protections or mechanisms for achieving organization.[19]

Despite the lack of sophistication in the new federal labor law, it resonated across the country, as over 1.5 million workers endorsed the idea of Section 7a by walking off the job in 1,900 different strikes in 1934. Emboldened by the premise that the federal government was now finally protecting the right to organize, workers poured into unions. "The President wants you to join a union," read United Mine Workers flyers with certain overstatement. In near-open class warfare in Minneapolis, running battles with the national guard in Toledo, a city-wide stoppage in San Francisco, and a regional revolt of countless isolated cotton mill villages across the Piedmont South, the strike wave of 1934 sought to breathe life into the legislative promises of the first New Deal. In each case, the answer was not a new day, but, in fact, the same litany of repression from state and local authorities that had plagued labor relations since the dawn of the industrial age. The scars of failure in the South, where workers were driven back into the mills by bayonets that had seen service in France, ran so deep that another such widespread industrial revolt would never again happen in the region. Rather than embracing a new day for the forgotten man, it appeared as though the nation clung to its anti-labor past. "Once again," writes historian Melvyn Dubofsky, comparing 1934 to the major strike waves in American history, "as in 1892, 1894, 1901, 1909, and 1919—the concentrated corporations in the basic industries had defeated trade unionism and maintained the open shop."[20]

The NIRA was the New Deal's false start: raising high hopes for working people in the 1934 strike wave only to smash them, and betraying the Democratic Party's anti-monopoly tradition with almost no political compensation. In *Schecter Poultry Corporation v. United States* (1935), the Supreme Court ruled unanimously that the act was unconstitutional, a mere month before it was set to expire. When the NIRA died, few mourned. It had not raised wages, its codes were never really enforced, and one part of the act often contradicted the other. It had not started the economy again, aside from providing a few direct relief efforts and the temporary illusion that the nation was on the move. The biggest corporations already held monopoly control over their industries, and though ineffectual, Section 7a and its ensuing waves of labor unrest challenged their ability to set the price of labor. Everyone, not least of all those in the Roosevelt administration itself, was relieved to see the NIRA pass into history. As an immigrant cook at the Brach Candy Company concluded, "NRA helpa the capitalist; didn't help the working-a people." Yet even in its failure, the NRA laid crucial groundwork for policies to come, as it raised hopes and gave the New Dealers another chance to get it right.[21]

More than five years into the global economic crisis, two years into Roosevelt's first term, and following a mixed bag of legislation successes, a rare political window opened in American politics. In the summer of 1935, with the economic crisis checked but unresolved, core pieces of first-round New Deal legislation found unconstitutional, and FDR's political capital still miraculously intact, the moment was ripe to advance the New Deal beyond its initial experimentation. The "second" New Deal proved a much more lasting transformation—the primary legislative scaffolding for the decades to come. Although far from cohesive, the second set of policies was more ideologically consistent, more pro-labor, more redistributive, and less concerned with the needs of business than large-scale legislative effort before—or since. The years between the National Labor Relations Act (or Wagner Act) in June 1935 and the Fair Labor Standards Act (FLSA) in June 1938 marked what one historian described as a rare, perhaps the sole, "working class interlude" in U.S. history.[22]

The belief that the moment was distinct and unique is not merely a product of hindsight. The sense of destiny was distinctly palpable, even at the time, among politicians, policymakers, and labor leaders. "Boys—this is our hour," Harry Hopkins exclaimed when the 1934 midterms achieved the unprecedented and increased the Democratic majority. "We've got to get everything we want—a works program, social security, wages and hours, everything—now or never." Senator Robert Wagner, realizing a unique moment was at hand, worked tirelessly on the National Labor Relations (or Wagner) Act, on the premise that the moment had arrived. "There would never have been a Wagner Act or anything like it at any time if the Senator had not spent himself in this cause to a degree which almost defies description," his aide Leon Keyserling explained. John L. Lewis, the mineworkers' leader who would launch a massive organizing drive in basic industry, also recognized the moment at hand. As he confessed to organizer Powers Hapgood, a drive in basic industry at any other time "would have been suicide for organized labor and would have resulted in complete failure. But now, the time is ripe; and now the time to do those things is here."[23]

With the crisis of the 1934 strike wave in need of a useful legal response, Congress started anew with labor legislation. The Wagner Act did not just honor the workers' right to organize but, unlike Section 7a of the NIRA, actually provided mechanisms and protections for doing so. The Works Progress Administration (WPA, 1935) expanded and nationalized unemployment relief. The National Youth Administration (NYA) offered work and training for the nation's youth. Arguably the most important act of the Depression Era, the Social Security Act (1935) provided for universal retirement, unemployment insurance, and welfare benefits for the poor and disabled. Though the so-called Wealth Tax was hardly the "soak-the-rich" effort it was attacked for being, it did raise important ideological points about the purpose of government in an unequal society. Finally, the Fair Labor Standards Act, rejected in the original wave of legislation, returned in a more tepid form in 1938 with national regulation of child labor, minimum wages, and legal provisions for overtime compensation. For generations to come, the FLSA would stand as the backbone of U.S. employment law—and marked the last of the major New Deal reforms.

Social security of some form had been a dream of progressives, including FDR, for decades. Of the major legislative accomplishments of the second New Deal, this one had the most substantial momentum prior to the crash. The United States entered the Great Depression as one of the very few advanced industrial nations without unemployment and old-age support. Like the opportunity for so much federal legislation in the 1930s, the moment appeared urgently at hand. As Roosevelt declared to Secretary of Labor Frances Perkins, "we have to get it started, or it will never start." Perkins concurred, telling her committee "this was the time, above all times." Yet the administration debates on Social Security, or what FDR called the "Big Bill," continued to be saddled with all sorts of particularly American problems: trying to find ways to leave the power with the states, trying not to have confiscatory taxes, trying to maintain work ethic and reward incentives by not paying the same amount to everyone, trying to appease the populist alternatives, trying to keep business ethics and individualism on the table, trying to keep private insurance ideas as models, and trying to appease white Southerners' fears about the economic empowerment of African Americans. The committee considered including health insurance (something only 6 percent of people had at the time) but feared provoking opposition from the American Medical Association that could scuttle the entire bill. Suggestions of federally funded old-age pensions met a similar fate, for similar reasons. In the end, the committee agreed on one of the most conservative options on the table—a program funded by both employee and employer contributions; this was, as Secretary of Labor Frances Perkins put it, "the only plan that could have been put through Congress."[24]

Madame Secretary, as Perkins was known, found the final product to be only "practical, flat-footed steps." The Social Security program's dependence on enrollee contributions meant that employers could, theoretically, pass the cost onto workers by taking it out of their wages. Enrollee contributions also served as a regressive tax; rather than the cost of care for the elderly being drawn from the national coffers, individuals paid for care themselves through payroll contributions. The limits on the Social Security Act were dramatic: there was no health care insurance, unemployment insurance was limited, contributory taxes were larger than hoped, and 9.4 million workers, including domestic and agricultural workers of whom so many were black, were left off the rolls. [25]

Debates over the bill featured the usual claims that it was socialism, class warfare, and the end of the American way of life. In contrast to his general indifference on labor matters, FDR took an active interest in Social Security and would have preferred cradle-to-grave coverage. Roosevelt may have sensed the vulnerability of his pet project, and therefore embraced the most conservative, but most durable, option. While flawed, the Social Security Act allowed for an American political miracle: it secured the legislation's survival by giving everyone a stake in its future. As FDR put it, "We put those payroll contributions there so as to give the contributors a legal, moral, and political right to collect their pension and unemployment benefits. With those taxes in there, no damn politician can ever scrap my social security program."[26]

Perhaps the second New Deal's most dramatic departure from historical legislative patterns was the Wagner Act, which not only guaranteed the right for workers to organize, but this time provided legal protections and mechanisms for doing so—finally enumerating "unfair labor practices" and establishing the National Labor Relations Board for oversight of the new system. The board would be an intermediary between business and labor by overseeing free and fair elections and doling out penalties for infractions.

The essence of the act, in some of the most unique language in U.S. legislative history, was to "encourage" collective bargaining as a way to right the power balance in American industry, maintain industrial peace, and, most importantly, boost consumption in order to stimulate the economy.

The moment of the Wagner Act's passage was a rare combination of raised expectations and labor unrest fostered by the promises of the NIRA's Section 7a. Ever since the Supreme Court found the NIRA unconstitutional, Senator Robert Wagner had been waiting in the wings with a more substantial bill to submit at just the right moment. Many on both the left and the right regarded the Wagner Act as an extreme piece of legislation. Critics from the right regarded it as class antagonism that violated the fundamental American value of individualism. Those on the left saw it as an attempt to control the unruly Depression Era working class, possibly even a step toward fascism. It was, however, labor's indisputable moment; debate in Congress lasted only two days. For the first and only time in American political history, the federal government actively supported—even promoted—the right of working people to organize into unions. There would never again be, in history to date, a piece of legislation that so advanced the collective interests of the American worker. Never again would there even be a real progressive reform of the act, as the generations to follow found themselves defending, not advancing, this one-time leap forward for private-sector workers.[27]

The Wagner Act spurred grander visions for organized labor that had already been in circulation since the 1934 strike wave. The industrial unions began to move from the obscure bailiwicks of craft to the mass production industries—especially in auto, rubber tire, electrical, and steel. The Committee for Industrial Organization (later the Congress of Industrial Organizations, or CIO), which broke dramatically with the American Federation of Labor (AFL), looked to organize all workers, including at times women and African Americans, whose exclusion had doomed earlier unionization efforts. With powerful new leaders and the promise of federal power, workers encircled the tire factories of Akron, sat down in a tactically ingenuous occupation of General Motors for forty-two days, and stared down one of the most powerful corporations in the world, U.S. Steel. In the face of challenges to the act, even the Supreme Court temporarily abandoned its own deep history of opposition to the collective interests of working people and upheld the Wagner Act in 1937.

A renewed sense of possibility among workers, new legislative support, and revived union leadership all commingled to produce a rare moment in the long struggle of organized labor when the unions won enormous, semipermanent, gains in basic industry. Unions recruited more than three million members in 1937 alone. By the end of World War II, the labor movement had stood up from its deathbed to fight and win over one-third of the nonagricultural labor force into its ranks.[28]

Roosevelt never developed much sympathy for unions per se, but he readily accepted them as allies of convenience. As industry and finance increased their opposition to the New Deal at mid-decade, the president turned to workers and organized labor for support. Clothing workers' union president and CIO leader Sidney Hillman recognized that, in order to face their shared enemies, the president and the unions needed each other. The president's political necessities thus shaped labor's opportunities. CIO chief John L. Lewis threw the full weight of the industrial unions behind Roosevelt in 1936, helping him to win the largest political landslide in history up to that date. Less class-based ideological reorientation than pragmatic political alignment, the

politics of 1936 nonetheless were a remarkable moment in
American political history in which the historically fractious working-class vote assembled en masse for one party
and one candidate.[29]

━━━━━━━━━━━━━━━━━━━━

The second New Deal consolidated Roosevelt's position as
one of the most popular presidents in history—and, for the
moment, the most economically radical of the industrial
age. At the Democratic convention in Philadelphia in 1936,
FDR indicted the "economic royalists" who had subverted
American democracy with political tyranny. "For too many
of us the political equality we once had won was meaningless in the face of economic inequality. A small group
had concentrated into their own hands an almost complete
control over other people's property, other people's money,
other people's labor—other people's lives. For too many
of us life was no longer free; liberty no longer real; men
could no longer follow the pursuit of happiness." To right
the subversion of American democracy, he declared, "This
generation of Americans has a rendezvous with destiny."
He proclaimed in Madison Square Garden on the eve of his
reelection, "I should like to have it said of my first Administration that in it the forces of selfishness and of lust for
power met their match. I should like to have it said of my
second Administration that in it these forces met their master." Never had such exceptional campaign rhetoric come
from a sitting president.[30]

When FDR won his 1936 reelection landslide—losing
only Vermont and Maine—he consolidated a political coalition that served the Democrats admirably for much of the
postwar era. Industrial workers, urban political machines,
labor unions, farmers, progressive intellectuals, African

Americans—and the segregationist Solid South wielding extraordinary power over the entire group—passed as common cause. The Democrats continued to hold their traditional sources of support in the North and the South, but FDR extended the coalition to include the farming West and, above all, consolidated the white "ethnic" populations (recently immigrated workers or their descendants) of the urban manufacturing centers. Middle-class voters, intrigued by the exciting new role for government and sympathetic to the theme of economic security, united behind Roosevelt. Progressive intellectuals and the militant left buried the hatchet of factionalism, and also got behind the president. The CIO, above all, threw in its lot with Roosevelt, and unlike the tepidly political AFL, became the backbone of the coalition.

By the dawn of Roosevelt's second term in 1937, the Democratic Party had enrolled millions of working-class and poor Americans together in a political coalition based on a new idea of collective economic citizenship and economic security. Discrimination and disenfranchisement continued, both within the ranks and at the level of legislation, and it was clear by this point that the New Deal had made a devil's pact not to challenge racial segregation in any meaningful way. Yet even so, the coalition was less divided by skill, region, and immigration status than any before. For the first time in American history, a diversity of working people appeared to be organized by party and union—organized, at least loosely, as a class. The apparent power of the Roosevelt coalition was such that some misguided pundits even began to speak of the extinction of the Republican Party. The historic fragmentation of urban working-class voters had become "a culture of unity"—a term that makes sense only when compared with what came before or after. As we shall see in the next chapter, however, race, religious culture, immigration, and individualism had conspired in very specific ways in the mid-1930s that made this moment possible.

The window of political opportunity that opened in 1935 quickly slipped shut again by 1938, bringing opportunities for labor and FDR's brief posture as a class warrior to a close. As the historian Nelson Lichtenstein argues, "industrial unionism's moment of unrivaled triumph proved exceedingly brief." It was only a matter of weeks after the CIO's famous victories at General Motors and U.S. Steel in 1937, he notes, that "the radical challenge posed by mass unions generated furious opposition: from corporate adversaries, Southern Bourbons, craft unionists, and many elements of the New Deal coalition itself." The passage of the 1938 Fair Labor Standards Act marked the end point in New Deal advances. As Melvyn Dubofsky concurs, for labor "the transformation ended almost before it began. By the spring of 1937 the militant unions in the CIO were in battle more to protect what they had just won than to conquer additional outposts. And by autumn many of their newly enrolled members had stopped paying dues, leaving the CIO with a total membership that surpassed the AFL's only on paper."[31]

When the Roosevelt administration failed to come to the aid of the steel workers during the "Little Steel" strike of May 1937, John L. Lewis and the CIO leadership were stunned. The bad old days had returned already. Ten protestors were shot and killed, seven shot in the back. Roosevelt, exhausted with strikes and nervous about attacks from the right, betrayed his new base by condemning both labor and capital: "the majority of the people are saying just one thing,

'A plague on both your houses.'" It foreshadowed the future of labor's frustrating relationship with the Democratic
Party for generations to come. Having done everything to
elect FDR, labor found itself alone in the cold during its
hour of need. As the steel workers lost their advance into
the collection of companies called Little Steel (that is, not
big U.S. Steel), the CIO leadership explained their disap-
pointment with the President:

> We don't want to "break" with the Administration.
> God knows we worked and sacrificed to keep it in of-
> fice. But we don't understand its attitude in the steel
> strike, and we are resentful to find that suddenly we
> are no longer politically respectable in the eyes of the
> Administration. Labor's money and labor's votes were
> welcome enough last fall, when the [steel executives
> like the] Girdlers and the Graces and the reactionary
> press were damning Roosevelt from hell to breakfast.
> But now, when Girdler and Grace have their claws in
> labor's throat, all we hear from the White House
> is—"A plague on both your houses!"

Tossed back into the industrial wilderness once more, labor
ceased its forward march. The 1938–1939 period marks the
years of defeat and retreat for the unions, which looked as
if the entire CIO project might end in yet another thwarted
advance for organized labor.[32]

Labor was hardly alone, as the entire New Deal began to
come under attack in 1937. Buoyed by his 1936 landslide,
Roosevelt overstretched himself politically, and his enemies
came in for the attack. He tried to pack the Supreme Court
with more justices in order to stop the court from blocking
his programs. He also attempted to purge the Democratic
Party, especially of conservative Southern Democrats who
were not loyal to the New Deal cause. And, finally, he tried

to reorganize the federal government—one of his most long-standing goals. Most of these efforts resulted in failure and accusations of dictatorial overreach.

Yet a once unimaginable sea change in the Supreme Court in 1937 saved many of the second New Deal's legislative advances. Just two months after FDR threatened to increase the size of the court as a way to drown out the conservative majority, the court upheld Washington State's minimum wage for women in a case that is often cited as the end of the *Lochner* era. The following month, in one of the most dramatic turns of the court, the justices voted 5–4 to uphold the Wagner Act, arguing that labor strife had an effect on interstate commerce and that industrial relations were therefore subject to regulation under the commerce clause. It was the end of what FDR had derided as the court's "horse-and-buggy definition of interstate commerce." The decision, *NLRB v. Jones & Laughlin Steel*, signaled what appeared to be the final end of the court's hostility to economic and business regulation in general and the New Deal in particular. Ending the ideology of "liberty of contract" for the foreseeable future, the 1937 cases made an unprecedented leap for the collective economic rights of working people to both state regulation and union recognition. As one of the most astute chroniclers of the New Deal framed it, the events were nothing short of the "Supreme Court reborn."[33]

The court's swing was one of the last pieces of good news for the New Dealers. The 1938 midterm elections went poorly, though Democratic majorities remained large. The House Committee on Un-American Activities set up shop to harass the leftism of the New Dealers; FDR's plan to pack the Supreme Court crumbled; his effort to cleanse the party failed. The New Deal barely declared victory before it was in retreat again. The economy had improved by mid-decade, but then, always concerned with balancing the books and under a new round of attacks from the right, FDR trimmed the budget and the economy once again tumbled into what was by then called the "Roosevelt recession." By the winter of 1938, the landscape of unemployment, poverty, and hunger looked a lot like it had in 1933—except that Roosevelt had no political capital left. The conservative coalition had successfully wrested legislative control from him. Both the liberal agenda and organized labor found themselves on the defensive after 1938, with no new initiatives and a great deal of defensive maneuvering ahead. The New Deal's momentum finally ran out; 1939 was the first year that Roosevelt proposed no new reforms.

Conservatives used the moment to redouble their forces. After 1938, the new system was at best checked and at worst under siege, as an alliance of Republicans, uneasy Southern Democrats, big business, and even the skilled workers of the American Federation of Labor began to build toward a political stalemate that meant neither advance nor retreat for the New Deal. FDR began to fire the reformers and replace them with more conservative administrators. Even the National Labor Relations Board appointments no longer went to the New Deal laborites, but to more cautious, centrist figures. Maury Maverick, outspoken Democratic representative from Texas, was one of the few who spoke openly of the exhaustion of New Deal efforts. "Now we Democrats have to admit that we are floundering," he told the House. "We have pulled all the rabbits out of the hat, and there are no more rabbits. . . . We are a confused, bewildered group of people, and we are not delivering the goods. The Democratic administration is getting down to the condition in which Mr. Hoover found himself."

After 1938, with prospects for further advance blocked, the liberals entered a phase of retrenchment that only the war would change.[34]

The trimming of sails applied to the labor movement as well. By funneling all working-class concerns through state mechanisms and the narrow confines of collective bargaining, the new relationship between state and society both legitimized and defused the conflict between labor and capital. Class and the "labor question" became less of a charged issue that challenged the fundamental arrangement of the political economy and more of an instrument for the rational order. As Steve Fraser put it, though the economic trauma of the 1930s "gave rise to a culture of resistance, that culture was itself often profoundly conservative even while ushering in a new age." What everyone said they wanted was "security." Sidney Hillman said that the "quest for security" was the "central issue in this life of modern man," and the CIO's project was to protect the individual male worker and the nuclear family from the instability of the market and the arbitrary forces of management. "For that, the moral and millenarian enthusiasms once invoked for the 'labor question' were no longer appropriate." The *raison d'être* of the Wagner Act was, after all, less about granting labor rights as a social good than providing increased wages to boost consumer demand in the nation's hour of need. It would not be long before working people's social identities as consumers trumped their identities as workers.[35]

The New Deal was more of a unique breakthrough than a product of a long political evolution. The necessary materials—progressive regulation, demands for labor rights, mothers' pensions, the analogue of war—were certainly loose in the political cosmos. Yet to see in those elements the coming New Deal is a teleological read that denies too much of the American past. Without the forces that pushed toward that single, short, dense, hot period of 1935–1937, from which the New Deal exploded into the future, it is imaginable that the postwar order would have been dramatically different. As we shall see in the next chapter, however, the configuration of key issues in the 1930s made the transformation possible—as well as unstable.

You're Next! "No greater wrong has been committed against the Negro than the denial to him of the right to work," proclaimed labor leader A. Phillip Randolph in 1944. Yet, as this poster argues, discrimination on the job posed a threat to the progress of all workers.
FEPC Poster, United Steel Workers of America Poster and Oversized Collection 1932–1982, Special Collections Library, The Pennsylvania State University.

CHAPTER FOUR

CONSTRAINTS AND FRACTURES IN THE NEW LIBERALISM

The New Deal appeared to sever abruptly many of the lingering ties that bound the nation to the political legacy of the nineteenth century. The long-standing debates about democracy and the corporation had ended in embracing big business and big labor both—if on unequal terms; in place of the liberty of contract, it introduced an idea of collective economic security and shared economic destiny. Yet the juggernaut had its fragilities. The developments that allowed the American population to overcome a history of social divisions were contingent, provisional, and dependent on specific historical circumstances. For all of its power, the New Deal never fully transformed American political culture.

As politically tenuous as the New Deal state transformations of the last chapter were, pulling the lens back to the broadest terrain of American history shows the fault lines that continued to run through the New Deal order. Potent cultural trends had ebbed, but their flow would again return: the ethos of "rugged individualism" and the closely associated ideology of liberal capitalism; the religious movements that remained both divisive and suspect of the state; the temporary cessation of new immigration into the United

States; and overlooked transitions in African American politics and Southern white party alignments. The New Deal
policy accomplishments tracked a precarious path through
these forces, one that involved evasions, exclusions, eli-
sions, and, above all, compromises that proved nearly fatal
to the project in the end. This chapter looks below the text-
book survey to see the continuities with the old order that
continued even at the height of the New Deal's growth.
Beneath the political revolution remained an older, powerful social order.

At the center of the New Deal's instability was the missing
place for the most forgotten "forgotten man": the African
American people. Well into the industrial age, the legacy
of slavery in the United States still crippled the advance of
modern politics. So entrenched was Jim Crow politics that
had the New Deal been committed to racial equality, had it
actually made any efforts to shatter the white consensus on
black racial inferiority, it is most likely that the New Deal
would not have happened. As far back as the end of Reconstruction, the two-party system depended on the subjugation of African American economic and political interests.
That pattern continued under the New Deal in order to
keep the Southern wing of the Democratic Party in the coalition. The ugly truth about the United States in the 1930s
was that without Southern white votes, nothing was going
to happen for the Democratic Party, and not challenging
Jim Crow was the only path to Southern white votes.

There could be no whisper of black participation in the
New Deal or there would be no political coalition, and no
New Deal. Yet nobody was even concerned there would be
whispers—the South was that sure of its power in the sys-

tem. Southern legislators had been baptized into, and their success tied to, a regional Democratic party that proudly proclaimed itself as the party of the white man. That perspective, which emphasized the maintenance of a low wage, nonunion, and racially stratified workforce "free" of Washington's regulation, contributed to a political imbroglio that even Democrats who wanted to change the system proved powerless to overcome. In fact, the Roosevelt administration's legislative strength rested directly on its Faustian pact with the Southern Democrats, whose representative power in Congress was buoyed numerically by people who were viciously disenfranchised, and in terms of seniority by longstanding control of the committee system due to the power of southern incumbency in a one-party system. Moreover, the Solid South's commitment to racial segregation was more powerful than most legislators' commitment to most any other cause—the single point of galvanizing unity in the fractious world of Washington.

Two political scientists place the political role of the Southern congressional delegation in sharp relief: "Chosen by an authoritarian, largely one-party political system, these members also enjoyed advantages of seniority, control of key committees, and the Senate's supermajority rules, most notably the filibuster. With these tools, the South possessed a structural veto over all New Deal and Fair Deal legislation at a time when Republicans alone could not sustain an effective opposition." Authoritarian, yes, but the white people they represented did not want to see equality in the labor market either. As the Jackson *Daily News* put it: "The average [white] Mississippian can't imagine himself chipping in to pay pensions for able bodied Negroes to sit around in idleness on front galleries supporting their kinfolks on pensions, while cotton and corn crops are crying for workers to get them out of the grass."[1]

The fight against racial segregation was simply beyond the political calculus, even the imaginations, of even the most progressive white politicians. "I've got to get legislation passed by Congress to save America," intoned the great liberal senator Robert Wagner. "If I come out for the anti-lynching bill, [the Southerners] will block every bill I ask Congress to pass to keep America from collapsing. I just can't take that risk." Harold Ickes expressed similar feelings about fighting Jim Crow. "While I have been interested in seeing that the Negro has a square deal," he had to admit that the issue of race would have to left to be left to the states. "I have never dissipated my strength against the particular stone wall of segregation."[2]

Southern congressmen united with Northern Democrats to create the New Deal, but the condition of that participation was simple: the exclusion of the occupations into which Southern blacks were segregated—agriculture and domestic service. The Southern economic and social order, which rested on low-cost, segregated labor, had to be preserved. The core, tragic dilemma of American class politics was that to include African Americans meant not to have "class" politics. Even hallmark pieces of legislation like Social Security, remarked one NAACP lawyer, worked "like a sieve with holes just big enough for the majority of Negroes to fall through." The cohesion necessary for broad working-class empowerment rested upon exclusion.[3]

As a coalition of African American advocacy groups summarized, "As far as the Negro is concerned, New Deal social planning generally has availed him little either because of its underlying philosophy, or because its administration has been delegated to local officials who reflect the unenlightened mores of their respective communities." As the report continues, "The Negro remains the most forgotten man in a program planned to deal new cards to . . . millions of workers. . . . The Negro worker has good reason to feel that his government has betrayed him under the New Deal." The National Urban League and the NAACP lobbied to make nondiscrimination and fair representation part of the New Deal, but with no success. The Agricultural Adjustment Act ended up helping to drive African Americans off the land as federal subsidies went to landowners rather than sharecroppers, and the National Recovery Administration earned the tag the "Negro Removal Act." Even in the North, where the CIO was committed to organizing without regard to race, the NAACP charged that the Wagner Act was being used "to organize a union for all the white workers, and to either agree with the employers to push Negroes out of the industry or, having effected an agreement with the employer, to proceed to make a union lily-white."[4]

Their racial position secured, the Southern Democrats embraced the early New Deal with enthusiasm. White Southern politicians voted strongly for the bold economic agenda of the first Roosevelt administration, especially since it offered to help pull up a deeply impoverished region in terms of infrastructure, agricultural techniques, jobs, and capital investment. The Southern congressmen enjoyed the new federal largesse as long as it did not upset the mythological combination of racial supremacy and defiant individualism that shaped Southern politics. While accepting federal dollars, they avoided the creation of a truly national, integrated labor market. As Texan congressman Maury Maverick put it, "the South is for the good old time virtues, but is not averse to taking a few billions of gold from the Federal till for the TVA, for cotton subsidies, WPA and others. . . . But when a general bill [such as the Fair Labor Standards Act] is offered, the South is liable to pull Thomas Jefferson from the grave, and swear it's coddling the people."[5]

While the exclusion of Southern African American occupations was central to the New Deal story, the politics of
race in the age of Roosevelt is more rich and complex than
a simple story of upholding segregation. The most interesting aspect of racial politics in the New Deal moment was
not just the subjugation of African Americans but also the
fact that black voters, attracted by the changes of the New
Deal, were moving away from their historic allegiance to
the Republicans toward the Democratic Party *despite* its
faults. Many, having come North toward greater freedom
and opportunity during World War I, looked favorably on
the New Deal's emphasis on social and economic citizenship. Others noticed FDR's "black cabinet," a collection of
informal advisors and administrators. Even those in the
South felt the change. The most dramatic and long-lasting
shift in voting patterns was among African Americans (of
those actually having the franchise), who cast a ballot for a
Democratic candidate for the first time. "My friends, go
home and turn Lincoln's picture to the wall," Robert L. Van
of the Pittsburgh *Courier* told black voters during the rise
of the New Deal. "That debt has been paid in full." The
complete realignment of African American voters would
have to wait until the war and beyond, but the days, as
Frederick Douglass put it in the nineteenth century, when
"the Republican Party is the ship; all else is the sea," were
over.[6]

Southern Democrats were still militantly committed to
Jim Crow, but many Northern Democrats were not, which
made for an awkward alliance. By the 1930s and 1940s, the
Democrats housed an untenable union of white suprema-
cists, tepid advocates for racial justice, and, increasingly,
African Americans themselves. It was a rare moment in
which the Democratic Party found itself "carry[ing] water
on both shoulders with regard to Negro voting," as one

contemporary put it. The mobilization of federal power was not, as during Reconstruction in the past and the Great Society to come, tagged as a racialized intervention. The Democrats, at least for a moment, were able to win the day for state intervention in the economy, not upset the politics of the racial status quo, and still win numbers of African Americans to their side. The political hat trick would prove too tenuous to sustain.[7]

In contrast to the New Deal's exclusions, the new labor movement staked its claim firmly on inclusion, declaring that the new unions would not discriminate on account of race, gender, or creed. In contrast to the old craft unions, many of which remained segregated if they let African Americans in at all, the CIO's very charter shows an aggressive posture toward the type of racism that had divided working people and hobbled organized labor since the dawn of the republic. This was a source of tremendous liberation for many black workers who had come North to find industrial jobs during the wartime migrations, but it was also frightening to many of the Northern white working class (as well as a reason the CIO could not crack the nonunion South). Still, no matter how checkered the story, the CIO offered the most important avenue for black empowerment until the 1960s. As W.E.B. Du Bois put it, as a result of the CIO, "numbers of men like those in steel and automotive industries have been thrown together, black and white, as fellow workers striving for the same objects. There has been on this account an astonishing spread of interracial tolerance and understanding. Probably no movement in the last 30 years has been so successful in softening race prejudice among the masses."[8]

Despite its break with the past, the CIO's successes remain imperfect. The leadership still had trouble with one of the thorniest issues of all: the racism of the Northern white rank and file. "The CIO unions themselves, though embracing a racially egalitarian ideology, were inconsistent when it came to battling discrimination against black workers and, constrained by the prejudices of the white rank and file, have failed to live up to their official principles," explain Meier and Rudwick in their study of race in the auto industry. "To advance the interest of black auto workers," they continue, "meant arousing the fears and prejudices of rank-and-file white members, and of the officers in the locals as well." The problem of the white rank and file, historian Bruce Nelson concludes, meant that the unions' "logic of solidarity came up against a different logic—of majoritarian democracy, which in the United States has always been deeply intertwined with racialized perceptions of self and society." The inclusion of black workers ran the risk of having white workers bolt from the union cause.[9]

The whiteness of the New Deal was only part of the politics of racial purity of the era; the other key element was immigration—or, more specifically, the cessation of nativism associated with immigration. Prior to the 1920s, waves of immigration in the late nineteenth and early twentieth centuries had fueled the factories and mills—as well as the nativist and racial antipathies of native-born workers—for generations. Advocates of immigration restrictions called it a "breathing space," while historians have variously referred to it as "hardening the boundaries of the nation" or a "retreat to restrictionism." Whatever the descriptor, the unintended result of a conservative racial immigration policy was the cohesion necessary for the most liberal period in American history.[10]

When first World War I and then the 1924 immigration act closed off the borders to Southern and Eastern Europeans, the gateway that would lead to white citizenship for those formerly deemed inferior was open. "Anglo-Saxon,"

once an exclusive racial identity, was being replaced by a
more cohesive pan-European whiteness. With the spigot of
immigration closed off, the latest generation of arrivals was
committed to staying in the United States, no longer "birds
of passage" or menacing throngs of cheap labor pouring off
the docks. Their claim to white citizenship became more
real. Simultaneously, the forced repatriation of hundreds of
thousands—perhaps millions—of Mexicans and Mexican-
American citizens through local and county initiatives also
helped unify the white population.

With the issues of ethnicity and immigrant status at bay,
and African Americans excluded, the new liberalism's exclusions passed for widespread working-class inclusion.
Scholars and activists have often pointed to race, ethnicity,
and immigration as some of the key dividing factors that
have prevented the kinds of homogenization necessary for
working-class solidarity and reform. For a brief moment, a
sort of "Caucasian" unity took place among a historically
divided working class, with the heterogeneity of American
experience transformed into a rare moment of homogeneity. By excluding blacks and immigrants, Americans could
define themselves as workers rather than make historic appeals to identities such as white or native born.[11]

The consolidation of the New Deal around a vague
Anglo-Saxon Americanism was at times a conscious strategy. In the 1930s, the term "Americanism" reverberated
throughout political discourse, but especially in organized
labor and the left. "I yield to no man the right to challenge
my Americanism or the Americanism of the organizations
which at this moment I represent," the magnetic CIO leader
John L. Lewis intoned. The Communists even made their
appeal based on their "Americanism," and the Popular
Front—the broad coalition of labor and the left—unified
around ideas of American traditionalism from Jefferson to

Lincoln. The Communist Party, as Irving Howe explained, "gave itself a remarkable paint job, changing from bright red to a lively red, white, and blue." The ubiquitous images of "the people" from Dorothea Lange's photographs to Frank Capra's movies to John Steinbeck's characters tended to be native-born whites (or at least interpreted that way—Lange's most famous photo, "Migrant Mother," was actually Native American).[12]

Even migrant labor in California became white, as Okies moving out of the Dust Bowl replaced Japanese, Filipinos, and Mexicans in the California fields. The working-class hero of American literature, Steinbeck's Tom Joad, was steeped deeply in the history of white Americana—his family tracing its lineage back to the Indian wars. Yet the iconography is fascinating given the fact that white workers played only a temporary role in California agricultural labor—the vast majority of the history of which involved people of color. In short, the civic nationalism of the forgotten man was white and native born. Not surprisingly, when conservatives attacked the New Deal, they did so by trying to tar it in old-school fashion as a "Jew Deal" to support immigrants and radicals.[13]

The political bridge between Southern and Northern Democrats was short lived. What became known as the "conservative coalition," anchored by Southerners along with the conservative wing of the Northern Republican Party, grew quickly to contest the power of the Roosevelt coalition. While the South was on board with the early New Deal, by late in the decade conservatives had turned toward engineering a sustained political attack on the New Deal.

As James T. Patterson described the thinking of members of the conservative coalition: "Some of these men might better be termed reactionaries, others moderates. Many spoke the language of Social Darwinism; others were Burkean conservatives. Some were agrarian conservatives; others were spokesmen for urban business interests." But the unifying factor "was opposition to most of the domestic programs of the New Deal."[14]

The South played a particularly important role in promoting the state as a tool for the defense of the independence of white working-class men. As Southern government officials became a bulwark against federal authority (though not monies), they checked the possibility that the Southern working class could ever be an integral part of the New Deal coalition. Such white working-class conservatism was less something inherent in the Southern workers' culture than it was learned. From the attempts at class-based populism to the destruction of the 1934 textile strike, Southern "workers drew a stark lesson from their defeats. Class politics, many concluded, promised more than it could deliver." The politics of race and reaction readily took their place.[15]

The tenuousness of the Democratic coalition remained obvious to all observers. When President Truman pushed for an anti-lynching bill, the elimination of the poll tax, and an end to discrimination in the armed forces after the war, the deep South fought back. Catalyzed by the introduction of a civil rights plank into the Democratic platform in 1948, the "Dixiecrats," the heart of the conservative coalition, bolted from the Democratic Party and nominated Strom Thurmond, segregationist governor of South Carolina, to be their presidential candidate. With the failure of the CIO's organizing drive, known as Operation Dixie, to bring the South under the New Deal/CIO umbrella, it was clear that white supremacy would continue to hobble the effective advancement of the shared economic agenda of the New Deal.

———————————

Religion hardly disappeared during the New Deal period, but the politics of religious values were certainly restrained and overshadowed by pressing economic concerns. In *Hellfire Nation,* James A. Morone shows how the old politics of moralism and piety faded away, leaving "not a hint about those past icons of depravity—lazy immigrants, undisciplined black men, or drunks lounging about the saloon." Instead, as FDR pointed out, the circumstances were "beyond the control of any individual." The public economic crisis trumped the need to redeem the nation from sin. As Morone continues:

> The general trend was vivid. Governments left the vice field, and they began withdrawing support from private purity campaigns. The secular motion ran right through the Roosevelt administration, Congress, the federal courts, and the special state constitutional conventions of 1933 that buried Prohibition.... The 1930s roiled with economic anxiety, class struggle, and New Deal frenzy. In contrast, religion faltered and traditional morality seemed to fade right out of politics. Personal behavior no longer held deep (much less dire) consequences for the republic.... Economic issues—fairness, inequality, hard times, self interest—turned moral.... The new piety demanded public action against private suffering.

With the civics of the social gospel momentarily triumphant, for a brief time, "competition, if not capitalism itself,
developed the vague odor of 'bad morals.' "[16]

The Great Depression delivered members of all religious
groups toward the Democratic Party, but mainline Protestants still remained politically less committed than did Catholics and Jews. Evangelical Protestants, a group that would
prove very volatile to Democrats later, went for Roosevelt
along with the Solid South. In the postwar era, the mainline Protestant faiths, and their pious reformism, tended to
meld into a blurry Judeo-Christian Cold War sensibility that
stretched over traditional hierarchies and hostilities, despite
the growing momentum of countercurrents.[17]

Outward religious expressions remained limited in the
Depression years: there was no great revival, little open political expressions of a fundamentalist turn to God as a result of the economic hardship. Following the humiliations
of the Scopes trial, evangelical and fundamentalist Christianity entered the Depression years seemingly exhausted and
underground, the revivalism of the 1920s appearing to have
been the last gasp of anti-modernism before the consolidation of the rational industrial order. As the great journalist
Walter Lippmann observed, Bible thumping no longer resonated with "the best brains and the good sense of the modern community," while Baptist leaders like Oliver W. Van
Osdel instructed his colleagues to reject the public sphere in
favor of modeling the struggles of "the rejected Son of God
in the days of declension and compromise." Those fundamentalist voices were not vanquished, but merely displaced.
They would resurface with renewed faith and vigor late in
the postwar era.[18]

People of faith, most of whom still lived in enclaves of
their own people, did turn to religious and ethnic institutions

for material support, which, like other local forms of charity and welfare, were rapidly drained of material resources. For the Catholic Church, Jewish welfare organizations, and Protestant denominations—both white and black—the Great Depression challenged organized religion's capacity to provide for its members: it undermined their position in the community and failed to provide protection in times of devastation and want. When ethno-religious groups could no longer take care of their hungry, their homeless, and their jobless, working people slowly turned to the state for the types of relief they once would have expected of their houses of worship.[19]

Nonetheless, foreshadowing the rise of a highly politicized Christianity in the 1970s and beyond, the seeds of a fundamentalist reaction against the New Deal were already being planted in the 1930s. In 1935, a political observer sent out into the country to gauge support for the president's bid in 1936, wrote back: "In my opinion, the strongest opposition to Mr. Roosevelt—in 1936—would come, not from the economic reactionaries, but from the religious reactionaries (if you can separate the two)." He continued to note that, "The opposition of what one can call the evangelical churches is growing steadily more bitter and open." Economic disaster, strikes, communists, and the global rise of dictators (a category that included FDR in the view of many) all fueled apocalyptic Christian thought. Then, in 1942, the National Association of Evangelicals was formed, giving legitimacy and national voice to evangelical concerns. Evangelism, while not as serious a threat to FDR as to future liberals, had hardly disappeared from the national stage but was slowing organizing for a forceful return to the political arena.[20]

Despite the muting of the evangelical tradition, the New Deal state still had to contend with a set of uprisings from a more visceral populist tradition—often tinged with religious overtones and calls to save the republic from the ruinous Roosevelt. Three in particular fought with and overlapped the New Deal: the California physician Francis Townsend, whose "Townsend Plan" for revolving old-age pensions helped fan the demand for Social Security; Father Coughlin, Detroit's "Radio Priest," whose massively popular weekly radio addresses criticized Roosevelt and pushed an anti-Semitic agenda; and Huey Long (the Louisiana "Kingfish"), whose "Share Our Wealth" programs promised to make "every man a king." In their own way, each populist sought to restore the republic to the little man, resurrect some version of traditional values, and deliver the individual from the crush of mass society.

Often ideologically fuzzy and sometimes contradictory, the Depression Era populists, as Alan Brinkley explains, "were manifestations of one of the most powerful impulses of the Great Depression, and of the many decades of American life before it: the urge to defend the autonomy of the individual and the independence of the community against encroachments from the modern industrial state." Followers of Long and Coughlin certainly did not look to a "collective future." As Brinkley continues, "They called, rather, for a society in which the individual retained control of his life and livelihood; in which power resided in visible, accessible institutions; in which wealth was equitably (if not necessarily equally) shared." FDR was well aware of the populist threat, often co-opting their topics and strategies, while staking out a position as the sober alternative. "I am fighting Communism, Huey Longism, Coughlinism, Townsendism," proclaimed the president. He needed to "save our system, the capitalist system" from "crackpot ideas." In most any other period in American history, these voices for the restoration of the populist-defined past would have, if not won out, been able to stymie or tip the balance against the reform process.[21]

Populism drew together the deepest currents of American history, making connections between individualism and mass movements, between fears of betrayal of the American cause and a sense of American destiny, and between the unknown future and the heroic ideas of the past. The fact that Roosevelt could manage and contain the wellspring of much of the populist discontent—as well as the religious dimensions of it—made the New Deal success all the more rare and all the more powerful. Whether it was the agrarian populists of the nineteenth century or the latter incarnations of the Tea Party in the early twenty-first century, the desire for restoration of an age of independence has held a magnetic draw for the American people. By opposing the New Deal from many perspectives, they were literally trying to conserve something: an old America that the New Dealers had consciously felt the need to vanquish.

There would, of course, be nothing approximating working-class political unity without the support of Catholic working people, who made up perhaps one-third of the CIO's membership. Between the empty coffers of many Catholic charities and the Catholic economic doctrines propounded by Pope Leo XIII in his 1891 encyclical *Rerum Novarum* and by Pius XI in his 1931 *Quadragesimo Anno*, a turn to the state for support made sense. While social justice appealed to the church, secularism and communism did not. It was a tenuous balance. Father Charles Rice, "Pittsburgh's labor priest," defended the unions and battled their Communists. Delivering the benediction at the CIO's first convention, Rice declared, "A victory for labor in its struggles for decent conditions is a victory for Americanism and Christianity."[22]

Yet for generations, American Catholics had grown to consciousness within a church tradition that identified individualism and secular modernity as mortal enemies. This was not simply the consequence of an arch-conservative, authoritarian hierarchy—although church leaders at every level tended to be just that; rather, this opposition to liberalism's secular individualism had complex roots in Catholic social teaching. In part, a long-held corporatist sensibility, which emphasized the centrality of the family over the autonomous individual, remained influential and found daily expression in the national system of parochial schools for generations of Catholic children. For American Catholics, that ethos both encouraged a "Catholic ghetto" mentality into the 1950s in response to secular culture *and* a serious social analysis of the political economy, which proclaimed social responsibility for poverty and other related problems. The very emphasis on family opened the door wide to demands for societal solutions to such structural inequalities. American Catholicism's leading progressive cleric, Father John Ryan, a Catholic champion of workers' rights, lamented the New Deal's shift to a Keynesian-inspired policy of consumer individualism that offered "new inventions to produce new luxuries" in lieu of economic planning that promoted communal well-being. Justice was embedded within that faith-based vision, perhaps secondary to it, but faith tended to provide the structure for Catholic social and economic concerns.[23]

Most importantly for political activity, the staunch anti-communism of the Catholic community had a pronounced impact on New Deal, working-class Catholics. Their faith precluded a ready acceptance of the rational-materialist vision of much of the CIO; their focus on family raised suspicions of a singular reliance on the state; their European ethnic heritage encouraged fear of Soviet intentions over the often mythic, and therefore all the more powerful, memories of original homelands; and their American patriotism alerted them to the need to defend the nation against subversion from within. In a way that particularly confounded many liberal and left commentators, these men and women could be deeply Catholic, active, even militant, trade unionists, and reject much of secular, liberal thought, while they simultaneously supported core economic aspects of New Deal policy.[24]

Civic faith was also a point of unity for many believers from a variety of denominations. The outward, political, expression of religious faith had a palliative in the alternative of a civic-religious framework—what FDR called "our covenant with ourselves." FDR's liberalism, argues Ronald Isetti, was not the secular liberalism to come, but something more transitional between the faith-based politics of William Jennings Bryan and the secular liberalism against which a religious backlash would eventually be mobilized. The New Deal, argues Isetti, was a "regulatory Progressive state based in political liberalism and Christian humanitarianism, which for Roosevelt were pretty much the same." Many working people of different faiths responded to the unifying symbolism of the president, placing his picture on mantels and claiming a personal relationship with him. His radio addresses turned him into a sort of secular, civic evangelical for many people. As the journalist Martha Gellhorn, sent out to canvas the land, reported back to the administration: "And the feeling of these people for the President is one of the most remarkable phenomena I have ever met. He is at once God and their intimate friend; he knew them all by name, knows their little town and mill, their little lives and problems. And though everything fails, he is there, and will not let them down."[25]

"With the shock of war," wrote Randolph Bourne during World War I, "the State comes into its own again." The return of one of the greatest continuities with the old order, war, revived the New Deal from its defensive doldrums in the late 1930s. World War II not only resurrected the economy in a way the New Deal could not, it also saved the Democratic Party and organized labor from attacks from the conservative coalition. The analogy of war had informed FDR's administration from the inauguration forward, but beginning in 1939 with the massive defense buildup through the Allied victory in 1945, war was no longer an analogy: the full mobilization of society made the analogy into a political reality. As New Deal champion William Leuchtenburg argued, historians have placed too much emphasis on progressivism and populism and not enough on war mobilization in understanding the origins of the New Deal. The metaphors for the first New Deal, after all, tended to be more martial than progressive. The organization of American economic and political life for a second total war provided a unique possibility for the incorporation of labor's otherwise tenuous success into the state. While bringing labor into the state machinery was a temporary move during World War I, during World War II the enabling legislature of the New Deal would have the illusion of permanence.[26]

In 1940, the biggest federal expenditure in American history was approved: $7 billion in lend-lease aid to the future allies of World War II. Workers flocked to the booming defense industries, the rich were taxed, controls were slapped on prices, women and minorities found new jobs and new status, and, under the massive spending of full mobilization, the Great Depression finally came to an end. When demobilization came after the war, the depression that so many feared to be a repeat of the aftermath of World War I did not return, since the postwar system rested on the legislative advances of the second New Deal and the power of the Democratic coalition. This time, although there were dramatic setbacks, unlike the social incorporation during World War I, working people would win the peace.

With the entire economy mobilized for war—the workers, the factories, the farms, and the citizenry—almost the entirety of the nation's manpower and ideas were directed toward an Allied victory. The system of central planning grew to become the closest thing to a state-run capitalist enterprise in American history. The government poured $350 billion into the war, which funded hundreds of thousands of planes, tens of thousands of tanks, a million and a half trucks, and millions of machine guns. The economy surged beyond imagination, and, quite simply, the Depression ended.[27]

When the war ended, Americans were protected by the unionization of one-third of the industrial workforce, unemployment compensation, Social Security, the Fair Labor Standards Act, the GI Bill, loans for housing, vocational training, remarkably high marginal tax rates, and a massive redistribution of wealth that prompted an enormous wave of consumer spending. The war created a ravenous appetite for labor—all of which flowed into the preexisting labor institutions and policy mechanisms created by the New Deal. Some call it the "third New Deal." As a result, the New Deal state created the foundation for the most equitable American economy since the beginning of the industrial age.

Prior to 1940, income tax was not a significant issue for the vast majority of Americans, but the war changed that, too. As late as the end of the 1930s, barely 5 percent of Americans paid income tax, and the amount of personal and corporate tax was actually below that of the 1920s. Even the Wealth Tax Act of 1935 (popularly know as the "soak-the-rich tax") ultimately did little soaking of the rich. The war, however, inflated the tax rolls to include 74 percent of the American people. What economists call the "Great Compression" in the American wage structure was the result. Economists Thomas Piketty and Emmanuel Saez have shown that "the twentieth century decline in inequality took place in a very specific and brief time interval." And the "surprising fact," Claudia Golden and Robert Margo argue, is that "top wage shares did not recover after the war." Why the wealthiest were not able to recoup their historic percentage of the pie in the immediate postwar era can be attributed to the New Deal policies and political culture that, in *maintaining* the pattern of redistribution that had been created during the wartime emergency, shared more widely the benefits of a booming economy.[28]

Yet the tremendous economic enfranchisement of working people did have its costs. Gone were the anti-monopoly fights, the Jeffersonian streak, the individualism, and the anti-statism that had defined Democratic politics for one hundred years. As Alan Brinkley explains, the final New Deal order was "a world in which large-scale bureaucracies were becoming ever more dominant and in which it was becoming increasingly difficult to imagine an alternative to them." Liberal political commentators and Democratic Party leaders alike would confine their policy aims to a single set of principles intended to regulate capitalism and macro-economic planning in order to increase consumption and maintain full employment. This new "set of liberal ideas," continues Brinkley, "essentially reconciled to the existing structure of the economy and committed to using the state to compensate for capitalism's inevitable flaws—a philosophy that signaled, implicitly at least, a resolution of some of the most divisive political controversies of the industrial era."[29]

After the war, labor would prove "scarce, expensive, and rebellious," in the words of *Fortune* magazine, launching the biggest strike wave in American history in 1946. Rather than defeat as in 1919, the postwar labor conflicts would prove the new system's mettle and durability, and the final consolidation of the New Deal order.[30]

The politics of the racial status quo also began to crack during World War II. The President of the Brotherhood of Sleeping Car Porters, A. Philip Randolph, along with other civil rights leaders, proposed a wartime March on Washington to protest occupational discrimination and segregation. To check the proposed march, Roosevelt issued Executive Order 8802, which instituted a Fair Employment Practices Committee to ensure there "shall be no discrimination in the employment of workers in defense industries or government because of race, creed, color or national origin." It was a tepid response, but it forestalled a domestic racial standoff with what might have been tens of thousands of African American protesters in the midst of a foreign war to defeat the idea of racial supremacy. Roosevelt's Executive Order kept the fragile and temporary balance of racial peace between, on the one hand, the recalcitrance of the white rank and file and the reluctance of the Democrats to politicize issues of racial equality directly, and, on the other, African Americans' demands for inclusion in the new booming economy.

The planned March on Washington would eventually see the light of day, but not until over two decades later in 1963, when its most memorable legacy was Martin Luther

King, Jr.'s dream of integration. The change is typically seen as the harbinger of the new rights-based liberalism away from the economics-based liberalism of the New Deal. Later, few would recall that the official title of the 1963 march was actually for "Jobs and Freedom." While most commentators tend to draw a sharp line of distinction between labor of the 1930s and 1940s and the civil rights of the 1950s and 1960s, they are connected. As the March on Washington's chronicler William P. Jones put it, "the civil rights movement was always closely linked to the social democratic politics of the New Deal." Without the New Deal, the forward advance of civil rights in the postwar era would have had a more uphill, desperate struggle.[31]

During the war, the establishment of the Fair Employment Practices Committee (FEPC) proved problematic for the stability of the Democratic coalition even in the North. As these policies were implemented in Detroit, Chicago, Cleveland, and other industrial centers, white workers, many in the United Auto Workers and other liberal unions, walked off the job rather than work with union "brothers" who were black. While segregation was often accepted as official practice within the AFL unions, the CIO was committed to racial equality. So pervasive were these actions, dubbed "hate strikes," and so committed were the strikers, that the national UAW joined forces with the federal government to strip their own locals of labor law protections if they persisted. Not even the wartime patriotism of Northern white workers could overcome embedded racial attitudes, and most unions could do little to alter rank-and-file thinking.[32]

The fact that the FEPC and future forms of racial justice on the job worked on a separate track from labor relations proved deeply problematic. As Paul Frymer argues, "the absence of a strong and racially diverse labor movement did not result because of the failures of a few or even many individuals within the labor and civil rights movements. Rather, it is the outcome of a political *system* that, in its effort to appeal to civil rights opponents, developed a bifurcated system of power that assigned race and class problems to different spheres of government." By the time that the civil rights struggles would be under way, there would be "two vectors of power involving labor and civil rights, created in different historical moments, in conflict with each other, leading to unintended consequences."[33]

Even amid the heyday of labor solidarity of the 1930s and 1940s, the nation remained rife with ethnic and racial tensions below the veneer of unity. Wide swaths of people found themselves tossed together in large manufacturing establishments in new ways. "Where logic and liberal theory had promised some sense of unity among the shipyard workers derived from their common interests and common status," explained Katherine Archibald in her ethnography of wartime shipbuilding, "I found in actuality differences and gaps—social abysses so deep that the possibility of spanning them never occurred, apparently, to right-minded people reared after a righteous custom." Shocked by the pettiness of internecine struggles, Archibald "found intolerance of slight linguistic and cultural differences so great that the ghosts of feudal snobbery seemed to have come alive. I found insularities so narrow as scarcely to be believed. Even among these people, for whose sake the liberal had contrived his dream of equalitarianisms, I found that the lesser inequalities were cherished, and the weaker suppressed by the less weak. Where I had confidently expected unity of purpose and of action, I found only antagonism and turmoil."[34]

The culture of the Depression decade and the war effort were awash in many forms of collectivism, seeming to trump the individualist streak in American culture. Whether it was the community saved by the goodness of one man in a Frank Capra movie, the mass experience of blended dance ensembles of a Busby Berkeley number, the rapid shift to the left of American intellectuals, the collective swing of the big band, the reality and metaphor of the assembly line, the lure of Soviet Russia, or the mass mobilization for the war, the 1930s and 1940s drew people together—ideologically and socially—in ways they had not been before. The old stories had fallen apart, and new stories began to be told— new stories about everyone being in the same boat with a shared fate.

Old forms of liberal individualism may have been at bay, but the confusion created by its absence never translated into a permanent realignment of political ideals about the individual in American life. The philosopher John Dewey searched for a solution for this as early as 1930 in his book *Individualism Old and New*. There he argued for a reconfigured liberalism, one that proclaimed the centrality of democratic debate and decision making, and one that derived its vitality from both the collective and individualistic values of a democratic nationalism. The atomistic individualism of classical nineteenth-century liberalism had grown obsolete and detrimental in an era of corporate capitalism, Dewey argued, but detrimental too was the embrace of bureaucratic organization and centralized planning implemented by "experts" who largely ruled apart from the people whose lives their decisions altered. Beyond problem solving by educated elites versed in the technology of management, Dewey asked, what did liberalism offer? His answer was not comforting: The "lack of secure objects of allegiance, without

which individuals are lost, is especially striking in the case
of the liberal." For a political movement, Dewey considered
this a tragedy: "For human nature is self-possessed only as
it has objects to which it can attach itself."[35]

The "old" individualism, for all of the political and cultural contradictions, had once connected many Americans
to the possibility of a broader collective identity, a path that
wove through Jeffersonian self-reliance to a concept of citizenship rooted in the social value produced for all by one's
individual work. At its most vibrant—in the abolitionist
movement, in populism, progressivism, the pre-1920 socialist movement, and the women's movement—these dissi-
dents expanded traditions of individualism into connections, albeit typically brief, to a common good. Dewey was
nonetheless right when he argued that the "old" individualism had outlived its usefulness in a corporate, consumer-
orientated society and economy whose domineering presence denied a political role for this ethos of individualism.

The New Dealers' turn away from anti-monopoly largely
eliminated the possibility of the old individualism transforming itself into a new fighting liberal faith. The *necessity*
of dissolving that earlier producer-based individualism in
socioeconomic national policies designed to work in concert with corporate development and, particularly after the
war, the consumer culture it encouraged, drained American
politics of a powerful dissenting tradition. As liberals dismissed most redistributive policies that significantly curtailed corporate prerogatives, the connection that had once
tied the individual to a communal vision sharply ebbed. In
the process, the "massification" of modern liberalism surrendered the Jeffersonian anti-statist tradition to the conservative cause.

Left-leaning New Dealer Rexford Tugwell, for one, grew
bitter about the limits individualism placed on politics in

the 1930s. As his biographer writes, Tugwell "learned that there would be no quick change from an individualist to a more collectivized society, that the New Deal would comprise measures which, from his standpoint, were essentially superficial." He thought that even when Roosevelt tried to construct a new vision of individualism suitable for modern, corporate society, those efforts "too had not been immune to our national myths. . . . [L]ike all of us," FDR "had a weakness for what was familiar and trusted which led him to overestimate their sufficiency and underestimate their irrelevant antiquity."[36]

The consequences were profound. Shorn as it was of a strong redistributive vision and lacking those "secure objects of allegiance," the New Deal proved to be a weak philosophical alternative to the dominant strain of individualism in the public arena. It would be only a matter of time before liberalism's more conservative opponents, artfully, and to a surprising degree, successfully, rearmed for battle between the people and the liberal elite. "Perhaps the chief impact of the Great Depression," writes historian Robert McElvaine, "was that it obliged the American people to face up to the necessity of cooperative action because it took away, at least temporarily, the easy assumption of expansion and mobility that had decisively influenced so much of past American thinking."[37]

The evolution of the term "liberalism" suggests the complexity of the transformation. The term had existed, intellectually, back to the first half of the nineteenth century to express two currents of meaning of individual freedom—a humanitarian reform impulse that freed people from state and religious restrictions, and a Manchesterian free trade impulse. But it hardly existed as a term in the American political vernacular prior to FDR. Democrats who began to use the term "liberal" for the new collective economic poli-

tics used the word for tactical cover—it tied their efforts to
nineteenth-century individualism as well as separated them
from the messiness and bipartisan understandings of "progressivism." "Liberalism" simultaneously helped to check
fears of creeping socialism by placing a collective economic
vision under a rubric that, at its core, resonated with individual liberty (now, the new breed argued, by guaranteeing
it through shared material security). In FDR's hands, however, the term became a transcendent symbol, a word that
could ward off attacks on collectivism as well as fend off
leaders like Hoover who longed to return "liberalism" to its
older, hard-nosed meanings. Tugwell, more sensitive to the
questions of individualism than most, explained that the
new liberalism was "a time of confusion, of trying to attain
collectivistic organization under individualistic labels."[38]

Much of the trajectory toward the New Deal's modern
form might have been predictable from the content of
FDR's famous 1932 Commonwealth speech in San Francisco, which offered insights beyond the "forgotten man."
Providing a cogent history of American individual drive
and the role of the state, he declared that it was time for "a
reappraisal of values" in American life. The industrial order
had delivered the nation to a new place. It was not just the
Great Depression, but the entire scope, scale, and concentration of economic power that had changed prospects for
individual uplift. "Equality of opportunity as we have
known it," FDR declared, "no longer exists." His answer to
that inequality was limited. "The government should as-
sume the function of economic regulation only as a last
resort, to be tried only when private initiative, inspired by
high responsibility, with such assistance and balance as government can give, has finally failed." A far more accurate
guide to the legacy of both FDR and New Deal liberalism
remained his call for an "enlightened administration" of the

corporate economy orchestrated by the state in concert with the business community.[39]

As Lawrence and Cornelia Levine have suggested, "the greatest irony" of the New Deal was that the Democratic coalition of industrial workers, labor unions, liberals, white Southerners, and African Americans remained "as inherently unstable and prone to ideological and political stalemate as the day Roosevelt became its leader." Yet the achievements for working people—especially the National Labor Relations Act, the Fair Labor Standards Act, the Social Security Act—were hardly the simple containment strategies for dissent that many criticize them for. They were, in fact, among the biggest, most important, and significant breakthroughs of twentieth-century history. The American working class was briefly at the center of American politics, the unrestrained power of business was momentarily in check, and the historic heterogeneity of the working class was diminished. Into that moment rushed the successful drive for industrial unionism and progressive legislation of the type the United States had not seen before or since.[40]

The great social critic Lewis Mumford once dismissed the New Deal as nothing but "aimless experiment, sporadic patchwork, a total indifference to guiding principles or definitive goals, and hence an uncritical drift along the lines of least resistance, namely the restoration of capitalism." That it was. We can add the deep ideological undercurrents of racism, cultural conflict, and individualism to this line of least resistance and admit that yes, the New Deal was all of these things. But it was also the foundation for the greatest age of equality in the United States since the onset of the industrial revolution.[41]

JFK Appeals to Organized Labor, 1962. In the commanding days of
American labor liberalism, President Kennedy addresses the convention of the United Auto Workers. Organized labor rocketed from
near-obscurity to a central role in the political and economic life of the
nation in the postwar era.
Courtesy of Walter P. Reuther Library, Archives of Labor and Urban Affairs, Wayne State University.

CHAPTER FIVE

THE GREAT EXCEPTION IN ACTION

The postwar era, the period of the "great exception" in action, was an extraordinarily good time to be a worker. This was not simply because wages were going up to unprecedented levels and inequality was going down but because the future was bright, work paid off, and there was tremendous promise for the next generation. Working people had achieved economic citizenship and found themselves grounded in an entirely different world than they had prior to the Great Depression. Wage earners were pushed up by union strength from below, drawn forward by the educational opportunities of the GI Bill, supported by macro planning for full employment and full consumption, made confident by Social Security, and buoyed by U.S. global economic dominance. Beyond a doubt, white, male industrial workers enjoyed the fruits of the new economic enfranchisement and women and minorities remained on the fringes of the postwar labor relations system, but there was an important spillover effect as well. Wages crept up for all workers—as did the attendant optimism. The welfare state remained limited, and many welfare services were tied to employment rather than simply citizenship. Yet, especially when compared to either the past or the future, the gains were real and exciting.

For the very first time in U.S. history, business, the government, and workers all accepted unions and collective bargaining as legitimate pillars of American working life. Organized labor could count 14.5 million members in its ranks after the war, about 35 percent of the labor force, a density of membership that would never be seen again after the mid-1950s. The pretax income of the bottom 60 percent of households more than doubled between 1949 and 1979, tracking neatly with rising productivity. Those earnings went up, while the number of hours worked fell. The high marginal tax rates instituted for the war, especially on unearned income from capital ownership, remained. The effect was to discourage runaway corporate pay. In the "confiscatory" days of taxation, the top marginal tax rate in the United States went up to 94 percent during the last two years of the war, a level it held until it dropped to 77 percent as a result of the Kennedy-Johnson tax bill in 1964 (and it was still at 70 percent when Reagan took office; when he left, it was down to 28 percent).[1]

Anti-communist sentiments helped provide an additional, if anxious, social unity, Keynesian economics gave a shared logic to economic growth, and the modern industrial labor movement appeared to have finally solved the "labor question" for the indefinite future. As a result, more income, more equality, more optimism, more leisure, more consumer goods, more travel, more entertainment, more expansive homes, and more education were all available in the postwar years to regular people than at any other time in world history. Rather than a limited victory, many, especially in the left-led unions, believed that the foundation had been laid for the expansion of the model into service work, white-collar work, and the range of occupations segregated as either black or female.[2]

The future was bright, but the entire system rested on a precarious edifice. FDR's landslide victory in 1936 served to realign the party system, drawing together a new coalition that for the first time placed American workers loosely in a single party. While this did not mean that "class" voting had come to America or that the Democrats had achieved the function of a labor party, it did mean that internecine hostilities were checked. Urban workers, many of whom were descendants of immigrants (called "the ethnics") but also those of "old stock" Protestants, African Americans, white Southerners, and a range of liberal and progressive intellectuals and party leaders, combined in an uneasy and unstable alliance. This was the social foundation for the Golden Age of the white, male industrial working class, as well as the foundation for an expansive set of possibilities for all. While FDR's ambitions for a "Second Bill of Rights" never materialized, this coalition was enough to stop a retrenchment of anti–New Deal forces—at least for a while.

Despite the dramatic changes, they did not liberate Americans from the historic constraints of their political culture. Indeed, the inherent limits that framed the New Deal were shared both by liberal elites and, to a significant degree, by a majority of working people as well. Union leaders, for example, operating with impressive rank-and-file support, largely avoided staking their legacy on racial justice, equal pay, quality of work life, or even the expansion of the movement beyond the white, male industrial sectors. The labor movement got stopped in its tracks trying to expand into the South under the battle cry "Operation Dixie," and by the end of the 1940s, labor fully embraced the Cold War ideology that constrained its options. What proved most attractive was less the forward march of equal empowerment than the welcome security the New Deal offered: rising wages that encouraged consumption and legal and economic policies that promised secure, continuous employment for nuclear families headed mostly by white, male industrial workers. Many union members, their local leaders, and their elected representatives believed that their success during the 1930s and 1940s had turned the house of labor into a permanent fixture in American life. Such satisfaction belied the fact that they were enjoying only a temporary, tactical, recognition of workers' needs rather than an enduring answer to the labor question.

─────────

While it lasted, though, the New Deal juggernaut was very effective. To be a steel worker before the coming of the CIO, for instance, was to be engaged in dangerous work, for low pay and long hours. By the 1950s, however, steel worker's son Jack Metzgar could point to a complete transformation in his family's fortunes—from their material well-being to his father's bearing toward supervisors on the shopfloor. Yet that new wealth meant more than simply working-class affluence; it was part of an expansive sense of possibility. Embracing the "moral injunctions to daily fortitude" involved in a life of hard industrial work "made so much more sense then when there were so many visible payoffs for doing so," explained Metzgar. "We were learning to tolerate less and less repression from anybody or anything. . . . If what we lived through in the 1950s was not liberation, then liberation never happens in real human lives." That Metzgar quite realistically framed his family's "liberation" as a product of home ownership, a new world of consumer

durables, and a lilting sense of hope built upon rising expectations—those expectations, in turn, buoyed by the cycle
of social Keynesianism fostered by collective bargaining—is
both honest and profoundly suggestive of the outer reaches
of American working-class politics.[3]

World War II consolidated working-class gains from the
1930s, but it also marked the slide toward bureaucracy and
the approach of seemingly inexorable political limits for
workers, policymakers, and union leaders. The immediate
postwar moment must be understood as both liberation
and limitation; both big wages and big bureaucracy; both
the dawning of an age of unprecedented legitimacy for
workers and the death rattle of labor as a social movement.
Yet we do a disservice to history if we look back to the
postwar moment and see only the coming specter of stasis
or decline. Most commentators at the time were stunned by
labor's rapid success and awed by its newfound power. The
labor intellectual J.B.S. Hardman noted that the meteoric
rise of unionism in this period "goes beyond anything ever
known."[4]

In 1946, U.S. workers made use of that power and walked
out in the biggest strike wave in its history. Unlike other
years of upheaval—like the momentous events of 1877,
1886, 1894, 1902, 1919, 1934, or 1936—this strike was
not a desperate gambit for union recognition, but a flexing
of the powers available to workers in the new labor relations system. Frustrated by wartime inflation and anxious
to settle down into a stable postwar order, workers went
out and demanded more—and got it. Organized labor even
contested the right to manage, including most dramatically
the UAW's demand that General Motors "open the books"
to prove it could not meet the 30 percent wage increase the
union believed it could afford without passing on price in-
creases to consumers. While labor lost battles for control

and planning, they did win fatter paychecks. By 1950, landmark negotiations in the auto industry had resulted in the security of a five-year contract with cost of living adjustments, health benefits, unemployment, pensions, and vacations. *Fortune* magazine called it "The Treaty of Detroit," and the agreement became a beacon for other industries and set the rules for the employment relationship—in both organized and unorganized industries.[5]

In the end, contracts ended up explicitly asserting a variety of "right to manage" clauses to check the power of unions to bargain for anything more than better wages, benefits, and working conditions, ceding management prerogatives—from the introduction of technology to the location of plants—to the corporations. An emerging deal became clear: more money for workers, but no new powers for unions beyond what they could wield in the narrow contractual world of the postwar bargaining table. As Michael Kazin argues, the end of the war marked "the last time that the men and women of organized labor could realistically imagine themselves to be combative and optimistic representatives of the ordinary people as a whole. The CIO was the last mass insurgency on the Left to argue the centrality of work to any notion of a democratic polity. When, for compelling reasons, the industrial labor movement embraced the new liberal order and got enmeshed in the coils of bureaucratic responsibility, there was no other force to carry on the tradition."[6]

————————

Historians have greatly debated the heady nature of labor's postwar moment. Some scholars have called the postwar era labor relations system a "liberation"; others see it as a "trap"; others a "counterfeit liberation"; and still others

as so limited by race, gender, and occupation as to barely
exist at all. Was it a labor-management "accord" or "com-
pact," in which labor, capital, and the state created a high-
wage social contract for the ensuing decades? Was it a liberal sellout by the labor leadership in a moment that, if
handled differently, might have had the potential to reframe
the postwar era in a more social democratic or corporatist direction? Was labor a victim of anti-communism and
postwar purges, forced into a more restrained role where it
might otherwise have continued labor's march into the service sector, into occupations held by minorities and women,
and into the South? Or, as others have contended, was it
a reasonable settlement, given fifteen years of depression
and war, in which working people were offered money and
security in exchange for industrial organization and peace?[7]

Given the very real obstacles that blocked the development of grander schemes, the war and postwar eras are best
seen as periods of working-class achievement rather than
compromise or sellout, a period in which the wartime emergency allowed unions to gain many of the advances they
were unable to achieve during the 1930s. Rather than seeing the postwar settlement as "a product of defeat, not victory," as the labor historian Nelson Lichtenstein and many
others have argued, we should see it as the best victory
available. To call it a "defeat" implies an array of strategic
options that probably did not exist. The political scientist
Tracy Roof clearly cuts through the ideological thicket surrounding this period, describing the period as "not a missed
opportunity as much as a missing opportunity." In the long
arc of American history, government endorsement of collective bargaining rights, embedded in a limited welfare state,
must be seen as a massive leap forward. Labor may have
rapidly waned as a social insurgency, but the presence and
power of unions in the postwar era did stand as institu-

tional proof of the far-reaching, if simple, idea that common people were entitled to a decent life.[8]

Consider, for instance, the Taft-Hartley Act (1947). In the year and a half after the war, seventy anti-labor bills were introduced into the House, and, when Republicans won the House and the Senate in 1946 for the first time since the Great Depression began, they got straight to work curbing labor's power. The result, labor's much-despised Taft-Hartley Act, posed a new, sharp set of constraints on working-class power. Taft-Hartley, which actually amended the Wagner Act, required union leaders to sign anti-communist affidavits, enumerated management's rights, allowed states to establish "right-to-work" laws, limited the unions' political powers, and eliminated secondary boycotts, in addition to a host of other curtailments. The results restricted labor liberalism geographically, ideologically, and politically. By purging the left from the labor movement, Taft-Hartley also sapped much of the energy and spirit around organizing women and minorities—the very groups labor would need to engage in the 1960s and beyond.

Rather than decry what was taken away by the act, one might, in retrospect, marvel at what remained. Given the unremitting pattern of hostility to collective bargaining that business and the state have demonstrated in U.S. history, the very fact that the act (derided as "fascist" and "slave labor" at the time) actually *maintained the bargaining rights in Wagner* reflected a unique moment in the organized power of workers. As the labor economist and historian Philip Taft (no relationship to Senator Taft) put it in 1948, "Recognition of the right to organize by a conservative Congress is an indication of the long distance we have traveled since the 1920s." Although the curtailments on the Wagner Act were significant and would prove difficult, unions nonetheless emerged from World War II with something tangible and, seemingly, durable. Unlike the aftermath of World War I, which ended in bitter repression, in the wake of World War II, labor had won a compromised peace.[9]

Labor had ambitious plans to repeal all or part of Taft-Hartley, and most presumed at some point that they would succeed. Yet it was not to be. While the Republicans' control of Congress lasted only until 1948, even with often strong Democratic majorities during the Truman, Johnson, Carter, Clinton, and Obama presidencies, repeal of Taft-Hartley (or other progressive reforms of private-sector labor law) never passed. With the coming of each Democratic administration since the New Deal, each legislative attempt ended by proving labor's inability to move Congress and the postwar presidents on labor law reform, revealing anew the constraints on labor's political power and the futility of reform efforts. Typically constrained by the Senate filibuster that was often used specifically to block labor and civil rights legislation in particular, efforts in labor's favor could never manage to expand beyond the one-time success of 1935.[10]

Despite the massive changes brought on by the New Deal and the CIO, as the historian David Brody points out, there was a haunting continuity with the deepest past in the guiding philosophies of the American labor movement.

> No one would want to equate the modern UAW-GM contract with any union agreement of the pre–New Deal era, or the role of the AFL-CIO inside the Democratic Party in 1968 with anything dreamt of by Samuel Gompers. . . . It is the underlying perspective that carried on, the assumption that labor's place was inherently limited, that its sphere was necessarily circumscribed in the nation's industrial life. And, if one listened closely, Gompers' words could be heard echoing long decades after his death. . . . If the [leaders like

UAW president] Walter Reuthers voiced a headier social rhetoric, if they grew restless under the burden of
[AFL-CIO president George] Meany's philosophy, in
practice they adhered to the same trade-union pre-
cepts confining the power of the labor movement.

The ghost of the narrow old philosophies of the American
Federation of Labor proved inescapable even at the height
of the CIO's power. *Fortune* magazine made the same point
with less subtlety: "American labor is not 'working-class
conscious;' it is not 'proletarian' and does not believe in
class war . . . today's successful, strong, and militant labor
movement is as little 'proletarian' or 'socialist' as the small
and unsuccessful labor movement of twenty years ago."[11]

In the decades following World War II, a booming domestic economy combined with a decline in partisanship
appeared to be confirmation that the new system worked.
The Cold War certainly raised tensions within liberalism,
and between liberalism and a conservative politics emerging
from its Depression Era dormancy, but it probably enhanced
the ideological and political strength of the New Deal order.
In fact, what was most impressive was the cohesive nationalism that formed public attitudes on this issue. Labor, too,
seemed ensconced as a staunch ally in a national anti-
communist crusade, and also wielded one of the most re-
spected, forceful, and effective lobbying operations in Washington. In the era of the "liberal consensus," to use Godfrey
Hodgson's formulation, those called "modern" Republicans
had adapted to the New Deal, relinquishing generations'
worth of fights against the progressive state. Though certainly uninterested in expanding it, they felt they could not
challenge the new pluralism. As President Dwight Eisenhower noted to his brother Edgar, "Should any political
party attempt to abolish social security, unemployment in-

surance, and eliminate labor laws and farm programs, you would not hear of that party again in our political history." In contrast to the conservatism before or that to come, Ike embraced much of the idea of a modern, reformed capitalism. Liberal intellectuals began to talk of the "end of ideology," of how the postwar system had ended class conflict by creating industrial pluralism, and how the unions were now simply junior partners to the corporations in the modern state's regulatory bureaucracy. The AFL and the CIO showed their Cold War unity and buried the hatchet to form the AFL-CIO in 1955.[12]

Not far below the patina of consensus, conservatives were mobilizing against the new order. The heated politics of domestic anti-communism often got inflated with, and at times actually served as a front for, an attack on the liberalism itself. Radical conservatism contained a number of ideological tenets that had little direct bearing on communism per se—there were, after all, very few domestic communists remaining in the United States and even fewer of any relevancy. Rather, it tended to contain political sentiments that sought to roll the nation's politics back to an early age. Nativism, religious fundamentalism, deep suspicions about organized labor, a defense of patriarchy, anti-cosmopolitanism, and an overall hostility to the modest collectivism of the New Deal swirled within the "paranoid style" of American politics. As Elizabeth Wickenden, welfare proponent and policy analyst from Roosevelt to Kennedy, framed it, one could envision the reactionary strains in search of an older, lost America:

> Right wing radicals are characterized in my observation by a virtually fanatical distaste for all popular

institutions of mutual support (from labor unions to
the United Nations). And a temperamental nostalgia
for an imagined lost society based on the virtues of
rugged individualism as they visualize them. This is
justified by a type of social Darwinism, doctrine of
self-regulating economic laissez-faire, and international isolationism which historical reality has long
since relegated to fantasy. Social security is, by any
functional definition, the pure prototype of institu-
tionalized mutual support, resting on a general recognition of the essential interdependence of modern life.
It is, therefore, a prime target for attack from the radical right.

Much of that "radicalism" would grow to become central
to the mainstream conservative movement during the 1980s
and beyond.[13]

High levels of religious faith in the postwar era were
largely subsumed within what Garry Wills calls an "interfaith amity." Despite the growing prominence of revivalists
like Billy Graham (a Democrat) and the reappearance of
morally engaged, grassroots, conservative activists, the primary current in American political life remained comfort-
ably in the cultured hands of mainline Protestants.

Even though overt religious conflict was limited, important changes in American religious identity were under way.
Seeking "A New Age, Not a New Deal," Baptists, Pentecos-
tals, and fundamentalists of a variety of stripes challenged
the secular authority of the New Deal and the labor movement with a belief in individual religious conversion and the
infallibility of the Bible. While their challenges remained
mostly below the national political radar, significant transformations in the map of religious identity were well under
way.[14]

As Southern workers moved west and north to work in defense industries, they brought their evangelical traditions with them and, in the process, began a slow transformation of working-class politics and identity. "Plain folk" migrants brought with them the mutually reinforcing ideologies of "Jefferson and Jesus," in which individual liberty and an individual's personal relationship with God were sacrosanct. The historian Darren Dochuk describes the tenets of evangelical Christian democracy as based in faith in "the efficacy of pristine capitalism, unbridled optimism about the freedom and power of the individual conscience, a belief in the rightness of government by popular consensus, and most importantly, a commitment to the sanctity of the community." In Southern California, defense workers first enrolled in the economic populism of the "Ham and Eggs" movement, which managed for a time to contain a political agenda broad enough to include both Christian Americanism and New Deal economic redistribution. Yet it was a big tent that would not long last. The movement, as Dochuk has shown, was "forced to confront a new political reality that compelled it to choose between rather than for Christ and the CIO." Feeling forced to select between their secular class identity and their faith and religious identity, many in Northern and Western industrial cities would eventually join the South in choosing their religious faith.[15]

Despite extraordinarily high levels of religiosity, the brewing fundamentalist movement, and emerging linkages between business elites and religious conservatives, postwar religion was more of a unifying force than one of dissent and division. Church and synagogue attendance boomed, and denominational adherence ran high, but few argued about it. In 1957, the census found that 96 percent of Americans said they belonged to a church or synagogue. Mutual respect for various faiths also ran extraordinarily high, and the idea that the United States was a "Judeo-Christian" nation held sway. Welded together by opposition to "Godless Communism," interfaith sensibilities endorsed the adding of "Under God" to the Pledge of Allegiance and making "In God We Trust" the nation's official motto. In what Wills has called a unique "era of good feelings" in the otherwise divisive history of American faith, it was enough for Dwight Eisenhower to claim, "Our government makes no sense unless it is founded in a deeply felt religious faith—and I don't care what it is." This contrasted dramatically with the drama of the Scopes trial before the New Deal and the coming radical politicization of religion that would form the Moral Majority in the 1970s.[16]

By the early 1960s, a true conservative movement began to emerge, though most liberals failed to take it seriously. Many, who were convinced that the "employers' paradise had been lost," sought to reclaim it. By 1960, the emerging conservative movement even had its own youth wing, Young Americans for Freedom, which predated the New Left. Conservatives also began to partner with slowly awakening religious communities long thought by liberal activists to have disintegrated. From the right, a deep distrust of liberalism, including its "modern Republican" variant, broadened into a popular movement. William F. Buckley's *National Review* helped move conservatism away from a "stuffy orthodoxy, Republican stand-pat-ism and economic self-interest," offering instead what Pat Buchanan called a "snapping pennant" of political faith. It would play a critical role in encouraging a variety of contentious conservative thinkers to reach ever more receptive audiences with a new vision. State after state in the South passed anti-union "right-to work" legislation, and sought to attract Northern industry with lower taxes and a variety of investment incentives.[17]

Conservatism again appeared irrevelant when Senator Barry Goldwater lost the 1964 election to Lyndon Baines Johnson in a landslide that echoed Roosevelt's in 1936. Liberals crowed loudly over the demise of a candidate and his movement that the historian Richard Hofstadter scorned as "so bizarre, so archaic, so self-confounding, so remote from the basic American consensus." Yet conservatives got busy planning for the future. Goldwater's more than 26 million voters proved a respectable base for future political organizing. The movement found its spokesman and, in 1966, a successful California gubernatorial candidate, in Ronald Reagan, an experienced conservative—and once a New Deal enthusiast and union leader. In but a few years, liberal exaltation at Goldwater's defeat proved to be as astute as an earlier liberal generation's complacent reaction to the Scopes trial.[18]

At the same time as the New Right got moving, the New Left was volubly dismissing the ideas and its institutions of liberalism (particularly the Democratic Party and its major ally, organized labor) as equally bankrupt. The rising social movements of the 1960s tended to see liberalism—and labor—at first as an ambivalent ally, their "social idealism waning under the tendencies of bureaucracy, materialism, business ethics," in the words of the New Left's 1962 "Port Huron Statement." By the latter half of the 1960s, both liberals and the unions grew to become the left's opponents— too bureaucratized, too slow on civil rights, too retrograde on women's issues, and, above all, among the staunchest supporters of the war in Vietnam.[19]

━━━━━━━━━━━━━━━━

Looking more closely at the postwar years, one can see that "consensus" looks more like stalemate. Congress remained

stuck between liberals and the combined forces of pro-
business Northern Republicans and Southern Democrats.
While nobody mounted a full-on attack on the New Deal,
it was hardly advanced in the nearly two decades after the
war. The entire system was enmeshed in a paralyzing web
of parliamentary rules, committee power, and filibusters—
most of which continued to be controlled almost exclusively by Southern Democrats dead set on maintaining Jim
Crow and their labor system. The cost of the political stalemate became obvious to Lyndon Johnson the night he took
office after the Kennedy assassination. "You know," LBJ
remarked to an aide, "when I went into that office tonight
and they came in and started briefing me on what I have to
do, do you realize that every issue that is on my desk tonight was on my desk when I came to Congress in 1937?"[20]

Yet that docket did not sit on his desk for long, as the
political logjam burst open on LBJ's watch. What rushed
through was one of the most active periods of federal legislation in American history. Acting on the double punch of
the Kennedy legacy and Johnson's genius for parliamentary
maneuvering, the Democrats were able to shake up their
right wing, add some moderate votes from the Republicans,
and work the entrenched rule and committee system with
enough acumen to get a wide array of bills passed, including
civil rights, transportation, Medicare, housing, anti-poverty,
and environmental protection. The legislative fury was such
that journalist James Reston quipped in 1965 that "Lyndon
Johnson is getting everything through Congress except the
abolition of the Republican party."[21]

Johnson envisioned his Great Society programs as "fulfilling FDR's mission," but the focus of those varied legislative acts differed sharply from Roosevelt's. Yet, even more
than the inchoate philosophy of the New Deal, Lyndon
Johnson's Great Society and the War on Poverty was a

hodgepodge of programs glued together by a couple of phrases. In his May 1964 speech, Johnson proclaimed that the century-long effort "to create an order of plenty for all of our people" had been successful. The current task, down into the coming century, would be "to use that wealth to enrich and elevate our national life, and to advance the quality of our American civilization." This was the moment for the nation to dedicate itself to reach beyond the "rich . . . and the powerful society . . . upward toward the Great Society," that place "where men are more concerned with the quality of their goals than the quantity of their goods." This was a vision for an age of affluence, quite different from Roosevelt's emphasis on fundamental material security, but it did result in an avalanche of social and cultural improvements aimed at a general uplifting of the nation.[22]

Johnson also declared an "unconditional war on poverty in America" in his January 1964 State of the Union speech and appointed Sargent Shriver, then the director of the Peace Corps, to head the effort. The creation of the Transportation Department; education bills, with their Pell grants and student loans; consumer protection acts; the Public Broadcasting System; the national endowments for both the humanities and the arts; and the beautification of the nation's highways did in fact greatly enhance American life, and all provided a thrilling sense of collective purpose and national greatness. Few innovations proved more popular than Head Start, which focused on the education of the nation's poor children. All of these programs would be attacked directly over the years, but as Robert Dallek has observed, their continued survival, and the broader spirit that motivated them, created a "hold on the public imagination that endures."[23]

Yet these were not the New Deal. Johnson was of the New Deal, yet the Great Society was not. Unlike his political hero FDR, LBJ was governing in the greatest economic success story in world history. For New Dealers, the problems of poverty and the labor market were structural. For Great Society liberals, they tended to be individual. The New Dealers believed that problems with the labor market—unemployment, poverty, even discrimination—boiled down to economic questions. Their answers tended toward macro regulation, planning, unionization, massive public works, and relief programs. But most Great Society liberals saw it differently. Rather than restructuring the economy and redistributing the wealth, the generation of the 1960s believed that labor market problems tended to be individual and personal—the limitations of the poor themselves. Although they often overlapped with the more structural view in large public works initiatives, by the 1960s, most policymakers came to believe that if one could not make it in the 1960s economy of abundance, then one simply needed help in doing so. Reform of the individual, not the society, thus became the focus.[24]

In a cabinet meeting a few weeks after LBJ's Great Society speech, Secretary of Labor Willard Wirtz suggested a massive jobs program similar to the New Deal's Works Progress Administration. Johnson's menacing glare foreclosed any movement in that direction: "I have never seen a colder reception from the president," a staff member at that meeting recalled. Johnson's "just—absolute blank stare—implied without even opening his mouth that Shriver should move on to the next proposal." Neither a jobs program nor direct relief, both echoes of a New Deal past, were on LBJ's agenda. The declarations of "unconditional war" on poverty, moreover, had always been grander than the actual funding could support. As Daniel Patrick Moynihan explained at the time, the "war" had been "oversold and underfinanced to the point that its failure was almost a matter of design." No sooner had the political dam broken in 1964–1965 than it began to re-form, blocking future liberal advances, while at the same time Johnson diverted the dollars he originally intended for his domestic war to the war in Vietnam.[25]

In addition, Great Society policymakers presumed that the main sectors of the economy would remain unionized indefinitely, and medical benefits would need to be provided only for those outside of the well-organized and well-remunerated "primary" sectors of the economy. Yet the sands were shifting under their feet. Of the flood of legislation that crossed Johnson's desk prior to the conservative turn of the 1966 midterm elections, Medicare (for the aged) and Medicaid (for the poor) stand out as promising the most in terms of collective economic rights. National health insurance had been on the progressive docket since the New Deal Era, but even at the apex of the liberals' postwar power, Johnson felt he did not have the votes to initiate a comprehensive national program of health insurance. By tactically choosing to provide protection to the poor and aged, the Great Society did help close some of the largest gaps in the semi-private welfare system created after World War II, but sacrificed the battle for universal coverage that had proven elusive from Roosevelt to Obama.

The Great Society was built on the premise that the New Deal generation had solved the major structural problems and that the New Deal order would persist—a juggernaut without the fragilities. The federal government's focus on limited welfare arrangements was intended simply to fill in the gaps for those outside unionized sectors of the economy. In reality, these arrangements were, as the historian Jennifer Klein put it, only "islands of security, with high waters all around." Within two decades, vast swaths of wage earners would qualify neither for the private welfare state of employer-provided health insurance nor for the federal programs. Medical benefits provided by a union contract would become an increasingly rare thing for working Americans after the 1970s. The optimistic premises of the New Deal order would lose both economic and political validity, leaving the very ideological foundations of the Great Society greatly weakened.[26]

Central to all developments in the 1960s was the black freedom struggle. One hundred years after the Civil War, civil rights legislation shook the political foundation of the New Deal coalition. The Civil Rights and Voting Rights Acts, pushed forward by ten years of an eloquent, patient, tactically brilliant struggle in the South, did not end discrimination, but they did end the formal commitment of one very important wing of the Democratic Party to white supremacy. But the morally compelling grassroots struggle to extend citizenship to all individual Americans also revealed the structural limitations of New Deal liberalism. Until the Kennedy and Johnson years, the Democratic Party largely continued to depend upon silence and denial of the race issue—and shuddered to its core whenever it came up. "We have lost the South for a generation," Johnson told an aide when he signed the Civil Rights Act. In fact, his assessment was optimistic; he had most likely lost the white South, a necessary if problematic part of the New Deal coalition, indefinitely. It must be noted that this cost was incurred against a simple commitment to basic constitutional rights—nothing more.

Yet, in the later phase of the civil rights movement, Martin Luther King, Jr., also began to face structural questions that went beyond individual rights. He knew the stakes were much higher than the formidable challenges he had already undertaken. As he explained to Congress in 1966: "It was easier to integrate public facilities, it was easier to gain the right to vote, because it didn't cost the Nation anything, and the fact is that we are dealing with [the economic] issue now that will call for something of a restructuring of the architecture of American society." Like so many of King's metaphors, this one was pitch-perfect. It is that very *architecture*—in both its grandeur and its formidable limitations—that presented more intractable problems. Attempts to storm that architecture or plans to redesign it mostly failed. Many bold attempts were made to meld the new politics of the 1960s with the old politics of the 1930s. Those efforts did not bend the arc of history, however; they were mostly bent by it.[27]

In a way that some still found counterintuitive, many of the most violent confrontations between blacks and whites occurred not in the South but in Northern cities. Early in the 1960s, before the passage of the Civil Rights Act in 1964 and the Voting Rights Act the following year, white trade unionists (particularly in the skilled building trades) often found themselves the target of picket lines and sit-ins for their practice of maintaining all-white applicant lists for required apprentice training programs. Their angry responses, sympathetically shared by many other union workers, were in part racially driven, but they were also a defensive reaction to a perceived economic threat. Organized workers, usually white and male, had achieved extraordinary victories in negotiations with employers over the previous decades and enjoyed the benefits of a semi-private welfare system. Nonunion workers, whether they had been excluded from existing unions appropriate to their occupa-

tions or labored in the burgeoning unorganized sectors of
the economy, were left out of the club. The fact that nonunion workers were so frequently women and people of
color in service occupations complicated the terms, and intensified the tensions, around economic inequality. Even
more explosive were the efforts by the civil rights movement
to expand housing options for blacks in Chicago, Detroit,
and other Northern cities. So violent and vitriolic was the
opposition in Chicago in the summer of 1966 that King
declared: "I think the people of Mississippi ought to come
to Chicago to learn how to hate."[28]

Many white workers felt they were becoming the new
forgotten men, a sentiment reinforced by the political drum-
beat of the remarkably strong presidential campaigns of
Alabama Governor George Wallace on the right. When racial equality became an explicit part of the Democratic
agenda, issues like school integration and busing generated
a white backlash and racialized populism evident in Wallace's presidential campaigns, the motifs of which were cautiously picked up by both Richard Nixon and Ronald Reagan. As Kevin Phillips famously suggested, the legions of
forgotten men among nominally Democratic Wallace voters—both North and South—were en route from a Democratic past to a Republican future.[29]

Figures such as George Wallace and Strom Thurmond
symbolized the nation's evolving political affiliations. The
states' rights Democratic senator from South Carolina, who
had bolted the party in 1948 to run as a Dixiecrat against
Harry Truman and the Roosevelt legacy, completed his
journey in 1964 by announcing his switch to the Republican Party and campaigned intensely for Barry Goldwater
throughout the South. After the success of the Civil Rights
and Voting Rights Acts, conservative Southern Democrats

rapidly began to change their registration and voting toward the Republican Party, driven by resistance to civil rights gains, federal enforcement of the Constitution, and a growing concern with the moral culture of American life. In one of the important—and ironic—realignments in politics, new Southern suburban Republicans joined to support Richard Nixon and ultimately Ronald Reagan in alliance with white working people in the North whose economic interests Southern politicians had consistently and effectively blocked for many generations.[30]

After World War II, talk of creating a third party drifted around left-leaning liberals and labor. Instead, the far-thinking minds of the time bet on what they called "realignment." As Walter Reuther, the dynamic head of the United Auto Workers, explained, "We felt that instead of trying to create a third party—a labor party . . . that we ought to bring about a realignment and get the liberal forces in one party and the conservative in another." Unfortunately, for liberals, a realignment did happen but not the one they had hoped for. The Southern Democracy did fall apart, but in so doing, white working-class voters shifted to the Republican Party rather than a (loose) class-based alignment with the Democratic Party. That form of realignment proved disastrous, as the liberal forces were overwhelmed beyond the 1970s. As the country moved right, even the Democrats became more conservative to keep up with the popularity of the new conservatism.[31]

The push for racial justice in the United States finally made the existing discriminatory immigration policy regime untenable—and created one of the greatest unintended policy outcomes of the twentieth century. The Immigration and Nationality Act of 1965 was meant merely to modify the existing immigration order by rectifying forty years of explicitly racist practice of the Johnson-Reed Act of 1924. Touted as a modest reform, it quietly and somewhat unceremoniously began a slow return to immigration patterns that would echo those of the late nineteenth century.

Debating the potential effects of the act on the Senate floor, Ted Kennedy argued,

> Under the proposed bill, the present level of immigration remains substantially the same . . . the ethnic mix of this country will not be upset. . . . Contrary to the charges in some quarters, [the bill] will not inundate America with immigrants from any one country or area, or the most populated and deprived nations of Africa and Asia. . . . In the final analysis, the ethnic pattern of immigration under the proposed measure is not expected to change as sharply as the critics seem to think.

His words proved almost completely wrong, as, fast-forwarding to the 1980s and beyond, new peoples from all over the world entered the labor market. In the process, though, immigration reemerged as a touchstone political issue. The immigration act of 1965 started by correcting a forty-year-old mistake but ended with a long slide into heated questions of racial identity and national citizenship. In a culture where racial tensions were once more overtly politicized and compounded by the continuation of intense immigration pressures from the southern border, these political currents fractured the polity and at times ignited passions that seemed to derive directly from nineteenth-century nativism.[32]

With immigration returning, racial issues no longer contained by repression and indifference of the white majority, and class only tenuously held together, the future of the

New Deal coalition began to appear shaky. By the 1970s, the politics of the left were avidly embracing the expansion of individual rights, and the religious right was mobilizing to redeem the nation from a culture of post-1960s sin. It would not be long before the fault lines of American politics began to look a lot like the New Deal *status quo ante*.

Protest for Immigrant Rights, 2006. Immigrant rights returned to the fore after being absent for generations. Here, Los Angeles workers and their allies claim their status as workers and citizens in enormous May Day demonstrations.
© David Bacon.

CHAPTER SIX

TOWARD A NEW GILDED AGE

Less than two generations after Franklin Roosevelt invoked his version of the famous "forgotten man," Richard Nixon turned the clock back on that mythological American figure. Accepting the 1968 nomination of the Republican Party, he recycled William Graham Sumner's original invocation by attempting to separate the nobility of the common person from the misguided pity of the do-gooders. Trying to rise above the turmoil of the 1960s, Nixon asked that the nation listen to the "quiet voice in the tumult of the shouting," where it could hear "the great majority of Americans, the forgotten Americans, the non shouters, the non demonstrators. . . . They work in American factories, they run American businesses. They serve in government; they provide most of the soldiers who die to keep it free. They give drive to the spirit of America. They give lift to the American dream. They give steel to the backbone of America. They're good people. They're decent people; they work and they save and they pay their taxes and they care." Taking his political tutorials from the realignments triggered by George Wallace, Nixon went on to give shelter to the disgruntled, confused, angry, and forgotten (white) working man. Like Sumner, Nixon sought to separate this honest worker from

threats perceived just below him in the economic pyramid—
as well as, more importantly, the meddlesome sympathies of
the reformers. In between the eras of Sumner and Nixon
was FDR's unique version of the forgotten man, rapidly
fading from the national consciousness.[1]

Nixon embodied many of the complex transitions in the
late postwar era. Watergate and Cambodia rightfully over-
shadow his presidency today, but if we take Nixon on his
own terms, then his overarching political goal was to build
a conservative answer to the Roosevelt coalition—what
Nixon liked to call the New Majority. He believed that his
1972 landslide electoral victory over outspokenly liberal
George McGovern was for the Republicans much like the
1936 election was for Roosevelt and the Democrats: it delivered the common man, somewhat narrowly defined, to
the party of Nixon. Although not ready to abandon workers to the free market—in fact still very much in a liberal
mode on domestic policy—Nixon's strategy was to shift the
electorate's allegiances from the shared material world of
the New Deal to the divisions of culture, social life, and
race. "The real issues of the election," he lectured his advisors, "are the ones like patriotism, morality, religion—not
the material issues. If the issues were prices and taxes, they'd
vote for McGovern."[2]

Riding high in the brief political triumph between Nixon's 1972 victory and the Watergate disaster, presidential
advisor Patrick Buchanan noted that "the ideological fault
that runs beneath the surface and down the center of the
Democratic Party is as deep as any political division in
America." The blue collar, lower middle-class ethnics and
white Southerners "who gave FDR those great landslides"
were in rebellion against the "intellectual aristocracy and
liberal elite who now set the course" of the Democratic

Party. The self-congratulations were premature, as the administration was on the verge of being taken under by the Watergate scandal. Buchanan missed only the degree and timing, though not the substance, of his point when he claimed that 1972 "makes the long-predicted 'realignment of parties' a possibility, and could make Mr. Nixon the Republican FDR" and the New Right "the successor to the Roosevelt coalition."[3]

Nixon and his advisors not only claimed credit prematurely, they also claimed too much of it. As Thomas Sugrue argues, the deeper impulses of American history had long been at work, slowly shaping this realignment. "The 'silent majority' did not emerge de novo from the alleged failures of liberalism in the 1960s; it was not the unique product of white rejection of the Great Society. Instead it was the culmination of more than two decades of simmering white discontent and extensive antiliberal political organization." In the aftermath of the Great Society, white working people felt themselves to be coughing up their taxes to support the poor minority—a very different formula than when the affluent few were being taxed to help support the working-class majority.[4]

After Richard Nixon's defeat of George McGovern in 1972, Democratic senator Eugene McCarthy pinpointed a key element of Nixon's victory: that as far as most voters were concerned, the Democrats had long been coasting on their old accomplishments. His party, lamented McCarthy, had not offered any real differences on major issues of collective welfare between themselves and the opposition since 1948. Rather, Democrats had pursued office in the postwar era "trying to get elected on the basis of our old achievements, running on the New Deal, what we did in the 1930s." We "were also running on the old failure of the Republicans," he concluded, reduced to digging up the corpse of Herbert Hoover to rattle voters' fears.[5]

Though liberals were able to recover from the 1972 electoral disaster and enjoy post-Watergate victories in the 1974 midterms, a messy, inflationary economy quickly destroyed the Democrats' last claim to leadership. The early 1970s inequality almost imperceptibly made the turn to begin its long climb back upward, individualism returned in what Tom Wolfe dubbed the "Me Decade," labor found itself embattled and in search of renewal, religious revivalism became an explicit part of the Republican Party in the "Moral Majority," and, by the 1980s, immigration returned as a core hot button issue.

At first, unemployment was at historic lows, and earnings were at their all-time high for male wage earners. But Vietnam spending launched an inflationary spiral, radically compounded by the price of oil during the embargo of the Organization of Petroleum Exporting Countries (OPEC). Then, beginning in 1973–1974, real earnings stagnated, advances driven down by the oil shocks and the ensuing double-digit inflation. Deindustrialization and plant closings proved to be the first harbingers of a global restructuring of work itself that would continue over the ensuing three decades. Neither the policies nor the political coalitions that had maintained the World War II era "great compression" proved tenable in the waning days of the "great exception." Well into the twenty-first century, earnings for working people continued to languish, rarely rising above the high achieved in the early 1970s. Levels of inequality long thought vanquished by the New Deal crept back up to 1920s levels by the 1990s. Liberals had a hard time identifying what they stood for, as they proved unable to withstand attacks from both the left and the right. Many then and since have pointed to the economic changes whirling about the 1970s and 1980s to explain the decline of liberalism, but the structural argument begs an important question: why was liberalism not able to mount a defense of its values or a counterattack with a new vision?[6]

———————

To be sure, the New Deal political coalition and its policy initiatives did not simply collapse of their own contradictions or of external economic forces. They were pushed—and pushed hard. The Business Roundtable, the revivification of free-market thinking, the conservative turn of the courts, the rise of union-busting law firms, well-financed conservative think tanks, and the rest of the New Right package actively sought its destruction. Yet, it was also *vulnerable* to attack. Too many of the analyses that try to account for the decline of the New Deal order fall into the liberal trap of presuming a static ideal of postwar liberalism and try to account for its fall. The New Deal order is in some sense both the object of study *and* the frame of reference in such accounts, when in fact it was too brief and too anomalous an episode in American history to be the norm against which twentieth-century declension narratives ought to be framed.

The one place both liberals and conservatives found traction was in advancing the cause of the deepest ideological wellspring in American political culture: the varieties of individual rights. The new post-1960s politics offered a desperately needed progressive version of individualism—often based on the rights of previously excluded groups—as well as a trenchant critique of the whiteness and maleness of the New Deal paradigm. The United States became more demo-

cratically inclusive during this period than any other time in
its history. The "movement of movements" of the 1960s and
1970s would eventually be called "rights consciousness" or
"identity politics" or even "post-material politics"—a
framework that contrasted with the economic liberalism of
the New Deal.

Reformed individualism was still individualism—a politics that discouraged broader economic solidarity in favor
of guaranteeing people an equal chance to compete in a
tightening labor market. Democratizing access to a market
is not the same as democratizing economic security. It was
the obverse of what the New Dealers had done: having
made great strides toward democratizing capitalism, the
generation of the 1930s had failed to democratize access to
the labor market (let alone the ballot). By the 1970s, the
opposite set of issues was in motion. Although unions tried
to resurrect the old system with labor law reform under
every Democratic president, the nearest miss coming under
Jimmy Carter for want of two votes for cloture, the old
system of labor rights was "fading away," legal scholar
Katherine Stone explains, subsumed by "a plethora of new
employment rights for individual workers" that promised
protection from issues such as discrimination and sexual
harassment.[7]

The revival of individualism since the decline of the New
Deal order developed in a radically expanded and much
healthier form. The promise of constitutional rights and liberties has been made much wider and more substantial by
the social movements of the twentieth century: there are no
segregationist state constitutions, a commitment to gender
equality is far broader, and the official forms of Jim Crow
are in their grave. The Civil Rights Act and the Voting Rights
Act are the most important political achievements of the

postwar era, and the transformation in gender relations is the most significant social transformation of the contemporary age. The current—and perhaps exhausted—debate between "class politics" and "identity politics" is a false one, as it overlooks the fragility of the one-time leap forward in class identity and how readily a reformed individualism adapted to American political and corporate culture. Above all else, any understanding of post–New Deal order individualism must place at the center of the discussion the problems involved with the restoration of the nearly uncontestable power of the fictitious, if legally protected, individual in American life: that of the corporation.[8]

The demand for social rights also had an odd twist, as it created a template for all groups to stake a claim in American politics. Irish, Italian, Greek, Jewish, and many others claimed political positions based on once submerged identities. After the scramble to fit in as "American" for generations, in the post–Civil Rights Era ethnicity became socially valuable. The "Ellis Island revivalism" put forward a history of hard work, the passage in steerage, and family uplift that served, often intentionally, to blunt the critique of the civil rights movement. Appeals to a generalized "whiteness" no longer worked, so the ethnic revival provided new claims on citizenship—and at times arguments for racial innocence. "Racists?" asked Michael Novak in his *The Rise of the Unmeltable Ethnics*. "Most of us ceased being serfs only the last two hundred years." Hardly a claim for interethnic solidarity, this was Nixon's "silent majority" setting the forgotten man beyond the reach of lower orders.[9]

The movements for gender and racial equality fundamentally transformed occupational life, expanding opportunity in revolutionary ways. Yet the underlying rationale was consistent with that "old" individualism that John Dewey had lamented. It could be perfectly aligned with enlightened corporate policy (not to mention a family wage economy that increasingly relied upon two breadwinners in the face of stagnating wages). There was no fundamental contradiction in the fact that a political demand that originated in a rhetorically left-leaning movement, but embedded its politics in an individualist vision, would find its most effective applications within major corporations and universities. Although blame for the decline of New Deal liberalism is sometimes laid on the table of post-1960s "rights consciousness," the draw of individual and group rights over collective material well-being actually speaks to more profound issues: the historical fragility of class identity in American politics, the exceptional nature of the New Deal order, and the powerful allure of individual rights in American culture. Perhaps most problematically, the new individualism often depended upon state support to rectify the historic forms of discrimination. Affirmative action and the Civil Rights Act's Equal Employment Opportunity Commission looked more like government bureaucracy than simple old-fashioned bootstrap individualism, a formula for further political divisions.[10]

The Democrats, in embracing the scope and scale of modern life and economy, faced a problem of which they were not yet aware. In choosing to regulate rather than fight the scale of the modern economy as they once had, in building the massive bureaucracies of the New Deal and the Great Society, they ceded claim to the most secure object of allegiance American culture had to offer—the tradition of Jeffersonian individualism—to the right. Even when liberals only sought to expand and democratize the individual rights tradition, they often leaned upon the new leviathan to do so. While conservatives became brilliant at manipulating a sense of individualistic defiance for corporate ends, the Democrats had nothing like "freedom" on which to rally the voters. Their old claim to "security" was turning into an empty promise, and they worked hard to be the party of access, multiculturalism, and, to a lesser degree, welfare. The Democrats were evolving into a hodgepodge of others, a collection of non-Republicans, much as they had been one hundred years prior—even if the geographic bases for that power had shifted dramatically.

As a conservative thinker argued in 1976, the Republican Party would have to become "the party of the working class, not the party of the welfare class." The rhetoric was not simply Wallace-like racial coding—it was gendered, too. The nineteenth-century roots of American social policy had often been about protecting women, whom even conservatives deemed outside of the individual liberties mythologies accorded male workers. The roots of the "maternalist" nature of American welfare would lead later to the derogatory attacks from the right as an attack on the "nanny state's" incursions on freedom.[11]

In this atmosphere, a struggle to define the meanings of individual rights commanded the dominant position in the public political discourse of both right and left. Conservatives, riding the wave of a grassroots movement that would bring Ronald Reagan to the White House, effectively pitted the rights of the forgotten man and woman against the controlling powers of the state bureaucracy and the courts. Liberals, too, built upon the success of the 1960s in expanding individual rights, even as they were reduced to defending rather than advancing the political and economic gains of the 1930s and 1940s. The slogans of the day suggest the new political battlefields: "right to choose," "right to life," "right to bear arms," "gay rights," "Equal Rights Amendment," "right to pray in school," "right to work," "welfare rights," "consumer rights," and even the claims to individual rights through a revival of dormant identities of white ethnic groups. The rights discourse, in the words of one critic, became "the near-invincible trump card in most debates regarding public policy." The specific applications of this renewed rights ideology served contradictory purposes. For liberals, it marked their growing distance from New Deal visions while simultaneously drawing them into the deepest currents in American history.[12]

———————

Meantime, the Wagner Act, the dramatic breakthrough in union rights from the 1930s, was slowly turning into an industrial artifact in a labor history museum. With serious, but failed, attempts to reform labor law under every Democratic administration from Truman through Obama, the Wagner Act sat rusting like abused machinery. Impervious to reform in the postwar era and irrelevant to much of the new politics of the 1960s and 1970s, labor law was further eroded by case law and increasingly aggressive employers who began to regard fines for unfair labor practices not as a serious deterrent, but as simply the cost of doing business. As labor law professor Cynthia Estlund put it, "The core of American labor law has essentially been sealed off—to a remarkably complete extent and for a remarkably long time—from both democratic revision and renewal and from experimentation and innovation," leaving it "frozen, or ossified, for over fifty years." While the Civil Rights Act's Equal Employment Opportunity Commission was doing a swimming business in fighting discrimination on the job, the Depression Era legal regime that protected the collective economic rights of workers, as one critic put it in 1983, had already been reduced to an "elegant tombstone."[13]

The witty labor lawyer Thomas Geoghegan stood by that elegant tombstone in the 1980s, waiting for the body to rise from underneath. But it would not. Perhaps it could not. His book *Which Side Are You On?* stands as labor's greatest and most melancholy eulogy. He noted that while unions had everything America had—diversity, upward mobility, patriotism—even shiny windbreakers covering doughy American bodies—he noted an important absence. Unions, he noted, display "all the American values except one: individualism. . . . Labor thinks of itself, consciously, as American as apple pie. But it is not. Go to any union hall, any union rally, and listen to the speeches. It took me years to hear it, but there is a silence, a deafening Niagara-type silence, on the subject of individualism. No one is against it, but it never comes up. Is that America? To me, it is like Spain."[14]

As a result, while gender and racial struggles fostered a fundamental transformation in equality and access on the job—however imperfectly—to the full diversity of the working class, inequality increased within the overall society. Access of people to occupations outside the New Deal paradigm grew at extraordinary rates, while much of organized labor failed to expand beyond its geographic or sectoral boundaries set in the 1940s. Men and women have become more equal in their abilities to negotiate the labor market, but that equality of individual access took place in a context of growing overall inequality. Even the measure of women's earnings—often communicated as a percentage of men's earnings—hid the fact that women's wages were benchmarked to a declining standard.

Although there had been a rich and vigorous history of "New Deal feminism" that focused on labor unions and workplace issues, second-wave feminism solidified around a different agenda. The 1963 Equal Pay Act, which amended the New Deal's Fair Labor Standard Act, was designed to abolish the gender wage gap. It had mixed results, but most of successive legislative energies and movements went into nonremunerative rights issues. With many new feminists rightfully regarding unions as too stodgy and male, and unions often fearful of the new feminism, a breach developed between labor liberalism and women's rights. Even the Equal Rights Amendment required great finagling to win labor's support. Just as race and gender became important axes around which politics turned in the 1970s and beyond, class as a central way of understanding civic life melted away as the economy soured, industry declined, questions of culture trumped economics, and business regained control of politics. The wealth pyramid may have become more diverse than ever, but it simultaneously increased in inequality. The tragedy of the occupational revolutions of the 1970s and 1980s was that just as new jobs opened up, so did low pay, vulnerability, and fragmented political power.[15]

There were some exceptions. The environmental movement grew significantly following the first Earth Day in 1970. In environmentalists' efforts to preserve the broadest common ground, the planet itself, a diverse and energetic network of activists grew and became a factor in American political culture. Environmentalists had significant success with the Clean Water and Clean Air Acts to preserve that common good, but continued to battle against the revival of conservative arguments, rooted in free-market thought, that decried the regulatory curtailment of corporate prerogatives. Other social movements with collective goals ranging

from saving manufacturing from the scourge of deindustrialization, to stopping American intervention in Central
America, to blocking nuclear proliferation, offered up visions that reached beyond individual rights and self-interest.
The outcomes often overwhelmed the intentions. And while
there is undoubtedly a collective betterment to many regulatory policies from the Great Society onward with cleaner air
and water, better transportation, and improved consumer
safety, none, with the exception of Medicare and Medicaid,
really redistributed corporate largesse to the people who
worked for them. Many of these efforts were more of the
"front porch politics" variety rather than federal government initiatives, the hopes for which had been truncated by
the disillusionments of Vietnam and Watergate. Post-1960s
liberalism, diverse and renewed, was looking more like pre–
World War I progressivism.[16]

By the time stagflation, the second greatest set of economic problems of the twentieth century, befuddled policymakers in its improbable combination of unemployment
and inflation, the New Deal coalition offered few answers
to the structural crisis of the 1970s. Given that the state had
provided the answers during the New Deal, and now state
intervention threatened to add to inflation, the liberals' core
weapon was sheathed. Old-school liberals tried to overcome the divisiveness of post-1960s America by rebuilding
a New Deal vision on a shared material platform that included labor law reform, full employment legislation, discussions over industrial policy, and debates over national
health insurance. All were stillborn. They scratched their
heads as the "presumed Weberian distinction between the
rational economic realm and the irrational social realm"
broke down into far more complicated axes of political and
social identity. Those dimensions of political identity with

the most traction for those on both the right and the left proved to be far from the workplace.[17]

The pre–New Deal system of corporate control of the "labor question" once dismissed as "welfare capitalism" returned to fill the breach. In lieu of the fading power of trade unions and the declining efficacy of the regulatory state, working people drifted back toward a corporate paternalism that reinforced employees' dependence upon the "largesse" of the private sector. Generations of analysts have typically believed that this limited system of worker benefits offered by employers in exchange for loyalty to the corporation of the 1920s broke down of its own accord with the inevitable rise of the welfare state and the modern union movement. Had it not been for the economic, and thus political, trauma of the 1930s, the course of corporate paternalism might well have continued uninterrupted as the main current of American industrial relations even in the postwar era. Sanford Jacoby builds on this, showing the enduring but overlooked legacy of welfare capitalism well after the height of the New Deal's powers and certainly long after their decline.[18]

As the 1970s turned into the 1980s and beyond, many New Deal liberals sensed that something had gone terribly wrong. In retrospect, one can see how liberals reached an impasse, proffering program after program to deal with social ills. This "seeing like a state," in the words of James Scott, was the only thing available that resembled John Dewey's "secure object of allegiance"—an enormous problem in a national culture suspicious of state action.[19]

The ensuing religiously infused culture wars continued the erosion of a collective economic vision. Advocates of a pro-choice position on abortion rights, shunning an electoral strategy, joined supporters of busing, affirmative action, and equal employment opportunity by leaning on the courts, which, for the new "forgotten Americans," many of whom were Catholics and evangelicals, smacked of a certain distrust of the majority's religiously informed attitudes. In one respect, liberalism had returned to the early dawn of its modern, twentieth-century roots, when it battled against William Jennings Bryan's evocation of community rule. This time, however, the forces of evangelical conservatism, widely, if differently, shared across the society, were harbingers of the future rather than ghosts of the past.

Back in the 1890s, the Republican Party melded pro-corporate policies with moral uplift and approbation of the moral life. The 1970s matched the combination and lit a fire under it with an injection of old-fashioned populism directed not against the financial and business elite, but against the cultural elite(ists). As the New Right's media guru Richard Viguerie noted about the 1970s, "We never really won until we began stressing issues like busing, abortion, school prayer and gun control. We talked about the sanctity of free enterprise, about the Communist onslaught until we were blue in the face. But we didn't start winning majorities in elections until we got down to gut level issues." In words that would have made the heart of William McKinley's strategist and financial backer Mark Hannah sing, 1970s conservative activist M. Stanton Evans noted that "The important thing . . . is not that some of them reach their political positions by reading Adam Smith while others do so by attending an anti-busing rally, but that all of them belong to a large and growing class of American citizens: those who perceive themselves as victims of the federal welfare state and its attendant costs."[20]

The 1960s countercultural challenge to American norms dissolved into some of the nation's most vaunted mainstream traits: consumption, religious revivalism, and antistatism. The Dionysian outlook readily melded with materialism and libertarianism, while America's consumer culture easily absorbed the 1960s' more commercially viable trends. The movement's famous search for authenticity and individual meaning had its most lasting *institutional* impact on American life less in the legacy of its multiple experiments with communal living than in the potent individualism of Protestant revivalism evident in the enormous growth of the "New Paradigm," nondenominational evangelical churches started in the late 1960s by converts from the hippie movement, the so-called Jesus people. As Michael Harrington lamented as early as 1973, "The cultural revolution has been subverted by the conservative society in which it is taking place."[21]

Religious values once again returned to center stage of the cultural struggle. A charged religious revival—"The Third Great Awakening," Tom Wolfe called it—reignited dormant political passions, which were then marshaled against the state's intrusion into the moral lives of Christian communities much like the days of Scopes. The postwar Judeo-Christian consensus was never as firm as many believed. It fell apart in the 1970s as people of faith questioned rendering unto Caesar what was Caesar's when the government was busy intervening in cultural questions like abortion, busing, prayer in school, pornography, and birth control—issues that repoliticized religion's place in American life and undermined the New Deal coalition in the 1970s and beyond.

Newsweek magazine called 1976 "The Year of the Evangelical." It snuck up on a lot of intellectuals who had long come to regard American religion as either a civil one or a broad and nonjudgmental commitment to Judeo-Christian values. Yet the widening stream of evangelical thought in the postwar era crested the banks in the 1970s to the shock of many. "As signs of America's growing irreligion and secularism multiplied," explains the historian Paul Boyer, "calls for political action intensified, and [Reverend Jerry] Falwell and others locked arms with politicians who professed to share their goals." Their messages were beamed into the living room, broadcast into new mega-churches, and, soon enough, made relevant in the polling booth. The new group that called itself the Moral Majority shattered the separation between religion and politics, mobilizing believers on issues of gender, sexuality, family, and tradition across the nation, proving their mettle as "pro-liberty, pro-family, pro-moral, and pro-America." As Falwell explained about his goals for increasing his flock: "Get them saved, baptized, and registered."[22]

Bolstering the fate of the GOP—especially the election of Ronald Reagan—the new revivalism and its anti-modern impulses resonated in important ways with an older America. Melding the moral reform dimensions of nineteenth-century America and the fundamentalism of a William Jennings Bryan, as the cultural historian Jackson Lears makes the comparison in his incomparable study, *No Place of Grace*, the new anti-modernism gained tremendous political traction in the last quarter of the twentieth century. Although conservatives might be "cynical or self-deceiving" at times, Lears argues, "the contemporary Right expresses some genuinely antimodern sentiments shared by many Americans and long epitomized in republican moralism and

Protestant fundamentalism." The anti-modern revival found voice in "tributes to family solidarity, the invocations of the work ethic, the idealization of the local community, the distrust of giant bureaucracies, even the pervasive religiosity" that those embedded in a secular, materialist, pragmatic perspective cannot ignore. "Beneath official pieties," Lears continues, "the Right embodies a wholly understandable yearning for an authentic, unchanging bedrock of moral values and beliefs that can withstand the disintegrative effects of modernization."[23]

When Ronald Reagan opened his 1980 campaign, one that would mark the effective closure of the New Deal order, he began at the Neshoba County fairgrounds in Mississippi. Not only was the site in the center of the old Dixiecrat culture, now leaning strongly Republican, but the town of Philadelphia, Mississippi, just a few miles away, was the spot where three civil rights workers were slain in 1964 while working for the voter rights and education campaign known as Freedom Summer. There Reagan flatly stated his approval of "states rights," a term that worked like a dog whistle to rally those who had yet to give up formal and informal faith in white supremacy or the semi-independence of the South and its values. The power of the appeal would help sweep the Southern electoral map (minus Georgia, home of Jimmy Carter) and the country in 1980, demonstrating the final end of the once solidly Democratic South.

Few people exemplify the massive realignment in politics better than Strom Thurmond—the South Carolina governor and senator, the man who carried the States' Rights Party standard out of the Democratic Party when a civil rights plank was introduced in 1948. He had once been an admirer of Franklin Roosevelt and, like so many in South Carolina, had counted on and cherished much of the early New Deal (all while ensuring that its bounty flowed almost exclusively to the white population). By the time of Reagan's election, Thurmond had long since switched parties, and saw a vindication of his extraordinarily long political career in the Reagan revolution of 1980. "President Reagan ran on practically the same platform that I ran on in 1948," Thurmond explained. "Less federal intervention, less federal control and less federal spending. I'm very pleasantly surprised. I didn't know it would come in my lifetime." Though Thurmond's words of celebration elided his overt commitments to everything connected to Jim Crow, the idea of more freedom and less government came cloaked in a thick racial ideology.[24]

The racial story was hardly just a Southern one. The integration of schools through federally mandated busing "fell like an axe" through the Democratic Party. Affirmative action on the job—in a period of high unemployment—helped push Northern white working-class voters to the right. Cartoonish rhetoric proliferated—for example, the suggestion that working peoples' taxes were being pipelined directly to black welfare recipients, a racist fantasy catalyzed by Reagan's Cadillac-driving "welfare queen" stories, which helped many people justify pulling the Republican lever for the first time in generations of their families' histories. Suburbanites squared off against the city, liberals against populists, and the government against the people. Pushed by a sense that the entire postwar success story was on the edge, it was easy to connect every problem to the new citizenship demands of African Americans. As one panicked white resident of Canarsie, Brooklyn, exclaimed as

African Americans were moving into his neighborhood, "The house you wanted is in danger, the kids are in danger, the neighborhood is in danger. It's all slipping away." Even if white populist anger was not directly pointed at African Americans, it would target what people believed to be sanctimonious social planners and government officials who appeared to think they knew better than regular folks.[25]

The revival of immigration fueled further discussions about patriotism, border security, national identity, and labor market regulation that resonated in a variety of ways with the century prior to World War I. The 1965 Immigration Act, which finally ended the racial quota system, remade American society in unintended ways. While reformers fixed the number of people who could enter the country, they had not grasped that each individual immigrant opened the door for an additional "nonquota" immigration based on family unification. Immigration delivered a chain of more immigration.

People from Asia and Africa entered the country both legally and illegally, as Americans dramatically found out when a ship named the *Golden Venture* ran aground in Queens with a cargo of 286 undocumented Chinese workers on board who had been sailing around the world for months. The garment sweatshop, a once-vanquished system of subcontracting and sweating profits out of immigrant workers, returned with a vengeance. New limits on immigration from the Western Hemisphere hardly stopped people from the Caribbean and Latin America from coming to the United States, but it did severely restrict their rights once they arrived. Midwestern meatpacking, formerly a stable source of high-wage, union jobs, returned to the days of Upton Sinclair's *The Jungle* (1906)—unions smashed, wages reduced, and worker safety imperiled. The firm Iowa Beef Packers (now Tyson) revolutionized the industry, moving production out of union strongholds, recruiting immigrant labor, manipulating federal subsidies, and transforming small towns throughout the Midwest. The firm sought out refugees and asylum-seekers from Eastern Europe and Asia, and kept a labor recruitment office in Mexico City, which they used to run help wanted radio ads and bus service to the United States—much like the old *padrone* labor recruitment system of the nineteenth century.[26]

The politics of immigration proved wide-ranging and politically divisive. Efforts ranged from the Immigration, Reform, and Control Act of 1986 to the 1994 passage of California's "Save Our State" (SOS) Proposition 187, which barred undocumented aliens from public education, health care, and welfare (voided by the courts in 1999), to a variety of English-only initiatives, calls to militarize the border, or demands to build an enormous fence between the United States and Mexico. The complexities of immigration were punctuated by perennial "amnesties" to all existing undocumented workers to stay in the United States, suggestive of how intractable and complicated immigration politics can be. At times, the hysteria over the fate of "America" in the popular press bordered on echoes of the 1916 anti-immigration polemic from eugenicist Madison Grant, *The Passing of the Great Race*, with but a few changes of subject and adjective. Yet the AFL-CIO, aware that new immigrant populations were completely restructuring the U.S. working class and were the future of the labor movement, finally changed its historic opposition to immigration in 2000. Reversing their long tradition of job-conscious nativism, the unions moved toward the spirit and energy of the immigrant communities by championing their rights rather than their restriction.[27]

The streets of American cities now pulse with immigrant cultures, but the industrial jobs that brought immigrants to the United States at the beginning of the last century are gone. Manufacturing employed one-third of all nonagricultural workers in 1960 but only one-eighth in 2010, and private-sector union density has fallen to 6 percent. Christine J. Walley's ethnography of southeast Chicago after the steel mills closed is telling. There she finds that although the industry is gone, the social dynamics "carry strong parallels with those of the past." "Just as the early steel industry pitted groups of workers against each other," explains Walley, so it is in the deindustrialized neighborhoods "for those holding the lower-end jobs . . . contemporary capitalism continues to create competition among ethnic groups." The low-wage service economy "targets new immigrants and that further destabilizes the shifting sands under the remaining working class." As before immigration restrictions of 1924, "now, few common experiences create a sense of mutual recognition across the divides. There is a fragmentation of experiences and also, for those who remember the old neighborhoods, a disconcerting fragmentation of community. While ethnic tensions reveal these economic and social fault lines, they fail to explicate the processes that got us, as a country, into such a position."[28]

After being absent in major political questions for generations, immigrant rights returned to the forefront of protest movements in the 1990s and beyond. In the Justice for Janitors campaigns, for instance, immigrant custodians from office buildings in cities across the United States joined in collaborations with labor, religious, and civil rights groups to win union contracts for tens of thousands of janitors. In 2006, enormous immigrant rights demonstrations across the country were organized on May Day, the international workers' day. Protest organizer Nativo Lopez saw the march as resurrecting the spirit and goals of working-class movements of the past. Posing an explicit comparison to Chicago's Haymarket affair, where May Day was born in 1886, he said, "They are rescuing from anonymity the struggle for the 8-hour day, begun in Chicago over a century ago by the immigrants of yesteryear. They are recovering the traditions of all working people." Some saw the marches as extensions of the civil rights movement, while others made the connection to labor, arguing simply "immigrant rights are worker rights."[29]

Claims for immigrant rights and citizenship have also fueled a backlash among white voters and other native-born groups. Fear and confusion over the state of employment and the United States' place in the world, according to political scientists, will most likely fuel "increased efforts at border enforcement, more migrant deaths, and strained relations between the nation's white (and primarily native-born) population along with its racial and ethnic minority groups." Three-fifths of Americans polled are in support of stricter immigration laws. The possibility of a "broad backlash" remains strong, but more importantly, subtler forms of policy questions get filtered through questions of immigration. Polling shows, for instance, that over two-thirds of those opposed to health care took the position because it might cover undocumented immigrants. Half of the white population believes that immigrants are a burden, add to crime, and take jobs from Americans. Nativism, as it did

prior to 1924, has proven to be a visceral political sentiment
that divides the electorate and hijacks policy discussions.[30]

In post-Nixon America, the corporations also succeeded in
their own counter-reformation of capitalism. This time,
however, they were less dependent on state-led redistribution to boost demand than on a global market for cheap
labor and an avidly consuming professional middle class.
Keynesian logic appeared to have died in the maelstrom of
1970s inflation. The answer to all social and economic
problems appeared to be, simply, less: less government,
less regulation, less unionization, and less wages. Inflation
seemed to turn everything upside down. Organized workers
protected contractually from inflation, no longer could claim
to be speaking for everyone. State spending seemed only to
exacerbate the problem. Economists who a generation earlier would have been pushing economic stimulus, higher
wage packages, and boosted consumption were now advocating deregulation, deunionization, and tightened budgets.
Ronald Reagan's favorite punch line, once political heresy,
began to gain traction: "The nine most terrifying words in
the English language," he loved to say, "are, 'I'm from the
government and I'm here to help.'" As the historian Angus
Burgin has explained, the old-school economic thinking
never fully went away; it had only been in exile since the
1930s. "Advocacy of free markets entered a period of reconsideration and retrenchment during the Great Depression," he explains, "but it by no means arrived at an 'end.'
Instead, the story of the half century after the onset of economic crisis is in part one of its triumphant return." This
was a great exception even in economic thought. It ended

when Keynesianism, rather than laissez-faire, had come to seem a relic of a rapidly receding economic world."[31]

A key turning point came in the summer of 1981, when one of Ronald Reagan's first presidential acts was to fire thousands of air traffic controllers for going on strike. Alan Greenspan described the destruction of the air traffic controllers' union as the "most important" of all of Reagan's domestic undertakings. The defeat of the Professional Air Traffic Controllers Organization (PATCO) during the first summer of the Reagan administration "gave weight to the legal right of private employers, previously not fully exercised, to use their own discretion to both hire and discharge workers." The renewal of employers' "freedom to fire" unleashed a new celebration of entrepreneurial initiative, a miraculous era of "low unemployment and low inflation." If we substitute Greenspan's phrase "freedom to fire" with "freedom to break unions, strip them of the right to strike, redistribute wealth upward, and create massive economic insecurity," then we have a story that also resonates with the labor movement. Indeed, PATCO has become the pivotal event—both symbolically and substantively—in almost everyone's understanding of the massive realignment of class power in the United States in the last few decades.

Yet the firing of the air traffic controllers was completely within the law. As public sector workers, they had no coverage under the Wagner Act, and no right to strike. Yet, here is a curious and puzzling thing: ever since the 1938 Supreme Court decision *NLRB v. Mackay Radio*, private-sector employers had the legal right to permanently replace strikers. This was a loaded gun that management rarely selected to use—until the 1980s. Whether because of the "gentlemen's agreement" between labor and industry, the remarkable levels of local solidarity that backed strikes, or other factors, for over forty years, business, except on rare occasions, did not fire striking workers. This was a great exception, indeed. After PATCO, however, private-sector employers received the signal that it was now acceptable practice to terminate striking workers—and they did. Labor lost its most valuable weapon in the 1980s, as firm after firm permanently replaced its striking workers until the fear of termination all but ended the right to strike in America.

———————————————

Smart, young, and pragmatic "New" Democrats, suspicious of the old backroom ways, tried to readjust to the new conservatism rather than fight back. Gary Hart, a young senator from Colorado who had run George McGovern's presidential campaign (where he learned to dislike organized labor), had already been talking about the "end" of the New Deal in the mid-1970s. Not surprisingly, it was a socially progressive and intensely pragmatic young Southern governor who rose to support another Southerner, incumbent president Jimmy Carter, at the 1980 Democratic convention with words rarely if ever heard in such a setting before that moment. The electorate "cannot be moved by the symbols and accomplishments of the Democratic Party of the past," the thirty-four-year-old Bill Clinton declared. He continued:

> We were brought up to believe, uncritically, without thinking about it, that our system broke down in the Great Depression, was reconstructed by Franklin Roosevelt through the New Deal and World War II, and would never break again. . . . [But] we must remember that we have no right to expect that this or

any system will be permanently prosperous, free of all crises. . . . We did not get into these difficulties overnight, and we will not emerge from them immediately. It is not in the cards.

A decade later, after the young governor had become president, this stream of logic would culminate with the rhetorical flourish, "the era of big government is over," albeit, one might add, over only for the forgotten Americans, not for the corporations.[32]

Many liked to call the postwar paradigm "pluralism," painting it as a political paradigm in which a variety of interests could organize and vie for political favor and attention. By the 1990s, one could say that it had been reduced to a conspicuous "singularism": whatever Wall Street wanted, it got—including the North American Free Trade Agreement, the World Trade Organization, deregulation, lower taxes, and fewer unions. By the 1990s, banking regulations had fallen to below pre–New Deal levels.[33]

Private-sector union density had also fallen to below that of the 1920s. Inequality too had jumped back to pre–New Deal levels. Clinton's secretary of labor, Robert Reich, would recall the president's frustration in this environment; "B[ill] is looking for scapegoats. . . . He stalks around the room, fuming. 'We're doing everything Wall Street wants! Everything Wall Street *doesn't* want gets slashed!' He takes another few steps. 'We're losing our *soul*!' He talks to no one in particular, but I can't help imagining he's yelling at Alan Greenspan. 'I can't do what I *came* here to do.' " With collective bargaining so deeply undermined, it is not surprising that when Al Gore ran for president in 2000, the core of his program was to protect middle-class entitlement programs like Social Security and Medicare in a "lock box," a phrase repeated so many times in Gore's campaign that defense of the remnants of the old order seemed his only strategy.[34]

Given the intense brevity of the "fragile juggernaut," it might be more accurate to think of the "Reagan revolution" as the "Reagan restoration," a return to the more sharply conservative, individualistic reading of constitutional rights and liberties that was prevalent before the New Deal. The elements of this restoration included a populace more stratified by economic distinctions and racial divides; a significantly more conservative interpretation of a host of social and cultural issues; a fragmentation of working people's collective agency and diffusion of their political voice; and a reuniting of religious and conservative activists in civic life. There are many reasons why this return to a new Gilded Age took the form it did, but we should be sure to count among them the profound fragility of New Deal liberalism itself.

We should also be clear about what this restoration is not: a return to small government, as Reagan so forcefully advertised. As David Stockman's lament about the Reagan administration's inability to truly roll back government suggests, a Hamiltonian structure—contra Louis Hartz—was the true vital center of twentieth-century American politics. Akin to post–Civil War America, the political discourse of the Reagan era celebrated the self-made man while denigrating the encroaching powers of government—all the while expanding those federal powers to new heights and engendering staggering levels of inequality that echoed, often superseded, that of the age of the Robber Barons. The

issue was never really whether that government was large
or small, as political campaign rhetoric might have us believe, but toward what ends and whose interest its massive
institutions would be driven.[35]

The New FDR?, 2008. When the 2008 Great Recession hit, commentators were quick to draw parallels between it and the Great Depression. Many imagined Obama as the new FDR, but the two presidents and their circumstances were dramatically different.
© Richard Thompson.

CHAPTER SEVEN

THE ERA OF BIG GOVERNMENT IS NOT OVER

(BUT THE NEW DEAL PROBABLY IS)

Spilled across the pages of journals of opinion are demands for a new New Deal, a global New Deal, a New and improved Deal, to reNew the Deal, and even New Deal 2.0. The excitement following Barack Obama's first election, just after the nation slipped into the abyss of a massive financial crisis, generated further New Deal analogies. Political cartoons with the new president posing as FDR sprang forth—an especially memorable example being the cover of *Time* magazine featuring a jubilant, toothy Barack Obama with cigarette holder posing confidently in an open limousine. Otherwise sober commentators began speaking of "Franklin Delano Obama." Meanwhile, among union watchers, minor twists of the labor movement seem to generate unrestrained proclamations of the second coming of the union movement that swept across the nation during the Great Depression. Even before the coming of the financial crisis of 2007–2008, the New Deal has been metaphor, analogy, political principle, and guiding light for all that must be returned to the progressive side of American politics.

Then, inevitably, comes the shock: the new Gilded Age seems to have a lot more traction in American political culture than did the hope of a new New Deal. The return of nineteenth-century-style plutocracy, crony capitalism, and shocking levels of inequality—disparities that continued even after the excitement of Obama's presidency—suggest a conscious, confident, and powerful ruling class that has largely separated itself from the concerns of the nation's working people. The fractious polity, in turn, has chosen quarrels over individual rights, ethnic and racial hostility, immigrant versus native, and crusades over moralism and piety in lieu of a politics of collective economic security.

These are not necessarily irrational choices. People stake out positions for many reasons, and cultural values are often among the most important beliefs people hold. They often offer more traction than an abstract gamble on shared economic or class interests—especially in the U.S. context. Sometimes those cultural interests and values do serve as a substitute for economic frustrations. Sometimes they're simply more important. Obama was playing with political fire when he oversimplified the relationship between social values and decades of economic decline:

> You go into these small towns in Pennsylvania and, like a lot of small towns in the Midwest, the jobs have been gone now for 25 years and nothing's replaced them. And they fell through the Clinton administration, and the Bush administration, and each successive administration has said that somehow these communities are gonna regenerate and they have not. And it's not surprising then they get bitter, they cling to guns or religion or antipathy toward people who aren't like

them or anti-immigrant sentiment or anti-trade sentiment as a way to explain their frustration.[1]

The tragedy of that now infamous quote lies not in its
condescension per se, but in the fact that the Obama administration ultimately offered precious little in terms of the
politics of material security. Part of that was President
Obama's unwillingness to make a bold, decisive break from
previous decades and make the case to the American people
that the state could help build economic security and opportunity for all. The first two years of the Obama administration was a lost opportunity for the American reform tradition—not just on policy grounds but in making the argument
that government had a role in helping regular people. Seemingly insecure in his position, the new president appointed
economic insiders, many of whom had played a role in
creating the crisis, while shying away from larger stimulus
packages or initiatives that would halt the decades-long
growth in inequality and wage stagnation. Banking, finance,
and important industries like auto were saved. Meanwhile,
working people continued to inhabit the exact same economy they had in the decades leading up to the crisis.

While Obama might have made more of his moment, I do
not believe he could come close to delivering the "next"
New Deal. The remarkable differences between the politics
of the crisis of 2008 and that of 1929 were too vast. When
FDR was inaugurated in March of 1933, the Depression
was already three and one-half years old. The mood of the
country was a peculiar combination of resignation and depression, anger and calls to action. Focusing his 1932 campaign against incumbent Herbert Hoover's inept handling

of the crisis—ultimately refusing to even meet with Hoover to discuss plans during the four months before he took office—FDR gathered around him a coalition that demanded change. One-quarter of the population was out of work, and there was no unemployment insurance, no social security, no deposit insurance, and what state and private charities existed had either collapsed or were teetering on the brink of bankruptcy. For three winters, the nation suffered untold misery, and major industrial cities had populations on the edge of starvation. Homelessness was rampant. By the time FDR took office, in the words of one historian, there had been "nearly four years for at least a segment of the population, which had been deeply socialized in the virtues of individualism, to come to the realization that the destitution they were experiencing was not their fault but that of some basic flaw in the system."[2]

Immediate federal action proved so popular that the Democrats gained a 3:1 majority in the House and Senate by the 1934 midterm elections—the only time in modern history that the party holding the White House had increased its midterm standing by such numbers. FDR's years also included the largest partisan majorities in American history. By the time the second New Deal came along, even 68 percent of Southern Democratic senators supported the Wagner Act (all of this before the mood changed in 1938). FDR eventually enjoyed a dramatic court reversal that sustained much of the second New Deal—the moment that ended the *Lochner* era and opened up a new period of court support for labor market regulations.

While horrific, the Great Recession of 2008 fell short of the full devastation of the Great Depression. Both the sense of panic and the unemployment rate were only a fraction of what they were in the 1930s. Although Obama entered office not long after the crash, he inherited a bailout engi-

neered by the previous administration, a trillion-dollar deficit, and a set of unpopular wars that proved to be the
economic and political opposite of the stimulus of World
War II. Because of Obama's almost militant commitment to
economic centrism and his unwillingness to confront the
political power of Wall Street, he immediately elected to
continue the policies (and even many of the players) from
the previous administration. That clouded the contrast with
the Republican he succeeded—a dramatic contrast that
FDR had used to superb effect. As compared to the era
when government hardly existed in the daily lives of regular
people, a safety net, under attack since 1981, still did exist
in 2008: Social Security, unemployment insurance, the Federal Deposit Insurance Corporation, Medicare, and Medicaid all helped cushion the blows of the financial crisis. Yet
there was also tremendous political activity, built up since
the 1970s, to *roll back* existing government activity that did
not simply serve business's interests. The Solid South that
FDR needed for his legislative successes had turned largely
Republican—and militantly so. The "modern" Republicanism of the postwar era, which had made its peace with the
New Deal, had already become a distant memory.[3]

While FDR enjoyed record majorities, Obama had only
a very brief and slender supermajority that could bring cloture to a now frequently invoked filibuster. Between contested elections, deaths, and party switching, supermajority
power barely existed. Then any hope completely disappeared for a supermajority in the 2010 midterm elections,
never to return. By Obama's reelection in 2012, the Democrats had again lost the entire South (minus Florida) and
most of the plains states and Rocky Mountain West—areas
the Democrats of FDR's generation could rely upon as long
as they did not threaten to undermine Jim Crow. The triumph of a black president may have been one of the most

important developments in American social and political history, but by the time of his second run, he could win only 39 percent of the white vote—a remarkable contrast to the 1936 landslide and the creation of the Roosevelt coalition.[4]

While the Roosevelt era Supreme Court reversed its historical commitment to affirming corporate rights by upholding much of the legislation of the second New Deal, Obama enjoyed no such support from the high courts. Quite the opposite. During his administration, the Supreme Court delivered the *Citizens United* decision (2010), which, by giving free (financial) speech to corporations, echoed the corporate personhood delivered in the Gilded Age's *Santa Clara* decision (1886). The *New York Times* editorial board called it "The court's Blow to Democracy." As they argued, "With a single, disastrous 5-to-4 ruling, the Supreme Court has thrust politics back to the robber-baron era of the 19th century." Legal scholars had already begun to talk of the courts' drift toward a neo-*Lochner* era. The *Hobby Lobby* decision (2014) affirmed not only corporate personhood, but that corporations could, like people, have religious beliefs and discriminate accordingly in their corporate practices.[5]

Hopes for a progressive revival faced further humiliation in the Obama years. The fate of the primary interest of unions, which had been reduced to below pre–New Deal levels of private sector density, was the Employee Free Choice Act (EFCA). The legislation was designed to end the tortured legal system of organizing and to increase workers' freedom to unionize. After untold millions of dollars of campaigning and lobbying in favor of EFCA and an endorsement by candidate Obama, it died in the Senate despite the high hopes generated by the supermajority moment. As journalist Harold Myerson put it, "for American labor, year one of Barack Obama's presidency has been close to an unmitigated disaster." It never improved. Given the failure of labor law reform in every Democratic administration since the Wagner Act was passed, however, the results of the EFCA battle, in the words of labor scholar Dorian Warren, were an "unsurprising failure."[6]

The failure to reform governmental policy over the decades presents a profound problem. As the president of the United Mine Workers, John Mitchell, admitted around the turn of the last century, the labor movement needs government support. "The trade union movement in this country," he argued, "can make progress only by identifying itself with the state." Yet the state's position on the collective interests of working people has remained unrelentingly hostile. What if, however, we are getting the state we've asked for? While the courts and elected officials have undoubtedly absorbed and promoted business's interest, the entire system rests on a much more problematic and still unresolved strain of individualism in American culture. As the historian Melvyn Dubofsky summarizes the problem, the arc of tension between labor rights and individual rights is a long one. "The right of individual workers to cross picket lines (even when they are members of the striking union) to serve as replacement labor (strikebreakers), and to claim a right to work regardless of union membership (right to work laws) remains alive and well," he writes. "It lives not because judges and the law that they declare create reality but because the appeal of individualism and the desire for liberty resonate across a wide spectrum of society."[7]

While a direct assault on public-sector collective bargaining in Wisconsin and Ohio sparked dramatic resistance, perhaps the most telling evidence of defeat of the New Deal paradigm was when the Michigan state legislature passed a right-to-work law right in the United Auto Workers' backyard, a painful affront to the birthplace of the modern industrial union movement. The days when a ragtag, but tactically brilliant, group of autoworkers emboldened by New Deal policy changed American history had been eclipsed by a piece of what the unions had once called the "slave labor" act. When Wisconsin passed a right-to-work law in 2015, it was the twenty-fifth state to do so, marking the fact that half the nation had fallen under what had once been thought of almost exclusively as a Southern issue. In 1968, when the United Auto Workers president Walter Reuther appeared at a rally in support of the Memphis sanitation workers strike, the dispute that led to the death of Martin Luther King, Jr., he declared that the labor movement was "going to bring Memphis kicking and screaming into the twenty-first century." It now appears the opposite is true: rather than the North transforming the Southern political economy, the South played an important role in transforming the North.[8]

All of this is not to say that Obama's presidency, especially his first two years, was a failure. It was not; it just was not a new New Deal. The failure rests more squarely in analysts' insistence in using the Depression Era analogy where it was not helpful. He did help dig the country out of the worst economic disaster in eighty years, pulled the United States back from a disastrous foreign policy, and renewed federal effectiveness in health and safety, immigration, and the environment. "Few new presidents have been greeted with so many crises at once," argue Theda Skocpol and Lawrence R. Jacobs, "and few have tackled so much so fast, whatever missed opportunities, political controversies, and maladroit steps there have been along the way."[9]

Candidate Obama campaigned mightily on behalf of the 49 million people without health insurance. The result was the biggest victory, and the most dramatic blow to inequality in over a generation, the Affordable Care Act (commonly known as Obamacare). The final legislation lacked the public option that had been a do-or-die aspect of the early bill for Democrats. In its place was simultaneously a weak system of health care reform that expanded Medicaid, regulated existing industries, offered public exchanges, and mandated individual coverage. The bill actually had conservative roots as an end run around more progressive ideas about national health insurance. Parts of Obamacare had been worked out at the Heritage Foundation, a conservative think tank, and it was closely related to a bill Nixon had put forth in 1974. There were cheaper and simpler approaches that would have worked through Social Security, Medicare, and payroll taxes, but, in typically American fashion, Obamacare neither competes with nor supplants existing systems but merely supports extant industry—no matter what the inefficiencies. While Obamacare made for the weakest health care system in the advanced economic world, it was a lot more than what had been there before and must therefore be seen as an important victory. Yet no sooner did it pass than lawsuits, impeachment threats, and conspiracy claims emerged along with the rest of the "paranoid style" of American politics.

The fundamental difference between the two eras was the place of the forgotten man and woman. FDR took office explaining that the "money changers had fled the temple" and that "the measure of the restoration lies in the extent to which we apply social values more noble than mere monetary profit." The unspoken mantra of the Obama administration, in contrast, was "Save Wall Street first," a symptom of, not a solution to, what political scientists Hacker and Pierson rightly call "the winner take all society." In the politics of the recovery after 2008, FDR's forgotten man remained trapped in the dustbin of history. In the politics of rage, however, he was the folk hero to conservative pundits and talk news shows that constructed a pot-boiling industry exploiting the mythology of the hijacking of the nation by various others—be they cultural elites, secular humanists, immigrants, or blacks. As conservative Fox News commentator Glenn Beck co-opted the discourse of the 1930s, "What happened to the country that loved the underdog and stood up for the little guy? What happened to the forgotten man? The forgotten man is you."[10]

It did not help that President Obama drew his advice from a narrow range of policymakers and lacked what FDR (and certainly LBJ after him) had in abundance—what George Packer called "a key element of presidential power, the ability to inspire fear." Even though he recognized, as he told investors, that he was "the only thing between you and the pitchforks," he never capitalized on that position. His commitment to political centrism was partially predetermined by a complex electorate that did not know what it wanted and a Republican opposition that remained steadfast in its determination to block the president at every turn. The fact that Obama failed to use the power of the bully pulpit—despite occasionally invoking Theodore Roosevelt's New Nationalism with a refreshing boldness—to change the discussion about the nature of the state in people's lives and the economy is probably the biggest difference, and the biggest failure, of the Obama administration.[11]

The rise of minorities to positions of power has been one of the great achievements of the post–Civil Rights Era. But, as Frank Rich explains, the "tsunami of anger" unleashed on Barak Obama was hardly a product of simple policy issues. Rather, it was a national projection of sociopolitical fragmentation by a set of increasingly bitter people who feel left behind. "The conjunction of a black president and a female speaker of the House—topped off by a wise Latina on the supreme court and a powerful gay Congressional committee chairman—would sow fears of disenfranchisement among a dwindling and threatened minority in the country no matter what policies were in play," Rich explains. "When you hear demonstrators chant the slogan 'Take our country back!' these are the people they want to take the country back from." We only need to think of how people's fears get expressed when they call Obama a socialist or a foreigner or a Nazi. President Obama's victory stirred up an intoxicating oppositional brew of libertarian, populist, conservative, racialist, and traditionalist elements that went into the Tea Party movement. There the baser instincts of American politics emerged with caricatures of American Christianity, nativism, racism, and individualism that helped to push an obstructionist-oriented Republican Party back to the forefront of American politics. Although the election of a black president suggests the broad, malleable, and multicultural range of opportunity in the post–Civil Rights Era, there remains a still powerful racial order that both denies its racism and compounds the problem with the widening gap of economic inequality.[12] Despite a new president of African descent, the United States remained tied to what Hofstadter once identified as "a larger complex of fear and suspicion of the stranger that haunted, and still tragically haunts, the nativist American mind."

At the upper echelons of economic leadership in the government and private sectors can be found a combination of cynicism and naïveté about inequality that is difficult to fathom. Market mechanisms, as if they existed in some untainted form, deliver the best—the only—possible outcome, goes the logic. As Treasury Secretary Henry Paulson put it, "our economy grows, market forces work to provide the greatest rewards to those with the needed skills in the growth areas." This formula, continues Paulson, "is simply an economic reality, and it is neither fair nor useful to blame any political party."[13]

Yet scholars interrogating the escalating levels of inequality, the hyperconcentration of income, and the shrinking share of reward that goes to working people find a more complex picture. They find that most of the usual answers for inequality—globalization, education, deindustrialization—do not hold water. The fact that fifty cents of every dollar of income gains were going to the top one percent of households in the lead-up to 2008 is not because of the efficient operation of a labor market that rewards skill and brilliance (especially since it was not working people who destroyed the economy).

The answer is simultaneously much simpler and far more complicated: *politics*. Context matters. Even Alan Greenspan has admitted as much. The problem is "not that humans have become any more greedy than in generations past," he explains, but that "the avenues to express greed have grown enormously." Those "avenues" were carved by politics. As Thomas Piketty has shown in his exhaustive work *Capital in the Twenty-First Century*, without government intervention, economic inequality will never be tamed—growth will naturally exceed distribution, and the regulatory and intellectual capture of the legislative process will continue without a strong set of alternative voices. That is one reason why a simple economic argument for the great exception is inadequate—the political culture explored here is pivotal. How sharp the elbows, how great the respect, how tight the social cohesion, and how much cultural authority all define a social group's capacity at the bargaining table.

Politics is one very important expression of workers' bargaining power. John Kenneth Galbraith called it "countervailing power" in his explanation of postwar industrial pluralism: the ability to offset business interests with the organized interests of other social groups. Yet there are few levers of countervailing power for working people in the United States today. In Piketty's study, war and taxation are the main levers, but tends to ignore social and political variables. Unions are another possible answer, as they once sat effectively at the governmental and business bargaining tables, but there could be many other forms of bargaining power from public policy, taxation, social mobilization, basic guaranteed income, or redefinition of rights.[14]

Unfortunately, the two-party system is hardly a competitive system seeking to draw in more voters of disenfranchised interests. Rather, it has relinquished all but the fight to define and control the center—thus marginalizing the economic interests of any but the most powerful. The bargaining power of working people—women and men; black, brown, and white; North and South—are not points of incorporation and mobilization except negatively. In a stunning exhaustive survey of independent influences by sets of actors on government policy outcomes in over 1,700 policy issues, political scientists Gilens and Page conclude "that majorities of the American public actually have little influence over the policies our government adopts." That process is controlled by the interests of a small number of elite Americans. While "regular elections, freedom of speech and association, and a widespread (if still contested) franchise" still exist, given the control over the process by the powerful few, "America's claims to being a democratic society are seriously threatened." We return to where we began: the 1889 cartoon image at the opening of chapter one called "The Bosses of the Senate." Meanwhile, high rates of inequality in a nation correlate to a host of negative outcomes, including shorter life expectancy, higher infant mortality, higher incarceration rates, lower levels of trust, higher rates of mental illness, more crime, and truncated social mobility. In this cluster of issues, the United States is an extreme outlier, having sacrificed the American dream of upward mobility in the name of anti-statism.[15]

Yet this is not simply a return to the past. As Steve Fraser only partially satirized the mapping of the first Gilded Age onto the second: "Crony capitalism, inequality, extravagance, Social Darwinian self-justification, blame-the-victim callousness, free-market hypocrisy: thus it was, thus it is again!" Admittedly, much of his hyperbole actually adds up to a valid comparison, as Fraser would be the first to admit, but differences are profound: one era is marked by the rise of manufacturing, the other by the consolidation of finance; one by massive changes wrought by industrialization, the other by the deflating expectations of deindustrialization; one by the exciting rise of working-class identity, the other by the demoralization of its decline; one by upward mobility, the other by stagnation; one by moving steel, the other by moving electrons; one by the consolidation of the assembly line, the other by the emergence of global production chains; one by unregulated capitalism, the other in the context of a rapidly weakening regulatory regime. Furthermore, missing today is the sense of political urgency and insurgency that defined the politics and social life of the first Gilded Age. In lieu of the social churn of the past, ours is a Gilded Age without a socialist like Eugene Debs, a plutocracy without a revolutionary like Big Bill Haywood, a betrayal of republican values without a populist firebrand like Mary Elizabeth Lease. Although radical and reformist politics roamed the land at the end of the nineteenth century, most working people remained mired in a crazy quilt of conflicting politics of religion, race, and sectionalism, tied up neatly in a rubbery ideology of individualism that could seemingly be stretched and molded to serve any and all needs.[16]

Caught up in the whirlwind of our present, we *overesti-*
mate how radically new the rate of change is in the global-
digital age. The sense of standing at the abyss of a new
world feels unprecedented. Yet when Henry Adams made
his prayer to the electric dynamo in 1900, he said that the
pace of technological change was so great that if left "his
historical neck broken by the sudden irruption of forces
totally new." In the creation of electric power, he saw the
emergence of a religious faith in the rational, sterile, and
technological future, which he regarded as "the break of
continuity," an "abysmal fracture" in everything he understood and trusted. Many would say the same about our
own time. This is not to say that history has started over or
is the same, but that our challenges are not unprecedented.
The arguments made here do not mean that politics is the
same as it was generations ago, only that the same issues
that are deeply ingrained in American history and culture
remain challenges for the past and the future.[17]

Our present time is not marked by the "era of big government" being over, but the better functions of the state have
become "submerged" below the waterline of national consciousness. As the political scientist Suzanne Mettler argues,
the government is still at work in the everyday lives of its
citizens but not in ways that are obvious to them. The fron-
tispiece of this book depicts a man examining his paycheck
while standing in front of a sign that clearly announces the
federal agency that employs him. The story of this man's job
and his relationship to the government is transparent. That
same individual today might receive an Earned Income Tax
Credit, which still costs the government revenue but plays a
much less bold ideological role in people's lives. The Earned
Income Tax Credit actually does positive good for poor
people, but most aspects of the submerged state—from
mortgage deductions to college savings accounts—function

as subsidies for the professional middle class more than the poor or working class.[18]

Policies that are largely invisible to the citizenry also seem more disposable. Compare for instance the much-celebrated GI Bill with the less obvious role of the 529 tax-free savings accounts for higher education. Both cost the government money, but one is the gold standard for what the government can do; the other is an unsung subsidy sopped up by the more affluent. In a survey, 57 percent of Americans reported that they used no government social programs. When respondents were presented with twenty-one different policies, from Social Security to the home-mortgage-interest deduction, 94 percent of those who did not identity themselves as recipients of government programs had, in fact, benefited from at least one. The average respondent had used four. The system obscures the meaningful role of government in people's lives, most of which falls to the upper classes, while simultaneously fueling demands for smaller government, the taming of deficits, and disdain for "government spending" (even though tax breaks are still a form of spending).[19]

━━━━━━━━━━━━━━━━━

Too often, political changes are seen as simple vacillating "cycles" of partisan history. While this might have some explanatory power when it comes to changes in what party is in charge, it fails to explain the underlying currents, coalitions, fractures, and agendas that run for longer periods. What replaces this generation of conservative, individualistic, "free-market" ideology, however, will not be some simple cycle back to a New Deal revival but will most likely be a much more chastened or radically different form of change that takes its cues from well outside of the New Deal paradigm.

Thus, we are left with a puzzle: on the one hand, we live with massive economic inequality; on the other hand, we have the argument that inequality has been tamed only under very rare circumstances. The path forward is not clear, but whatever successful incarnation of a liberal "social imaginary" might follow will not look like the New Deal, and it might be best to free ourselves from the notion that it will. Recognizing a "great exception" allows us to look beyond the static political solutions that emerged in the uniquely traumatic circumstances of the Roosevelt years and begin to consider what Barrington Moore has called "suppressed historical alternatives" that might help to (re) imagine contemporary bridges between the individualist strains in our public culture and a vision of the common good.[20]

Today, labor activists, for instance, succeed, when they do at all, by using tactics that stay far away from the once-promising mechanisms of the National Labor Relations Act. The workers' collective economic voice, gone from the state, has returned to the immigrant ethnic enclave, the church, the workers' center, and the occasional union. Hopes of decent pay for the working poor turn away from Congress and toward local living wage coalitions, city ordinances for higher minimum wages, immigrant rights groups, and workers' centers. Many of these efforts have been put under the heading "alt labor," the name of which alone is telling. The vibrant Occupy movement, with its wide ideological net, helped change the national discussion about inequality in the United States and the world, but had a hard time—or refused to try—making the leap to formal policy or politics.[21]

Looking beyond the New Deal, modern-day reformers might find more potent historical analogies for contemporary dilemmas in the fluid alliances of the Progressive Era rather than in the administration of Franklin Roosevelt. The ill-defined "kaleidoscopic" nature of local and state actions,

shifting alliances, diffuse leadership, cross-class identifica-
tions, and general social ferment might be a more useful
model or historical analogue for the future. A return to the
pre-Depression, pretrauma outlines of progressive-style politics, albeit updated for the global age, would suggest a politics of reform and regulation both moral and pragmatic;
spurred by local and state sites of innovation; bolstered by
cross-class alliances and enlightened elite leadership; focused on immigrant rights, consumer safety, corporate regulation, and occupational justice; advocating gas and water
(and perhaps health care) socialism; and even promoting the
types of militant voluntarism that originally grew in the
shadow of a state hostile to the collective interests of workers. This neo-progressivism is obvious in labor organizing,
where debates have even turned toward a renewed anarcho-
Gomperism once thought forever vanquished by the broader
vision of the CIO in the 1930s. While criticized for being
vague, individualistic, fluid, and lacking a core of class-
based vision, the Progressive Era's strengths may have rested
in the exact sort of things for which it has been criticized.[22]

At their best, the progressive reformers made the best of
the power of individualism in American political culture,
affirmed a vision of democratic life across class (if decidedly
not always racial) lines, and sought a bridge between that
individualism and a common good. That approach, with all
of its potential for mixed results, is worth revisiting to consider if, and how, it might provide insight on the new problems of our own time. Obviously, the racial politics of the
Progressive Era offer nothing but descent into some of the
most heinous aspects of American political culture but, in
the messy and often irresolute politics of the first decades of
the twentieth century, might actually be the most promising
historical analogy—if they are necessary at all—for the future of progressive politics.

The broad historical canvas of American politics might be imagined as a bright burst of economic experimentation set against a background of enduring themes of moral reform and corporate power. That preoccupation with morality, often twisted in its expression, touches all the American conflicts in this book: struggles to control immigrants, subjugate African Americans, revive religious faith, or escape the strictures of the state. Perhaps above all, it colors the deep longing to restore the values of individual freedom, vigor, and sovereignty to a mass society—the preoccupation with which, ironically, aids the power of corporate capitalism by letting it off the hook. Even at the height of the New Deal order, writing in 1955, historian Richard Hofstadter penetrated the mid-century bustle and found that "much of America still longs for—indeed, expects again to see—a return of the older individualism and the older isolation and grows frantic when it finds that even our conservative leaders are unable to restore such conditions." Hofstadter identified a vision eerily similar to that illusory "nation of small proprietors, of corner grocers and smithies under spreading chestnut trees" that Brain Truster Ray Moley perceived as the primary obstacle to the New Deal's traction in the 1930s.[23]

A large measure of the electorate, Hofstadter argued, still believed that "somewhere in the American past there was a golden age whose life was far better than our own. . . . Actually to live in that world," however, "actually to enjoy its cherished promise and its imagined innocence, is no longer within our power." If it ever was. As always, the distance between lost garden and experienced reality produces an endless wellspring of anxiety ripe for political mobilization—witness the rise of the Tea Party and the various military adventures to regenerate American greatness.[24]

Perhaps even Hofstadter underestimated the power of
the themes he analyzed, given the world that would unfold
beyond his lifetime. Although his critique targeted the populist right, and goes a long way toward offering context for
the "great exception," perhaps the tables might also be
turned. Hofstadter's words could also well apply to much
of the left, trapped in its own longing for the faded days of
the rationalism of New Deal order.

To reframe the New Deal order as a great exception, I
must emphasize, is not to take a jaundiced view of American history, but rather urges a more thorough and realistic
understanding of our recent past in the hope that it can
provide a more stable intellectual foundation for discussions of present and future politics. I recognize the contested
nature of American politics and social life that have informed a wide variety of dissenting movements that reshape
our politics and discourse, but I also understand that the
most powerful aspects of American political culture have
often proved resistant to these protests. My aim is also not
to diminish the vision or values of those dissenters, but
rather to resituate and rethink the New Deal Era in the
broader terrain of U.S. history. Our founding mythos of individualism has structured our collective life, created much
of value, and become so intimately intertwined with the
very essence of the nation itself that its limitations become
most difficult to perceive and discuss. If this argument is
correct, then conservative victories are more understandable and progressive victories all the more precious.

Despite the New Deal's many flaws and fissures, the programs of the 1930s represent the best of what the United
States can be as a nation—caring, sharing, secure, and occasionally visionary. Few issues seem more important today
than the need to bring the concerns of working people out
of the shadows and into the political and economic light.

But bad history makes for weak political strategy. While it is useful and hopeful to imagine that the United States can take the issue of collective economic rights as seriously as it did in the 1930s and 1940s, our present politics ought not be misled by freewheeling historical analogies based on an extraordinarily unique period in American history.

Max Weber suggested that culture works like loaded dice. It does not necessarily mean that the dice will always turn up a certain way, but it does mean they are more likely to do so. There have been times, and more will occur, when change is possible, when the burden of experience offers new insight even as human contradictions remain a constraint. Critical engagement with the past prepares us to move forward, allows us to parse the messiness of history and perhaps come to the present fully prepared, as well as fully humbled, for the task ahead. As the sociologist Ulrich Beck argues, "Skepticism . . . makes everything possible again: ethics, morality, knowledge, faith, society, and criticism, but differently—a few sizes smaller, more tentative, more revisable and more capable of learning and thus more curious, more open to the unexpected."[25]

Thus, this critical gallop through a century and a half of history should not be taken as an exercise in cynicism but as a project to strengthen the imagination for the work that lies ahead. It is my belief that the strongest political commitments are those that embrace the challenge of clear historical analysis. There is more hope to be found in historical clarity, after all, than there is in chasing ghosts.

ACKNOWLEDGMENTS

My biggest debt in this project, by a long shot, is to my friend and colleague Nick Salvatore. While I hope the dedication says enough, for the record: this book began as the Krieger Lecture in American Political Culture, which we gave together in 2007 at Cornell University. The product of rich, long conversations about history, politics, and American culture in our offices after our classes, that lecture had an electrifying urgency, as people seemed to feel a pressing need to figure out where they stood on the ideas and problems we presented. In 2008, we then published an early version, "The Long Exception: Rethinking the Place of the New Deal in American History," in *International Labor and Working-Class History* (with five commentaries and a response). We also sharpened our arguments in at least a dozen scholarly talks alone and together, and dozens more casual conversations across the country.

Although we picked this project back up and put it down a number of times, Nick ultimately, and probably wisely, decided to move on to other projects. In so doing, he graciously and without hesitation bequeathed all of our collective efforts to me. I finally decided to pursue our original idea in this book format. Nick still read an entire draft of the early manuscript. He had many criticisms and disagreements with that draft, some of which have been incorporated and some of which I have selected not to change. In sum, this is my book and any mistakes in interpretation and evidence are mine. Yet most of the core ideas in this book were developed in sustained, fascinating discussions with my dear friend. His name may not appear on the cover, but these ideas (and still even some of the words) are as much his as mine. Nick makes working at Cornell a joy.

Years ago, Bill Serrin, the *New York Times* labor beat reporter turned journalism professor, asked me if I thought the CIO ever would have happened had it not been for the Great Depression. I've been pondering a version of that question ever since. I first thought of this argument while trying to account for the decline of the New Deal while teaching my Recent History of American Workers course, and I am indebted to all the students who have taken that course and given me a run for my intellectual money. I would also like to thank Dean Harry Katz for making the ILR School at Cornell University a dream of a place to work, and Sandy and Carol Krieger for their generous support of the Cornell American Studies Program. Every day I am grateful that I work with Rhonda Clouse, who has had my back at all times (and has only occasionally thrown things at me when it is turned). At Princeton University Press, I thank Eric Crahan, who has shepherded this book through the process, Edward Berkowitz for a particularly fine close read, and Gary Gerstle, who both read the manuscript and set the bar quite high with his model of historical thinking. Rob Vanderlan and Joel Dinerstein could be counted on for lightning-fast reads, penetrating criticism, and invaluable advice. Finally, the extraordinary support of the Andrew J. Nathanson Professorship made this book, and so much more, possible.

For important comments, criticism, and assistance, I would like to thank Glenn Altschuler, Larry Bartels, Kevin Boyle, Robert Bussel, Wynndam Curtis, Derek Chang, Dorothy Sue Cobble, Samuel Flaks, Maria Cristina Garcia,

Rebecca Givan, Robert Hutchens, Louis Hyman, William P. Jones, Michael Jones-Correa, Michael Kazin, Jennifer Klein, Isaac Kramnick, Kevin Kruse, Adam Litwin, Nelson Lichtenstein, Nancy MacLean, Joseph McCartin, Jack Metzgar, David Montgomery, Aaron Sachs, Michael Smith, Jason Sokol, Ann Sullivan, Michael Trotti, Clarence Walker, Julian Zelizer, and Robert Zieger.

The highlight of my writing time was always when one of two teenagers wandered up to my study, plopped down in the big overstuffed chair, and told me about the important stuff—or sometimes, nothing at all. Aidan and Aliya continue to make my life a joy. Welcome to the early onset of adulthood—stave it off as long as you can.

Being with Mickey has been the great exception of my life. No two people can locate the profound in the absurd, the joy in the mundane, or the love in the everyday like the two of us. Time to reload. The raucous view from a Buick Six continues.

NOTES

PROLOGUE. PHILADELPHIA, 1936

1. The prologue is drawn from Franklin D. Roosevelt, "Acceptance Speech for the Renomination for the Presidency," Philadelphia, PA, 27 June 1936. Available at website of The American Presidency Project, www.presidency.ucsb.edu/ws/?pid=15314 (accessed 2 June 2015); David Kennedy, *Freedom from Fear: The American People in Depression and War, 1929–1945* (New York, 1999), 280–281; Arthur Schlesinger, *The Politics of Upheaval, 1935–1936* (Boston, 1960), 583–584; Raymond Moley, *The First New Deal* (New York, 1966), 551; Adam Seth Cohen, *Nothing to Fear: FDR's Inner Circle and the Hundred Days That Created Modern America* (New York, 2009), 293; William E. Leuchtenburg, *The White House Looks South: Franklin D. Roosevelt, Harry S. Truman, Lyndon Johnson* (Baton Rouge, LA, 2005), 123–124; Roger Biles, *The South and the New Deal* (Lexington, KY, 1994), 140.

INTRODUCTION. RETHINKING THE NEW DEAL IN AMERICAN HISTORY

1. Gary Gerstle, "The Protean Character of American Liberalism," *American Historical Review* 99 (October 1994): 1043–1073.

2. Robert Zieger, *The CIO: 1935–1955* (Chapel Hill, NC, 1995), 1.

3. Paul Krugman, "For Richer," *New York Times Magazine*, 20 October 2002. See Colin Gordon, *Growing Apart: A Political History of American Inequality*, at http://scalar.usc.edu/works/growing-apart-a-political-history-of-american-inequality/index (accessed 3 June 2015).

4. Richard Kirkendall, "The New Deal as Watershed: The Recent Literature," *Journal of American History* 54 (March 1968): 839.

5. Lionel Trilling, *The Liberal Imagination: Essays on Literature and Society* (New York, 1950), xv; William Leuchtenburg, *In the Shadow of FDR: From Harry Truman to Barack Obama*, 4th ed. (Ithaca, NY, 2009), 2.

6. Barton J. Bernstein, ed., *Towards a New Past: Dissenting Essays in American History* (New York, 1968), 264–265; see, especially, Frances

Fox Piven, *Poor People's Movements: Why They Succeed, How They Fail* (New York, 1977).

7. Milton Friedman and Anna Schwartz, *A Monetary History of the United States, 1867–1960* (Princeton, NJ, 1963); Amity Shlaes, *The Forgotten Man: A New History of the Great Depression* (New York, 2007), 7.

8. Thomas Piketty, *Capital in the Twentieth Century* (Cambridge, MA, 2014); John Kenneth Galbraith, *American Capitalism: The Concept of Countervailing Power* (Cambridge, MA, 1956).

9. Anthony J. Badger, *FDR: The First Hundred Days* (New York, 2008), xv, 61; Ira Katznelson, *Fear Itself: The New Deal and the Origins of Our Time* (New York, 2013), 162; Richard Hofstadter, *The Age of Reform: From Bryan to FDR* (New York, 1955), 303, 316–317.

10. Lizabeth Cohen, *Making a New Deal: Industrial Workers in Chicago, 1919–1939* (New York, 2008), explains the role of commercial culture, mass production, and welfare capitalism for the rise of the New Deal; for the best single essay on the power of corporate paternalism, see David Brody, "The Rise and Decline of Welfare Capitalism," in Brody, *Workers in Industrial America: Essays on the 20ᵗʰ Century Struggle*, 2nd ed. (New York, 1993), 48–81; the often overlooked continued power of welfare capitalism is covered in Sanford Jacoby, *Modern Manors: Welfare Capitalism since the New Deal* (Princeton, NJ, 1997); Herbert Croly, "The Eclipse of Progressivism," *New Republic* 27 (October 1920), at www.newrepublic.com/article/politics/the-eclipse-progressivism (accessed 4 June 2015); on "significant emancipation," see Geoffrey Blodgett's review of John Braeman, Rober H. Bremner, and Everett Walters, eds., *Change and Continuity in Twentieth-Century America*, in *New England Quarterly* 38 (December 1965): 562.

11. Alan Brinkley, *End of Reform: New Deal Liberalism in Recession and War* (New York, 1996), 3–4.

12. Benjamin Franklin, *The Writings of Benjamin Franklin*, vol. 3, ed. Albert Henry Smyth (New York, 1907), 139–141.

13. Matthew Frye Jacobsen, *Whiteness of a Different Color: European Immigrants and the Alchemy of Race* (Cambridge, MA, 1998), 93, 109.

14. James T. Kloppenberg, "In Retrospect: Louis Hartz's *The Liberal Tradition in America*," *Reviews in American History* 29 (September 2001): 464; James A. Morone, *Hellfire Nation: The Politics of Sin in American History* (New Haven, CT, 2003), 350; Garry Wills, *Head and Heart: American Christianities* (New York, 2007), 451–453.

15. Katznelson, *Fear Itself*, 25, 149.

16. "Culture of unity" is a phrase used by Lizabeth Cohen in *Making a New Deal*.

17. David Brody, "Labor vs. the Law: How the Wagner Act Became a Management Tool," *New Labor Forum* 13 (Spring 2004): 9–16.

18. "Individualism for the masses" is from Nancy L. Green, *Ready-to-Wear and Ready-to-Work: A Century of Industry and Immigrants in Paris and New York* (Durham, NC, 1997), 15.

19. On Tugwell, see Lawrence W. Levine and Cornelia R. Levine, *The People and the President: America's Conversation with FDR* (Boston, 2002), 219–220. For an analysis of Tugwell, see Kirkendall, "New Deal Watershed," 846. FDR also rhetorically evoked a more collective vision, but without consistent effort. For an effort to revive it, see Cass R. Sunstein, *The Second Bill of Rights: FDR's Unfinished Revolution and Why We Need It More Than Ever* (New York, 2004).

20. The massive literature on the decline of the New Deal order is beyond the scope of a single footnote. No attempt has been made to be exhaustive. For the decline of New Deal liberalism, see Steve Fraser and Gary Gerstle, eds., *The Rise and Fall of the New Deal Order* (Princeton, NJ, 1989); Thomas J. Sugrue, *The Origins of the Urban Crisis: Race and Inequality in Post War Detroit* (Princeton, NJ, 1996); Mathew D. Lassiter, *The Silent Majority: Suburban Politics in the Sunbelt South* (Princeton, NJ, 2006); Michael Goldfield, *The Decline of Organized Labor in the United States* (Chicago, 1987); Todd Gitlin, *Twilight of Common Dreams* (New York, 1995); Thomas Byrne Edsall with Mary D. Edsall, *Chain Reaction: The Impact of Race, Rights, and Taxes on American Politics* (New York, 1991); Robert M. Collins, *More: The Politics of Economic Growth in Postwar America* (New York, 2000); Richard Oestreicher, "The Rules of the Game: Class Politics in Twentieth-Century America," in *Organized Labor and American Politics, 1894–1994: The Labor-Liberal Alliance*, ed. Kevin Boyle (Albany, NY, 1998), 29.

21. Jacob S. Hacker and Paul Pierson, *Winner-Take-All Politics: How Washington Made the Rich Richer—and Turned Its Back on the Middle Class* (New York, 2010), 99; Jefferson Cowie, *Stayin' Alive: The 1970s and the Last Days of the Working Class* (New York, 2010).

22. "Difference," Daniel T. Rodgers writes, "requires contrast; exceptionalism requires a rule. Difference claims feed on polarities and diversity; exceptionalist claims pin one's own nation's distinctiveness to every other people's sameness—to general laws and conditions governing everything but the special case at hand." What makes the United States different was mollified during the New Deal. Rodgers, "Exceptionalism," in *Imagined Histories: American Historians Interpret the Past*, ed. Anthony Molho and Gordon S. Woods (Princeton, NJ, 1998), 22–23; see Daniel T. Rodgers, "Contesting Inequality," *Raritan Review* (Spring 2014): 24.

23. Richard Hofstadter, *The Age of Reform* (New York, 1955), 308.

24. See Eric Foner, *Nothing but Freedom: Emancipation and Its Legacy* (Baton Rouge, LA, 1983). This is not to criticize the fact that abolition is what David Brion called the "greatest landmark of willed moral progress in human history," in Brion, *The Problem of Slavery in the Age of Emancipation* (New York, 2014).

25. Van Wyck Brooks, "On Creating a Usable Past," *The Dial* 64 (11 April 1918): 337–341; Barrington Moore, *Injustice: The Social Bases of Obedience and Revolt* (New York, 1987), 376; George Lakoff and Mark Johnson, *Metaphors We Live By* (Chicago, 2003); George Lakoff, *Moral Politics: How Liberals and Conservatives Think* (Chicago, 2002).

26. Eugene O'Neil, *More Stately Mansions* (New Haven, CT, 1964), 140, 195.

CHAPTER ONE. THE QUESTION OF DEMOCRACY IN THE AGE OF INCORPORATION

1. Quoted in Sven Beckert, *The Monied Metropolis: New York City and the Consolidation of the American Bourgeoisie, 1850–1896* (New York, 2001), 279.

2. Thomas K. McCraw, *Prophets of Regulation: Charles Francis Adams, Louis D. Brandeis, James M. Landis, Alfred E. Kahn* (Cambridge, MA, 1984), 64–65; John M. Cooper, *Pivotal Decades: The United States, 1900–1920* (New York, 1990), 134; David Nasaw, *Andrew Carnegie* (New York, 2006), 513–523; Ron Chernow, *The House of Morgan: An American Banking Dynasty and the Rise of Modern Finance* (New York, 1990), 85–86; Leon Fink, *Workingmen's Democracy: The Knights of Labor and American Politics* (Urbana, IL, 1983), xii.

3. *Santa Clara County v. Southern Pacific R. Co.* 118 *U.S.* 394 (1886) in U.S. Supreme Court JUSTIA, at https://supreme.justia.com/cases/federal/us/118/394/ (accessed 3 June 2015); John C. Coffee, Jr., " 'No Soul to Damn: No Body to Kick': An Unscandalized Inquiry into the Problem of Corporate Punishment,' " *Michigan Law Review* 79 (1981): 386; John A. Powell and Caitlin Watt, "Corporate Prerogative, Race, and Identity Under the Fourteenth Amendment," *Cardozo Law Review* 32 (2010): 885.

4. Judge quoted in Melvyn Dubofsky, "The Federal Judiciary, Free Labor, and Equal Rights," in *The Pullman Strike and the Crisis of the 1890s: Essays on Labor and Politics*, ed. Richard Schneirov, Shelton Stromquist, and Nick Salvatore (Urbana, IL, 1999), 170; see also Cedric de Leon, *The Origins of the Right to Work: Antilabor Democracy in*

Nineteenth-Century Chicago (Ithaca, NY, 2015); Christopher Tomlins, *The State and the Unions: Labor Relations, Law, and the Organized Labor Movement in America, 1880–1960* (New York, 1985).

5. Daniel T. Rodgers, *Work Ethic in Industrial America, 1850–1920* (Chicago, 1978), 35.

6. Mark Twain and Charles Dudley Warner, *The Gilded Age: A Tale of Today* (New York, 1904 [1873]); Vernon Louis Parrington, *Main Currents in American Thought: An Interpretation of American Literature from the Beginnings to 1920*, vol. 3 (New York, 1930), 25; Nell Irvin Painter, *Standing at Armageddon* (New York, 1987).

7. Alan Trachtenberg, *The Incorporation of America: Culture and Society in the Gilded Age* (New York, 1982).

8. See Harry L. Watson, *Liberty and Power: The Politics of Jacksonian America* (New York, 1991).

9. Herron quoted in Nick Salvatore, *Eugene Debs: Citizen and Socialist* (Urbana, IL, 1982), 191.

10. *Atlantic*, quoted in Lears, *Rebirth of a Nation*, 191; see also Rodgers, *Work Ethic in Industrial America*.

11. Leon Fink, "The New Labor History and the Powers of Historical Pessimism: Consensus, Hegemony, and the Case of the Knights of Labor," *Journal of American History* 75 (June 1988): 124.

12. Josiah Bartlett Lambert, *"If the Workers Took a Notion": The Right to Strike and American Political Development* (Ithaca, NY, 2005), 57. "Corporations," explains Joyce Appleby, "made their moves toward consolidation before the era of big government began." Appleby, *The Relentless Revolution: A History of Capitalism* (New York, 2010), 263.

13. Eric Foner, *Fiery Trial: Abraham Lincoln and American Slavery* (New York, 2010), 112.

14. Foner, *Fiery Trial*, 115; see also David Montgomery, *Beyond Equality: Labor and the Radical Republicans, 1862–1872* (Urbana, IL, 1981); Eric Foner, *Free Soil, Free Labor, Free Men: The Ideology of the Republican Party before the Civil War* (New York, 1970).

15. de Leon, *Origins of the Right to Work*, 106–110.

16. Leon Fink, *The Long Gilded Age: American Capitalism and the Lessons of a New World Order* (Philadelphia, 2015), 31.

17. Joel Williamson, "The Meaning of Freedom," in *Reconstruction: An Anthology of Revisionist Writings*, ed. Kenneth M. Stampp (Baton Rouge, LA, 1969), 218; W.E.B. Du Bois, *Black Reconstruction in America* (New York, 1935), 26.

18. Heather Cox Richardson, *The Death of Reconstruction* (Cambridge, MA, 2001), 245.

19. See Mathew Frye Jacobson, *Whiteness of a Different Color: European Immigrants and the Alchemy of Race* (Cambridge, MA, 1999).

20. Mike Davis, *Prisoners of the American Dream: Politics and Economy in the History of the U.S. Working Class* (New York, 1986); Bruce Nelson, *Divided We Stand: American Workers and the Struggle for Black Equality* (Princeton, NJ, 2001); Richard Jules Oestreicher, *Solidarity and Fragmentation: Working People and Class Consciousness in Detroit, 1875–1900* (Urbana, IL, 1986); Alexander Saxton, *The Indispensable Enemy; Labor and the Anti-Chinese Movement in California* (Berkeley, CA, 1971); David Roediger, *The Wages of Whiteness: Race and the Making of the American Working Class* (New York, 1991); Gwendolyn Mink, *Old Labor and New Immigrants in American Political Development: Union, Party, and State, 1875–1920* (Ithaca, NY, 1986); Mae M. Ngai, *Impossible Subjects: Illegal Aliens and the Making of Modern America* (Princeton, NJ, 2004); Jacobson, *Whiteness of a Different Color*; David Gordon, Richard Edwards, and Michael Reich, *Segmented Work, Divided Workers: The Historical Transformation of Labor in the United States* (New York, 1982); John R. Commons, *Races and Immigrants in America* (New York, 1907), 150; David Roediger and Elizabeth D. Esch, *The Production of Difference: Race and the Management of Labor in U.S. History* (New York, 2012).

21. Edward Blum, " 'Paul Has Been Forgotten': Women, Gender, and Revivalism in the Gilded Age," *Journal of the Gilded Age and Progressive Era* (July 2004): 250, 251.

22. Garry Wills, *Head and Heart: American Christianities* (New York, 2007), 341–350; Richard Hofstadter, *Anti-Intellectualism in American Life* (New York, 1963), 110; William G. McCloughlin, *Modern Revivalism: Charles Grandison Finney to Billy Graham* (New York, 1959).

23. Henry Adams, *The Education of Henry Adams* (Boston, 1918), 7.

24. Martin Shefter, "Trade Unions and Political Machines: The Organization and Disorganization of the American Working Class in the Late Nineteenth Century," in *Working-Class Formation: Nineteenth-Century Patterns in Western Europe and the United States*, ed. Ira Katznelson and Aristide R. Zolberg (Princeton, NJ, 1986), 208–210.

25. Montgomery, *Beyond Equality*, 195.

26. Robin Archer, *Why Is There No Labor Party in the United States?* (Princeton, NJ, 2007), 240–241.

27. Rudyard Kipling, *From Sea to Sea: Letters of Travel, Part II* (New York, 1900), 58–59.

28. Dana Frank, *Buy American: The Untold Story of Economic Nationalism* (Boston, 1999), 45–46; Melvyn Dubofsky, *State and Labor in Modern America* (Chapel Hill, NC, 1994), 25.

29. Patten quoted in Eric Foner, *The Story of American Freedom* (New York, 1998), 133; Archer, *Why Is There No Labor Party*, 1.

30. See Rosanne Currarino, "The Politics of 'More': The Labor Question and the Idea of Economic Liberty in Industrial America," *Journal of American History* (June 2006): 17–36.

31. William E. Forbath, *Law and the Shaping of the American Labor Movement* (Cambridge, MA, 1991), 2, 3; his chapter on "Government by Injunction" starts on p. 59.

32. Salvatore, *Debs*, 135; see Karen Orren, *Belated Feudalism: Labor, the Law, and Liberal Development in the United States* (New York, 1991).

33. Salvatore, *Debs*, 177.

34. Charles Postel, *The Populist Vision* (New York, 2007), 2; Michael McGerr, *A Fierce Discontent: The Rise and Fall of the Progressive Movement in America, 1870–1920* (New York, 2003), 3; Beckert, *Monied Metropolis*, 9.

35. Shefter, "Trade Unions and Political Machines," 230.

36. David Montgomery quoted in Eric Foner, "Why No Socialism in the United States?" *History Workshop Journal* 17 (Spring 1984): 59.

37. Michael Kazin, *American Dreamers: How the Left Changed a Nation* (New York, 2011), 93.

CHAPTER TWO. KALEIDOSCOPE OF REFORM

1. Steve Fraser, "The Labor Question," in *The Rise and Fall of the New Deal Order*, ed. Steve Fraser and Gary Gerstle (Princeton, NJ, 1989), 55–84.

2. Paul Boyer, *Urban Masses and Moral Order in America, 1820–1920* (Cambridge, MA, 1978), 196. See Walter Lippmann, *Drift and Mastery: An Attempt to Diagnose the Current Unrest* (Madison, WI, 1985 [1914]). For a fresh look at the middle class in the Progressive Era, see Robert D. Johnston, *The Radical Middle Class: Populist Democracy and the Question of Capitalism in Progressive Era Portland, Oregon* (Princeton, NJ, 2003). A useful survey that puts the middle class at the center of the story is Michael McGerr, *A Fierce Discontent: The Rise and Fall of the Progressive Movement in America* (New York, 2003), xv.

3. James T. Kloppenberg, *Uncertain Victory: Social Democracy and Progressivism in European and American Thought, 1870–1920* (New York, 1986), 410.

4. Richard Hofstadter, *The Age of Reform: From Bryan to F.D.R.* (New York, 1955), 266.

5. On the "language of class," see Shelton Stromquist, *Re-Inventing 'The People': The Progressive Movement, the Class Problem, and the Origins of Modern Liberalism* (Urbana, IL, 2006), 4. Historiographic surveys of the period must begin with Peter G. Filene, "An Obituary for 'The Progressive Movement,'" *American Quarterly* 22 (Spring 1970): 20–34; Daniel T. Rodgers, "In Search of Progressivism," *Reviews in American History*, 10 (December 1982); Alan Brinkley, "Richard Hofstadter's *The Age of Reform*: A Reconsideration," *Reviews in American History* 13 (September 1985): 462–480; Robert D. Johnston, "Re-Democratizing the Progressive Era: The Politics of Progressive Era Political Historiography," *Journal of the Gilded Age and Progressive Era* 1 (January 2002): 68–92.

6. Christopher L. Tomlins, *The State and the Unions: Labor Relations, Law, and the Organized Labor Movement, 1880–1960* (New York, 1985), 58, 76, 32; Forbath, *Law and the Shaping of the American Labor Movement*.

7. Theda Skocpol, *Protecting Soldiers and Mothers: The Political Origins of Social Policy in the United States* (Cambridge, MA, 1992), 2.

8. Skocpol, *Solidiers and Mothers*, 52; Linda Gordon, *Pitied but Not Entitled: Single Mothers and the Origins of Welfare* (New York, 1994).

9. Skocpol, *Soldiers and Mothers*, 37.

10. Linda Gordon, "Gender, State, and Society: A Debate with Theda Skocpol," *Contention* 2, no. 3 (Spring 1993): 139–156.

11. Theodore Roosevelt, "The New Nationalism," Osawatomie, Kansas, August 31, 1910, in *Theodore Roosevelt: Letters and Speeches*, ed. Louis Auchincloss (New York, 2004), 799–814. On the issues in the 1912 campaign, see John Milton Cooper, *The Warrior and the Priest: Woodrow Wilson and Theodore Roosevelt* (Cambridge, MA, 1983), 187–227 (Wilson is quoted on 203); Lewis L. Gould, *America in the Progressive Era, 1890–1914* (New York, 2001), 58–66; Lewis L. Gould, *Grand Old Party: A History of the Republicans* (New York, 2003), 153–192.

12. Jackson Lears, *Rebirth of a Nation: The Making of Modern America, 1877–1920* (New York, 2009), 316–317.

13. Walter Lippmann, *Drift and Mastery: An Attempt to Diagnose the Current Unrest* (New York, 1914), 146.

14. Joseph McCartin, *Labor's Great War: The Struggle for Industrial Democracy and the Origins of Modern American Labor Relations, 1912–1921* (Chapel Hill, NC, 1997), 120–172; Fraser, "The 'Labor Question,'" 56.

15. Quoted in Melvyn Dubofsky, *The State and Labor in Modern*

America (Chapel Hill, NC, 1994), 77; McCartin, *Labor's Great War*, 12, 95, 185.

16. See Gary Gerstle, *American Crucible: Race and Nation in the Twentieth Century* (Princeton, NJ, 2001), Woodrow Wilson with Mario R. Dinunzio, ed., *Woodrow Wilson: Essential Writings and Speeches of the Scholar-President* (New York, 2006), 202; on Wilson and segregation, see Karin L. Stanford, ed., *If We Must Die: African American Voices on War and Peace* (Lanham, MD, 2008), 106.

17. David M. Reimers, *Unwelcome Strangers: American Identity and the Turn against Immigration* (New York, 1998), 114–116.

18. Gary Gerstle, "The Protean Character of American Liberalism," *American Historical Review* 99 (October 1994): 1045. Gerstle's idea of the "protean" character, the "malleability" of American liberalism, differs from the one argued for here. I see more continuity in the long run around moralism, individualism, and race than an ongoing evolution. The 1930s gives the impression of a changing and evolutionary model, but it stands out. Otherwise, continuity might be fairly dominant though hardly determinative.

19. Gerstle, *American Crucible*, 105, 107.

20. Mae Ngai, *Impossible Subjects: Illegal Aliens and the Making of Modern America* (Princeton, NJ, 2004), 27.

21. Daniel J. Tichenor, *Dividing Lines: The Politics of Immigration Control in America* (Princeton, NJ, 2002); Ngai, *Impossible Subjects*; Jacobson, *Whiteness of a Different Color*; Lizabeth Cohen, *Making a New Deal: Industrial Workers in Chicago* (New York, 1991); Vernon M. Briggs, Jr., *Immigration and American Unionism* (Ithaca, NY, 2001).

22. Quoted in Richard Pells, *Radical Visions and American Dreams: Culture and Thought in the Depression Years* (New York, 1998), 54.

23. Grant McConnell, *Private Power and American Democracy* (New York, 1966), 38.

24. Edward Larson, *Summer for the Gods: The Scopes Trial and America's Continuing Debate over Science and Religion* (New York, 1997), 36.

25. Larson, *Summer for the Gods*, 39; the unity of Jefferson and Jesus is explored in Michael Kazin, *A Godly Hero: The Life of William Jennings Bryan* (New York, 2006).

26. For the resilience of the evangelical movement after Scopes, see Joel Carpenter, *Revive Us Again: The Reawakening of American Fundamentalism* (New York, 1997).

27. Gerstle, "Protean Character," 1058, n. 38.

28. Mark Hendrickson, *American Labor and Economic Citizenship: New Capitalism from World War I to the Great Depression* (New York, 2013), 297–298; Daniel Rodgers, *Atlantic Crossings: Social Poli-*

tics in a Progressive Age (New York, 1998), 371–374; on postwar "growthsmanship," see Robert Collins, *More: The Politics of Economic Growth in Postwar America* (New York, 2000).

29. This is largely the argument of Cohen, *Making a New Deal*, which is excellent in its analysis of changing regimes of production yet does not rely enough on the simple fact of immigration restrictions as a unifying factor in the culture, perhaps overdeveloping its other points about consumption.

30. David Brody, *Workers in Industrial America: Essays on the Twentieth Century Struggle*, 2nd ed. (New York, 1993), 78; Sanford M. Jacoby, *Modern Manors: Welfare Capitalism since the New Deal* (Princeton, NJ, 1998).

31. Daniel Nelson, *Frederick W. Taylor and the Rise of Scientific Management* (Madison, WI, 1980).

32. See John Dewey, *Individualism Old and New* (New York, 1930), 5, 14; see also Gholamreza Sami, *Ragged Individualism America in the Political Drama of the 1930s* (Bloomington, IN, 2011).

33. Hofstadter, *Age of Reform*, 307.

34. The phrase "big bang" is used in the welfare literature; see Skocpol, *Soldiers and Mothers*, 4; William Graebner, "A 'Big Bang'—or a Whimper?," *Berkeley Journal of Sociology* 36 (1991): 57–63.

CHAPTER THREE. WORKING-CLASS INTERREGNUM

1. *New York Times*, 8 April 1932; Franklin D. Roosevelt, "The 'Forgotten Man' Speech," radio address, Albany, NY, 7 April 1932, *The Public Papers and Addresses of Franklin D. Roosevelt*, vol. I, comp. Samuel L. Rosenman (New York, 1938), 625.

2. Raymond Moley, *The First New Deal* (New York, 1966), 341; William Graham Sumner, *The Forgotten Man and Other Essays*, ed. Albert Galloway Keller (New Haven, CT, 1919), 476, 493, 494.

3. Christopher M. Finan, *Alfred E. Smith: The Happy Warrior* (New York, 2002), 276.

4. Franklin D. Roosevelt, Acceptance Speech, Democratic National Convention, 1932. FDR Library, at https://fdrlibrary.wordpress.com /tag/democratic-national-convention/ (accessed 3 June 2015).

5. Franklin D. Roosevelt, Address at Oglethorpe University in Atlanta, 22 May 1932, at www.presidency.ucsb.edu/ws/?pid=88410 (accessed 3 June 2015).

6. The Brain Trust is covered in David M. Kennedy, *Freedom from Fear: The American People in Depression and War, 1929–1945* (New York, 1999), 120–122.

7. Franklin D. Roosevelt, Inaugural Address, 4 March 1933, The American Presidency Project, at www.presidency.ucsb.edu/ws/?pid =14473 (accessed 4 June 2015). Al Smith and other traditionalists again shuddered at Roosevelt's promise of a new Leviathan. "What does a democracy do in a war?" he asked. "It becomes a tyrant, a despot, a real monarch. In the World War we took our Constitution, wrapped it up and laid it on the shelf and left it there until it was over." The shadow of dictatorship—though not yet the darkest shades of fascism—cast over Europe, and to many at the time American history seemed to lay in the balance. Was Roosevelt poised to save American democracy or destroy it? Smith quoted in William E. Leuchtenburg, *The FDR Years: On Roosevelt and His Legacy* (New York, 1997), 48.

8. Isaiah Berlin, *The Proper Study of Mankind: An Anthology of Essays* (New York, 1949), 636.

9. Kennedy, *Freedom from Fear*, 167.

10. T. H. Watkins, *The Hungry Years: A Narrative History of the Great Depression* (New York, 1999), 70.

11. Richard Lowitt and Maurine Beasley, eds., *One Third of a Nation: Lorena Hickok Reports on the Great Depression* (Urbana, IL, 1983), 158–159.

12. Robert S. McElvaine, *The Great Depression in America, 1929–1941* (New York, 1984), 172, 174–175.

13. Robert S. McElvaine, ed., *Down and Out in the Great Depression: Letters from the Forgotten Man* (Chapel Hill, NC, 2008), 56; Bryant Simon, *A Fabric of Defeat: The Politics of South Carolina Millhands, 1910–1948* (Chapel Hill, NC, 1998), 82.

14. Arthur Schlesinger, *The Coming of the New Deal, 1933–1935* (New York, 1958), 22; Jonathan Alter, *The Defining Moment: FDR's Hundred Days and the Triumph of Hope* (New York, 2006), 225. There is a useful timeline of the first hundred days in Anthony Badger, *FDR: The First Hundred Days* (New York, 2008), ix–x; Kennedy, *Freedom from Fear*, 154.

15. Schlesinger, *The Coming of the New Deal*, 5.

16. Quoted in Roger Biles, *A New Deal for the American People* (DeKalb, IL, 1991), 36.

17. Alter, *Defining Moment*, 301.

18. Badger, *FDR*, 98; Elliot A. Rosen, *Roosevelt, The Great Depression and the Economics of Recovery* (Charlottesville, VA, 2005), 94.

19. Quoted in Biles, *A New Deal*, 45; Dubofsky, *The State and Labor in Modern America*, 112.

20. Dubofsky, *State and Labor*, 118–119; Badger, *FDR*, 155, says "labor was consistently outgunned by business."

21. Quoted in Lizabeth Cohen, *Making a New Deal: Industrial Workers in Chicago, 1919–1939* (New York, 1990), 277.

22. J. David Greenstone, *Labor in American Politics* (New York, 1969), 71.

23. Hopkins quoted in Gertrude Schaffner Goldberg, "The New Deal and the Creation of an American Welfare State," in *When Government Helped: Learning from the Successes and the Failures of the New Deal*, ed. Sheila D. Collins and Gertrude Schaffner Goldberg (New York, 2014), 187; Keyserling quoted in Biles, *A New Deal*, 161; Lewis quoted in Brody, *Workers in Industrial America*, 99.

24. Kennedy, *Freedom from Fear*, 249, 258, 266–273.

25. Kennedy, *Freedom from Fear*, 271; Frances Perkins, *The Roosevelt I Knew* (New York, 1946), 281; James T. Patterson, *America's Struggle against Poverty in the Twentieth Century* (Cambridge, MA, 2000).

26. FDR quoted in W. Andrew Achenbaum, *Social Security: Visions and Revisions* (New York, 1986), 22–23.

27. This is not to overlook both the Railway Labor Act (1926) and the Norris LaGuardia Act (1932).

28. Dubofsky, *State and Labor*, 137. On new union leadership, see Melvyn Dubofsky and Warren Van Tine, *John L. Lewis: A Biography* (New York, 1977); Steven Fraser, *Labor Will Rule: Sidney Hillman and the Rise of American Labor* (New York, 1991); Nelson Lichtenstein, *The Most Dangerous Man in Detroit: Walter Reuther and the Fate of American Labor* (New York, 1995). On the changing role of the state, see Dubofsky, *State and Labor*; Christopher L. Tomlins, *The State and the Unions: Labor Relations, Law, and the Organized Labor Movement in America, 1880–1960* (New York, 1985); Robert Zieger, *The CIO, 1935–1955* (Chapel Hill, NC, 1995); David Brody, *Workers in Industrial America: Essays on the 20th Century Struggle*, 2nd ed. (New York, 1993).

29. Dubofsky, *State and Labor*, 133.

30. Franklin Roosevelt, Acceptance Speech for the Renomination for the Presidency, Philadelphia, 27 June 1936, at www.presidency.ucsb.edu/ws/?pid=15314 (accessed 4 June 2015); Roosevelt, Address at Madison Square Garden, New York City, 31 October 1936, www.presidency.ucsb.edu/ws/?pid=15219 (accessed 4 June 2015).

31. Nelson Lichtenstein, *State of the Union: A Century of American Labor* (Princeton, NJ, 2002), 52–53; Dubofsky, *State and Labor*, 137–138.

32. Benjamin Stolberg, "Big Steel, Little Steel, and the C.I.O.," *Nation*, 31 July 1936, 119–123.

33. William E. Leuchtenburg, *The Supreme Court Reborn: The Constitutional Revolution in the Age of Roosevelt* (New York, 1995), 90.

34. Christopher L. Tomlins, *The State and the Unions: Labor Relations, Law, and the Organized Labor Movement in America, 1880–1960* (New York, 1985), 230–243, calls it "Thermidor." Brinkley, *End of Reform*, 30.

35. Steve Fraser, "The Labor Question," in *The Rise and Fall of the New Deal Order, 1930–1980*, ed. Steve Fraser and Gary Gerstle (Princeton, NJ, 1990), 78.

CHAPTER FOUR. CONSTRAINTS AND FRACTURES IN THE NEW LIBERALISM

1. Sean Farhang and Ira Katznelson, "The Southern Imposition: Congress and Labor in the New Deal and Fair Deal," *Studies in American Political Development* 19 (Spring 2005): 1; Robert S. McElvaine, *The Great Depression, 1929–1941* (New York, 1984), 257.

2. Katznelson, *Fear Itself*, 160, 164; Ickes quoted in Philip A. Klinkner and Rogers M. Smith, *The Unsteady March: The Rise and Decline of Racial Equality* (Chicago, 2002), 130.

3. Sieve remark in Jason Scott Smith, *A Concise History of the New Deal* (New York, 2014), 91; James Gregory, *The Southern Diaspora: How the Great Migrations of Black and White Southerners Transformed America* (Chapel Hill, NC, 2005); St. Clair Drake and Horace R. Cayton, *Black Metropolis: A Study of Negro Life in a Northern City* (New York, 1945); Patricia Sullivan, *Days of Hope: Race and Democracy in the New Deal Era* (Chapel Hill, NC, 1996); Ira Katznelson, *When Affirmative Action Was White: An Untold History of Racial Inequality in Twentieth Century America* (New York, 2005).

4. Michael Hiltzik, *The New Deal: A Modern History* (New York, 2011), 308, 320; Katznelson, *When Affirmative Action Was White*, 29; Paul Frymer, *Black and Blue: African Americans, the Labor Movement, and the Decline of the Democratic Party* (Princeton, NJ, 2008), 29.

5. Ira Katznelson, *Fear Itself: The New Deal and the Origins of Our Time* (New York, 2013), 159; Maverick quoted in Tracy Roof, *American Labor, Congress, and the Welfare State, 1935–2010* (Baltimore, MD, 2011), 32.

6. Smith, *A Concise History*, 74; Steven A. Reich, *A Working People: A History of African American Workers since Emancipation* (New York, 2013), 9, 87–100.

7. Quoted in Sullivan, *Days of Hope*, 7.

8. Quoted in Michael Goldfield, "Race and the CIO: The Possibilities

for Racial Egalitarianism during the 1930s and 1940s," *International Labor and Working-Class History* 44 (Fall 1993): 2.

9. August Meier and Elliott Rudwick, *Black Detroit and the Rise of the UAW* (New York, 1979), 4, 109; Bruce Nelson, *Divided We Stand: American Workers and the Struggle for Black Equality* (Princeton, NJ, 2001), xxxiii.

10. See Gary Gerstle, *Working-Class Americanism: The Politics of Labor in a Textile City, 1914–1960* (Princeton, NJ, 1989), ch. 5.

11. Gary Gerstle, "The Protean Character of American Liberalism," *American Historical Review* 99 (October 1994): 1068.

12. Gerstle, *Working-Class Americanism*, 5; Michael Kazin, *American Dreamers: How the Left Changed a Nation* (New York, 2011), 171, 181; Gary Gerstle, *American Crucible: Race and Nation in the Twentieth Century* (Princeton, NJ, 2001), 160; Linda Gordon, *Dorothea Lange: A Life beyond Limits* (New York, 2009), 235–236; James N. Gregory, *American Exodus: The Dust Bowl Migration and Okie Culture in California* (New York, 1989).

13. Gerstle, *American Crucible*, 160.

14. James T. Patterson, *Congressional Conservatism and the New Deal: The Growth of the Conservative Coalition in Congress, 1933–1939* (Lexington, KY, 1967), vii–viii; Clinton Rossiter, *Conservatism in America: The Thankless Persuasion* (New York, 1962); Roof, *American Labor*.

15. Bryant Simon, *A Fabric of Defeat: The Politics of South Carolina Millhands, 1910–1948* (Chapel Hill, NC, 1998), 9.

16. James A. Morone, *Hellfire Nation: The Politics of Sin in American History* (New Haven, CT, 2003), 365–366, 376.

17. Lyman Kellstedt, John Green, Corwin Smidt, and James Guth, "Faith Transformed: Religion and American Politics from FDR to George W. Bush," in *Religion and American Politics*, ed. Mark A. Noll and Luke E. Harlow, 2nd ed. (New York, 2007), 270; Gary Scott Smith, "Religion and the Presidency of Franklin Delano Roosevelt," in *Religion and the American Presidency*, ed. Gaston Espinosa (New York, 2009), 185–210; Gerstle, *American Crucible*, 185.

18. Joel Carpenter, *Revive Us Again: The Reawakening of American Fundamentalism* (New York, 1997), 14.

19. Lizabeth Cohen, *Making a New Deal: Industrial Workers in Chicago, 1919–1939* (New York, 1991), 221.

20. Matthew Avery Sutton, "Was FDR the Antichrist? The Birth of Fundamentalist Antiliberalism in a Global Age," *Journal of American History* 98, 4 (March 2012): 1052.

21. Alan Brinkley, *Voices of Protest: Huey Long, Father Coughlin,*

and the Great Depression (New York: Knopf, 1982), xi. Even then, he had to fight off the left, the right, and, most importantly, edge above the fray of populist movements that continued their historical grip on American politics. See also David M. Kennedy, *Freedom from Fear: The American People in Depression and War, 1929–1945* (New York, 1999), 242.

22. John P. Hoerr, *Harry, Tom, and Father Rice: Accusation and Betrayal in America's Cold War* (Pittsburgh, 2005), 5.

23. John McGreevy, *Catholicism and American Freedom: A History* (New York, 2003), 105–114, 130–131, 164. See also the discussion of Baltimore's working-class Catholics during the 1940s in Kenneth D. Durr, *Behind the Backlash: White Working-Class Politics in Baltimore, 1940–1980* (Chapel Hill, NC, 2003), esp. chs. 1–3.

24. Neil Betten, *Catholic Activism and the Industrial Worker* (Gainesville, FL, 1976), 108–123, esp. 110–112; Frank Walsh, *Sin and Censorship: The Catholic Church and the Motion Picture Industry* (New Haven, CT, 1996). See also Kenneth J. Heineman, *A Catholic New Deal: Religion and Reform in Depression Pittsburgh* (University Park, PA, 1999), 133–143, 165–169. On the issue of Catholic sexual practices, see Leslie Woodcock Tentler, *Catholics and Contraception: An American History* (Ithaca, NY, 2004). On the broad outlines of Catholic popular social thought, see McGreevy, *Catholicism and American Freedom,*127–165; John McGreevy, *Parish Boundaries: The Catholic Encounter with Race in the Twentieth Century Urban North* (Chicago, 1996); Durr, *Behind the Backlash*; Jay Dolan, *In Search of American Catholicism: A History of Religion and Culture in Tension* (New York, 2002), 127–190.

25. Ronald Isetti, "The Moneychangers of the Temple: FDR, American Civil Religion, and the New Deal," *Presidential Studies Quarterly* 19 (Summer 1996): 686; William E. Leuchtenburg, "Franklin D. Roosevelt: The First Modern President," in *Leadership in the Modern Presidency*, ed. Fred I. Greenstein (Cambridge, MA, 1988), 15.

26. Randolph Bourne, "The State," unpublished manuscript, 1918, at http://fair-use.org/randolph-bourne/the-state/ (accessed 4 June 2015); see William E. Leuchtenburg, "The New Deal and the Analogue of War," in *Change and Continuity in Twentieth-Century America*, ed. John Braeman, Robert H. Bremner, and Everett Walters (Columbus, OH, 1964), 81–143.

27. Katznelson, *Fear Itself*, 345–346.

28. Roger Biles, *A New Deal for the American People* (DeKalb, IL, 1991), 231; Claudia Goldin and Robert Margo, "The Great Compression: The Wage Structure in the United States at Mid-century," *Quar-*

terly Journal of Economics 107 (1992): 1–34. Thomas Piketty and Emmanuel Saez, "Income Inequality in the United States, 1913–1998," *Quarterly Journal of Economics* 118 (2003): 1–39.

29. Brinkley, *End of Reform*, 6.

30. Quoted in Katznelson, *Fear Itself*, 391.

31. William P. Jones, *The March on Washington: Jobs, Freedom, and the Forgotten History of Civil Rights* (New York, 2013), xv.

32. August Meier and Elliott Rudwick, *Black Detroit and the Rise of the UAW* (New York, 1979). On Randolph, FDR, and fair employment, see Paula F. Pfeffer, *A. Philip Randolph: Pioneer of the Civil Rights Movement* (Baton Rouge, LA, 1990); Merl E. Reed, *Seedtime for the Modern Civil Rights Movement: The President's Committee on Fair Employment Practice, 1941–1946* (Baton Rouge, LA, 1991). For a sampling of the racial politics in northern cities during the 1940s, see Thomas J. Sugrue, *The Origins of the Urban Crisis*; Arnold Hirsch, *Making the Second Ghetto: Race and Housing in Chicago, 1940–1960* (New York, 1983); Martha Biondi, *To Stand and Fight: The Struggle for Civil Rights in Postwar New York City* (Cambridge, MA, 2003); Robert O. Self, *American Babylon: Race and the Struggle for Postwar Oakland* (Princeton, NJ, 2003).

33. Paul Frymer, *Black and Blue: African Americans, the Labor Movement, and the Decline of the Democratic Party* (Princeton, NJ, 2008), 2–3, 9. Emphasis added.

34. Katherine Archibald, *Wartime Shipyard: A Study in Social Disunity*, ed. with an introduction by Eric Arnesen and Alex Lichtenstein (Urbana, IL, 2006 [Berkeley, CA, 1947]), 6.

35. John Dewey, *Individualism Old and New* (New York, 1930), 30, 59–61, 93; for a fuller exploration, see Robert B. Westbrook, *John Dewey and American Democracy* (Ithaca, NY, 1991).

36. On Tugwell, see Bernard Sternsher, *Rexford Tugwell and the New Deal* (New Brunswick, NJ, 1964), 328; Lawrence W. Levine and Cornelia R. Levine, *The People and the President: America's Conversation with FDR* (Boston, 2002), 219–220. FDR also rhetorically evoked a more collective vision, but without consistent effort.

37. McElvaine, *Great Depression*, 337.

38. Ronald D. Rotunda, "The 'Liberal' Label: Roosevelt's Capture of a Symbol," *Public Policy* 17 (1968): 377 at 380. As the *New York Times* journalist Arthur Krock put it, "The word 'liberal' in its present meaning was then [around 1933] only beginning to supplant the old word 'progressive' " (379). See also John Dewey, "A Liberal Speaks Out for Liberalism," *New York Times*, 23 February 1936. Moley, noting the rise of the second New Deal, put it similarly: "And with the change there came into use the word 'liberal' to describe an ideology based on

the enlargement of the power of the Federal government and an abundance of welfare programs" (Rotunda, 401).

39. For Roosevelt's Commonwealth Club address, see the American Rhetoric On-Line Speech Bank, at www.americanrhetoric.com /speeches/fdrcommonwealth.htm (accessed 4 June 2015); Alan Brinkley, *End of Reform: New Deal Liberalism in Recession and War* (New York, 1995), 4–7; Jack Metzgar, *Striking Steel: Solidarity Remembered* (Philadelphia, 2000), 62, 146–147. James MacGregor Burns discusses the ambiguities of that 1932 speech in *Roosevelt: The Lion and the Fox* (New York, 1956), 142, 180. For FDR's 1936 speech, see *The Public Papers and Addresses of Franklin D. Roosevelt, with a Special Introduction and Explanatory Note by President Roosevelt*, 13 vols., comp. Samuel I. Rosenman (New York, 1938), vol. V, 230–236. As is evident in the Commonwealth speech, FDR delivered two messages, one stressing efficient administration and the other an "economic constitutional order." But the bottom line, as David M. Kennedy notes, was ultimately to provide security for the vulnerable, but also for working people, investors, and the corporations. See David Kennedy, *Freedom from Fear: The American People in Depression and War, 1929–1945* (New York, 1999), 364–365.

40. Levine and Levine, *The People and the President*, 250–256.

41. Pells, *Radical Visions and American Dreams*, 84.

CHAPTER FIVE. THE GREAT EXCEPTION IN ACTION

1. W. Elliot Brownlee, *Federal Taxation in America: A Short History* (Washington, DC, 2004); Thomas Piketty, *Capital in the Twenty-First Century* (Cambridge, MA, 2014).

2. Robert H. Frank, *Falling Behind: How Rising Inequality Harms the Middle Class* (Berkeley, CA, 2007), 6–14.

3. Jack Metzgar, *Striking Steel: Solidarity Remembered* (Philadelphia, 1999), 6, 39.

4. David Brody, *Workers in Industrial America: Essays on the 20th Century Struggle* (New York, 1993), 157.

5. Nelson Lichtenstein, *The Most Dangerous Man in Detroit: Walter Reuther and the Fate of American Labor* (New York, 1995).

6. Michael Kazin, *The Populist Persuasion: An American History* (New York, 1995), 162–163.

7. See, for instance, Bruce Nissen, "A Post-World War II 'Social Accord,'" in *U.S. Labor Relations, 1945–1989: Accommodation and Conflict*, ed. Bruce Nissen (New York, 1990), 191–193; Nelson Lichtenstein, "From Corporatism to Collective Bargaining," in *The Rise and*

Fall of the New Deal Order, 1930–1980, ed. Steve Fraser and Gary
Gerstle (Princeton, NJ, 1989), 122; David M. Gordon, "Chickens Home
to Roost: From Prosperity to Stagnation in the Postwar U.S. Economy,"
in *Understanding American Economic Decline,* ed. Michael A. Bernstein and David E. Adler (New York, 1994); Kevin Boyle, *The UAW
and the Heyday of American Liberalism* (Ithaca, NY, 1998). See my
own perspective of the instability of the postwar order in Jefferson
Cowie, *Capital Moves: RCA's Seventy-Year Quest for Cheap Labor*
(New York, 2001).

8. Nelson Lichtenstein, *State of the Union: A Century of American
Labor* (Princeton, NJ, 2002), 99; Tracy Roof, *American Labor, Congress, and the Welfare State, 1935–2010* (Baltimore, MD, 2011), 216.

9. Taft quoted in Robert Zieger, *American Workers, American
Unions: The Twentieth Century,* rev. ed. (Baltimore, MD, 2002), 156.

10. Taylor E. Dark, *The Unions and the Democrats: An Enduring Alliance* (Ithaca, NY, 1999); Zieger, *American Workers,* 153.

11. Brody, *Workers in Industrial America,* 220–221. Sean Farhang
and Ira Katznelson, "The Southern Imposition: Congress and Labor in
the New Deal and Fair Deal," *Studies in American Political Development* 19 (Spring 2005): 3.

12. See H. W. Brands, *The Strange Death of American Liberalism*
(New Haven, CT, 2001); Daniel Bell, *The End of Ideology: On Exhaustion of Political Ideas in the Fifties* (New York, 1960); Godfrey Hodgson, *America in Our Time: From World War II to Nixon—What Happened and Why* (New York, 1976), 74–79; Clark Kerr, *Industrialism
and Industrial Man: The Problems of Labor and Management in Economic Growth* (Cambridge, MA, 1960); Derek Bok and John T. Dun-
lop, *Labor and the American Community* (New York, 1970); Katherine
Stone, "The Post-War Paradigm in American Labor Law," *Yale Law
Journal* 90 (June 1981): 1509–1580. On the merger, see Robert Zieger,
The CIO, 1935–1955 (Chapel Hill, NC, 1995), 305–371.

13. Landon R. Y. Storrs, *The Second Red Scare and the Unmaking of
the New Deal Left* (Princeton, NJ, 2013), 6, 249, 261.

14. On the emerging challenge to the mainline Protestant establishment, see William Martin, *A Prophet with Honor: The Billy Graham
Story* (New York, 1991); Joel A. Carpenter, *Revive Us Again: The Reawakening of American Fundamentalism* (New York, 1999). On racial
issues, see Kevin Kruse, *White Flight: Atlanta and the Making of Modern Conservatism* (Princeton, NJ, 2005); Taylor Branch, *Parting the Waters: America in the King Years, 1954–1963* (New York, 1988).

15. Darren Dochuk, *From Bible Belt to Sunbelt: Plain-Folk Religion,
Grassroots Politics, and the Rise of Evangelical Conservatism* (New
York, 2011), xvii, xix, 103.

16. Garry Wills, *Head and Heart: American Christianities* (New York, 2007), 451–464.

17. Buchanan is quoted in John A. Andrew, *The Other Side of the Sixties: Young Americans for Freedom and the Rise of Conservative Politics* (New Brunswick, NJ, 1997), 63. "Paradise lost" is from Kim Phillips-Fein, *Invisible Hands: The Making of the Conservative Movement from the New Deal to Reagan* (New York, 2009), 9. On the origins of the conservative movement, see Lisa McGirr, *Suburban Warriors: The Origins of the New American Right* (Princeton, NJ, 2001); Rick Perlstein, *Before the Storm: Barry Goldwater and the Unmaking of the American Consensus* (New York, 2001); John Micklethwait and Adrian Wooldridge, *The Right Nation: Conservative Power in America* (New York, 2004); George H. Nash, *The Conservative Intellectual Movement in America since 1945* (New York, 1976).

18. Richard Hofstadter, "A Long View: Goldwater in History," *New York Review of Books*, 8 October 1964, as quoted in Perlstein, *Before the Storm,* 452.

19. Students for a Democratic Society, "The Port Huron Statement" (1962), in James Miller, *"Democracy Is in the Streets:" From Port Huron to the Siege of Chicago* (New York, 1987), 344; Jefferson Cowie, *Stayin' Alive: The 1970s and the Last Days of the Working Class* (New York, 2010), 23–74.

20. Calvin Mackenzie and Robert Weisbrot, *The Liberal Hour: Washington and the Politics of Change in the 1960s* (New York, 2008), 82.

21. Mackenzie and Weisbrot, *Liberal Hour*, 7; Roof, *American Labor*, 83–111, does an excellent job of dissecting the politics of Congress.

22. Lyndon B. Johnson, "Great Society Speech," University of Michigan, 22 May 1964. Downloaded 5 June 2015, http://www.pbs.org /wgbh/americanexperience/features/primary-resources/lbj-michigan.

23. Robert Dallek, *Lyndon B. Johnson: Portrait of a President* (New York, 2004), 155–157, 234–239, 373–374; Bruce J. Schulman, *Lyndon B. Johnson and American Liberalism: A Brief Biography with Documents* (New York, 1995), 99–102 (Johnson's Great Society speech is reprinted at 174–177); Barbara C. Jordan and Elspeth D. Rostow, eds., *The Great Society: A Twenty Year Critique* (Austin, TX, 1986), particularly the comments of Bill Moyers (35–37, 171–179) and Ray Marshall (53–56). For a detailed narrative of the Great Society's legislative efforts, see Irving Bernstein, *Guns or Butter: The Presidency of Lyndon Johnson* (New York, 1996).

24. Mackenzie and Weisbrot, *The Liberal Hour*, 101.

25. Randall B. Woods, *LBJ: Architect of American Ambition* (New

York, 2006), 449, 451. See also Robert Dallek, *Flawed Giant: Lyndon Johnson and His Times, 1961–1973* (New York, 1998), 79; James T. Patterson, *America's Struggle against Poverty, 1900–1985* (Cambridge, MA, 1986), 141. In his footnote (p. 259), Patterson identifies the staffer as Adam Yarmolinsky and quotes his recollections from the unpublished transcript of a 1973 panel discussion at the John F. Kennedy Library, "Poverty and Urban Policy" (287); Maurice Isserman and Michael Kazin, *America Divided: The Civil War of the 1960s*, 3rd ed. (New York, 2007), 110, 192; Patterson, *America's Struggle against Poverty*, 151. Had the money spent on the war on poverty in the 1960s gone directly to those living below the poverty line, it has been calculated that everyone would have received a mere $70 per year.

26. Jennifer Klein, *For All These Rights: Business, Labor, and the Shaping of America's Public-Private Welfare State* (Princeton, NJ, 2003), 257. On the unique aspects of the U.S. welfare state, see Jacob S. Hacker, *The Divided Welfare State: The Battle over Public and Private Social Benefits in the United States* (New York, 2002); Peter A. Swenson, *Capitalists against Markets: The Making of Labor Markets and Welfare States in the United States and Sweden* (New York, 2002).

27. Testimony of Martin Luther King, Jr., *The Federal Role in Urban Affairs: Hearings before the Subcommittee on Executive Reorganization of the Committee on Government Operations*, U.S. Senate, 89th Cong., 2nd Sess., 14–15 December 1966 (Washington, 1967), 298. Nancy MacLean uses part of this quote in her excellent *Freedom Is Not Enough: The Opening of the American Workplace* (Cambridge, MA, 2006), 7, but misses the point that King is speaking of economics and not simply the "culture of exclusion." See Martin Luther King, Jr., "A Time to Break Silence" and "Black Power Defined," both delivered in 1967, in James M. Washington, ed., *A Testament of Hope: The Essential Writings of Martin Luther King, Jr.* (San Francisco, 1986), 231–244, 303–312, respectively; Taylor Branch, *At Canaan's Edge: America in the King Years, 1965–68* (New York, 2006), 581–604, 625. On King and Debs, see Thomas F. Jackson, *From Civil Rights to Human Rights: Martin Luther King, Jr., and the Struggle for Economic Justice* (Philadelphia, 2007), 320.

28. Branch, *At Canaan's Edge*, 511; Thomas J. Sugrue, "Affirmative Action from Below: Civil Rights, the Building Trades, and the Politics of Racial Equality in the Urban North, 1945–1969," *Journal of American History* 91 (June 2004): 145–173; Dennis A. Deslippe, " 'Do Whites Have Rights?': White Detroit Policemen and 'Reverse Discrimination' Protests in the 1970s," *Journal of American History* 91 (December 2004): 932–960; Kenneth D. Durr, *Behind the Backlash: White Working-Class Politics in Baltimore, 1940–1980* (Chapel Hill, NC, 2003); Jonathan Rieder, *Canarsie: The Jews and Italians of Brooklyn*

against Liberalism (Cambridge, MA, 1985); Robert Self, *American Babylon: Race and the Struggle for Postwar Oakland* (Princeton, NJ, 2003).

29. Kevin Phillips, *The Emerging Republican Majority* (Garden City, NY, 1970).

30. See Cowie, *Stayin' Alive*; Numan V. Bartley, *The Rise of Massive Resistance: Race and Politics in the South during the 1950s* (Baton Rouge, LA, 1997/1969); Phillips, *Republican Majority*; Dan T. Carter, *The Politics of Rage: George Wallace, the Origins of the New Conservatism, and the Transformation of American Politics* (Baton Rouge, LA, 1995); Earle Black and Merle Black, *The Rise of Southern Republicans* (Cambridge, MA, 2002); Ronald P. Formisano, *Boston against Busing: Race, Class and Ethnicity in the 1960s and 1970s* (Chapel Hill, NC, 1991).

31. Reuther quoted in Roof, *American Labor*, 232 n. 10.

32. Daniel J. Tichenor, *Dividing Lines: The Politics of Immigration Control in America* (Princeton, NJ, 2002), 219–241.

CHAPTER SIX. TOWARD A NEW GILDED AGE

1. Richard Nixon, Acceptance Speech, Republican National Convention, 1968; see Rick Perlstein, *Nixonland: The Rise of a President and the Fracturing of America* (New York, 2008), 433–435. On his adoption of Wallace, see Jefferson Cowie, "Nixon's Class Struggle: Romancing the New-Right Worker, 1969–1973." *Labor History* 43 (Summer 2002): 257–283.

2. Raymond Price, *With Nixon* (New York, 1977), 121–122; Robert Mason, *Richard Nixon and the Quest for the New Majority* (Chapel Hill, NC, 2004); Jefferson Cowie *Stayin' Alive: The 1970s and the Last Days of the Working Class* (New York, 2010), 125–166.

3. Patrick J. Buchanan, *The New Majority: President Nixon at Midpassage* (Girard Bank, 1973), 63–64; Cowie, *Stayin' Alive*, 161–162.

4. Thomas Sugrue, *The Origins of the Urban Crisis: Race and Inequality in Postwar Detroit* (Princeton, NJ, 1996), 268; Thomas Byrne Edsall and Mary D. Edsall, *Chain Reaction: The Impact of Race, Rights, and Taxes on American Politics* (New York, 1992).

5. McCarthy speech in *Proceedings of the 46th National Convention of the United Mine Workers of America* (Indianapolis, 1973), 276. A similar argument about coasting on one-time success is in Rick Perlstein, *The Stock Ticker and the Superjumbo: How the Democrats Can Once Again Become America's Dominant Political Party* (Chicago, 2005).

6. Daniel H. Weinberg, "A Brief Look at Postwar U.S. Income In-

equality," *Current Population Reports*, June 1996, Bureau of the Census (P60–191); Daniel H. Weinberg, Charles T. Nelson, and Edward J. Welniak, Jr., "Economic Well-Being in the United States: How Much Improvement—Fifty Years of U.S. Income Data from the Current Population Survey: Alternatives, Trends, and Quality," *American Economic Review* (May 1999): 18–22; *Wall Street Journal*, 12 October 2007; Francine D. Blau and Lawrence M. Kahn, "Gender Differences in Pay," *Journal of Economic Perspectives* 14 (Fall 2000): 84–85; Claudia Goldin and Robert A. Margo, "The Great Compression: The Wage Structure in the United States at Mid-Century," *Quarterly Journal of Economics* 107 (February 1992): 1–34.

7. Alan Brinkley, *The End of Reform: New Deal Liberalism in Recession and War* (New York, 1996), 3–10, 268–271; Katherine Van Wezel Stone, "The Legacy of Industrial Pluralism: The Tension between Individual Employment Rights and the New Deal Collective Bargaining System," *University of Chicago Law Review* 59 (Spring 1992): 576; Michael J. Piore and Sean Safford, "Changing Regimes of Workplace Governance, Shifting Axes of Social Mobilization, and the Challenge to Industrial Relations Theory," *Industrial Relations* 45 (July 2006): 299–325. For the post–civil rights opening of the workplace, see Nancy MacLean, *Freedom Is Not Enough: The Opening of the American Workplace* (Cambridge, MA, 2006); Edsall and Edsall, *Chain Reaction*, 95. William Saletan discusses the role of individualism in the pro-choice movement in *Bearing Right: How Conservatives Won the Abortion War* (Berkeley, CA, 2003). For an incisive critique of liberalism in this era, see Michael Sandel, *Democracy's Discontent: America in Search of a Public Philosophy* (Cambridge, MA, 1996); alternatively, see Michael Walzer, *Politics and Passion: Toward a More Egalitarian Liberalism* (New Haven, CT, 2004), and Walzer, "The Communitarian Critique of Liberalism," *Political Theory* 18, 1 (February 1990): 6–23.

8. "Rights consciousness" is critiqued in Nelson Lichtenstein, *State of the Union: A Century of American Labor* (Princeton, NJ, 2003), 209–211. For the tension between competing versions of the women's movement, see Dorothy Sue Cobble, *The Other Women's Movement: Workplace Justice and Social Rights in Modern America* (Princeton, NJ, 2004); see also Todd Gitlin, "Beyond Identity Politics: A Modest Precedent," and the response of Michael Eric Dyson, "The Labor of Whiteness, the Whiteness of Labor, and the Perils of Whitewashing," in *Audacious Democracy: Labor, Intellectuals, and the Social Reconstruction of America*, ed. Steven Fraser and Joshua B. Freeman (New York, 1997), 153–172.

9. Michael Novak, *The Rise of the Unmeltable Ethnics* (New York, 1972), 71–72; Matthew Frye Jacobson, *Roots Too* (Cambridge, MA,

2006); Thomas J. Sugrue and John D. Skrentny, "The White Ethnic Strategy," in *Rightward Bound: Making America Conservative in the 1970s*, ed. Bruce J. Schulman and Julian E. Zelizer (Cambridge, MA, 2007), 192.

10. Lichtenstein, *State of the Union*, 178–203; MacLean, *Freedom Is Not Enough*.

11. Quoted in Kim Phillips-Fein, *Invisible Hands: The Businessmen's Crusade against the New Deal* (New York, 2010), 216; Theda Skocpol, *Protecting Soldiers and Mothers: The Political Origins of Social Policy in the United States* (Cambridge, MA, 1992); George Lakoff, *Moral Politics: How Liberals and Conservatives Think* (Chicago, 1996).

12. Premilla Nadasen, *Welfare Warriors: The Welfare Rights Movement in the United States* (New York, 2005); Jane J. Mansbridge, *Why We Lost the ERA* (Chicago, 1986); Matthew Frye Jacobson, *Roots Too: White Ethnic Revival in Post-Civil Rights America* (Cambridge, MA, 2006); Jonathan Rieder, *Canarsie: The Jews and Italians of Brooklyn against Liberalism* (Cambridge, MA, 1987).

13. Cynthia Estlund, "The Ossification of Labor Law," *Columbia Law Review* 102 (October 2002): 1530; Paul Weiler, "Promises to Keep: Securing Workers' Rights Under the NLRA," *Harvard Law Review* 96 (June 1983): 1769.

14. Thomas Geoghegan, *Which Side Are You On? Trying to Be for Labor When It's Flat on Its Back* (New York, 1991), 5.

15. See Dorothy Sue Cobble, *The Other Women's Movement: Workplace Justice and Social Rights in Modern America* (Princeton, NJ, 2004); Alice Kessler Harris, *In Pursuit of Equity: Women, Men and the Quest for Economic Citizenship in Twentieth Century America* (New York, 2001). My exchange with Jennifer Klein on this is illustrative; see Jefferson Cowie, "Red, White, and Blue Collar," *Democracy: A Journal of Ideas* 20 (Spring 2011), at www.democracyjournal.org/20/red-white-and-blue-collar.php (accessed 3 June 2015).

16. Michael Stewart Foley, *Front Porch Politics: The Forgotten Heyday of American Activism in the 1970s and 1980s* (New York, 2013).

17. There was precious little history of planning in the postwar era to build upon when the crisis of the 1970s hit. Margaret Weir, *Politics and Jobs: The Boundaries of Employment Policy in the United States* (Princeton, NJ, 2002); Otis L. Graham, *Toward a Planned Society: From Roosevelt to Nixon* (New York, 1976); quote on Weberian rationality from Piore and Safford, "Changing Regimes of Workplace Governance," 319.

18. David Brody, *Workers in Industrial America* (New York, 1993),

78; Sanford M. Jacoby, *Modern Manors: Welfare Capitalism since the New Deal* (Princeton, NJ, 1998).

19. James Scott, *Seeing Like a State: How Certain Schemes to Improve the Human Condition Have Failed* (New Haven, CT, 1998).

20. Richard Viguerie quoted in *Guardian*, 1 April 1981, 5. Evans quote, Phillips-Fein, *Invisible Hands*, 216.

21. Chuck Smith began his ministry to former hippies, surfers, and other countercultural types in Southern California in 1966, and membership doubled almost monthly at first. Thirty years later, the Calvary Chapel movement Smith started had sponsored more than 600 loosely affiliated domestic churches, another 200 abroad, and a splinter movement, the Vineyard Church, with another 600 congregations. See Randall Balmer, *Mine Eyes Have Seen the Glory: A Journey into the Evangelical Subculture in America* (New York, 2000/1993), 12–30; Donald E. Miller, *Reinventing American Protestantism: Christianity in the New Millennium* (Berkeley, CA, 1997), 17–20, 29–34. On the continued dramatic growth of these and other, similar, congregations in the decade following 1996, see Lauren Sandler, *Righteous: Dispatches from the Evangelical Youth Movement* (New York, 2006); Jeffrey L. Sheler, *Believers: A Journey into Evangelical America* (New York, 2006); Michael Harrington, *Fragments of the Century* (New York, 1973), 231.

22. Paul Boyer, "The Evangelical Resurgence in 1970s American Protestantism," in Bruce J. Schulman and Julian E. Zelizer, *Rightward Bound* (Cambridge, MA, 2008), 29–51, esp. 41.

23. Jackson Lears, *No Place of Grace: Antimodernism and the Transformation of American Culture, 1880–1920* (New York, 1981), 307.

24. Joseph Crespino, *Strom Thurmond's America* (New York, 2012), 297.

25. Rieder, *Canarsie*, 147, n. 47; Godfrey Hodgson, *The World Turned Right Side Up* (New York, 1997).

26. Peter Kwong, *Forbidden Workers: Illegal Chinese Immigrants and American Labor* (New York, 1998); Eric Schlosser, *Fast Food Nation: The Dark Side of the All-American Meal* (New York, 2001), 161–162; Daniel J. Tichenor, *Dividing Lines: The Politics of Immigration Control in America* (Princeton, NJ, 2002), 242–288. See also Cowie, "A Century of Sweat: Subcontracting, Flexibility, and Consumption," *International Labor and Working-Class History* 61 (Spring 2002): 128–140.

27. Madison Grant, *The Passing of the Great Race* (New York, 1922). For a modern contemporary, see Samuel Huntington, *Who Are We? The Challenges to National Identity* (New York, 2004).

28. Christine J. Walley, *Exit Zero: Family and Class in Postindustrial Chicago* (Chicago, 2013), 156.

29. Kevin R. Johnson and Bill Ong Hing, "The Immigrant Rights Marches of 2006 and the Prospects for a New Civil Rights Movement," *Harvard Civil Rights-Civil Liberties Law Review* 42 (2007): 99–138; comparison with Haymarket is at photographer David Bacon's website, http://dbacon.igc.org/PJust/mayday06-la08.html (accessed 3 June 2015); *Los Angeles Times*, 25 April 2000.

30. Most immigration scholars do not take into account the effect on the native-born population and only occasionally take into account black-immigrant relations. For a useful corrective, see Marisa Abranjano and Zoltan L. Hajnal, *White Backlash, Immigration, Race, and American Politics* (Princeton, NJ, 2015), 1–22.

31. Angus Burgin, *The Great Persuasion: Reinventing Free Markets since the Depression* (Cambridge, MA, 2012), 4–5.

32. E. J. Dionne, Jr., "Gary Hart, the Elusive Front-Runner," *New York Times Magazine*, 3 May 1987; Governor William Jefferson Clinton, "We Must Speak to America," Democratic National Convention, 14 August 1980, reprinted in Stephen A. Smith, ed., *Preface to the Presidency: Selected Speeches of Bill Clinton, 1974–1992* (Fayetteville, NC, 1996), 24–25. William Jefferson Clinton, "State of the Union Address," 23 January 1996, Washington, DC, at http://clinton4.nara.gov/WH /New/other/sotu.html (accessed 27 November 2007).

33. Jacob S. Hacker and Paul Pierson, *Winner-Take-All Politics* (New York, 2010), 69.

34. Robert Reich, *Locked in the Cabinet* (New York, 1997), 105.

35. David A. Stockman, *Triumph of Politics: How the Reagan Revolution Failed* (New York, 1986); Theodore J. Lowi, *The End of the Republican Era* (Norman, OK, 1995), 25. On Louis Hartz and "American exceptionalism," see Hartz, *The Liberal Tradition in America* (New York, 1955); Seymour Martin Lipset, *American Exceptionalism: A Double-Edged Sword* (New York, 1996); and the enormous literature that has grown around Hartz's analysis. On the contradictions of disparaging the state while expanding it in the Reconstruction and Gilded Age, see Heather Cox Richardson, *West from Appomattox: The Reconstruction of America after the Civil War* (New Haven, CT, 2007).

CHAPTER SEVEN. THE ERA OF BIG GOVERNMENT IS NOT OVER (BUT THE NEW DEAL PROBABLY IS)

1. *New York Times*, 3 April 2008.

2. Sheila D. Collins, "Public Attitudes toward Government: The So-

cial and Political Context of the Great Depression and Great Recession," in Collins and Gertrude Schaffner Goldberg, eds., *When Government Helped: Learning from the Successes and the Failures of the New Deal* (New York, 2014), 2.

3. Gertrude Schaffner Goldberg, "The New Deal and the Creation of the American Welfare State," in Collins and Goldberg, eds., *When Government Helped*, 181.

4. The window was tiny, if it existed at all. Al Franken won his eight-month battle to affirm his razor-thin majority for the Senate seat in Minnesota; Arlen Specter switched his party affiliation to Democrat; and then there was Republican Scott Brown's surprising victory in the race to replace liberal stalwart, Senator Ted Kennedy, in the February 2010 election. On the supermajority math, see Governor Jennifer M. Granholm, "Debunking the Myth: Obama's Two Year Supermajority," *Huffington Post*, 1 October 2012, at www.huffingtonpost.com/jennifer-m-granholm/debunking-the-myth-obamas_b_1929869.html (accessed 2 June 2015).

5. *New York Times*, 21 January 2010; *New York Times*, 22 July 2014.

6. *Washington Post*, 10 February 2010; Dorian T. Warren, "The Unsurprising Failure of Labor Law Reform and the Turn to Administrative Action," in *Reaching for a New Deal: Ambitious Governance, Economic Meltdown, and Polarized Politics in Obama's First Two Years*, ed. Theda Skocpol and Lawrence R. Jacobs (New York, 2011), 191–229.

7. Melvyn Dubofksy, "The Federal Judiciary, Free Labor, and Equal Rights," in *The Pullman Strike and Crisis of the 1890s: Essays on Labor and Politics*, ed. Richard Schneirov, Sheltom Stromquist, and Nick Salvatore (Urbana, IL, 1999), 173.

8. Reuther quoted in the documentary *At the River I Stand*, dir. David Appleby, Allison Graham, and Steven Ross, California Newsreel, 56 minutes, 1993.

9. Theda Skocpol and Lawrence R. Jacobs, "Reaching for a New Deal: Ambitious Governance, Economic Meltdown, and Polarized Politics," in Skocpol and Jacobs, *Reaching for a New Deal*, 2.

10. Skocpol and Jacobs, *Reaching for a New Deal*, 15; Beck quoted in Thomas Frank, *Pity the Billionaire: The Hard-Times Swindle and the Unlikely Comeback of the Right* (New York, 2012), 137.

11. See David Leonhardt, "Theory and Morality in the New Economy," *New York Times*, 23 August 2009. George Packer, "Obama's Lost Year: The President's Failure to Connect with Ordinary Americans," *The New Yorker*, 15 March 2010; Frank Rich, "The Rage Is Not about Health Care," *New York Times*, 27 March 2010.

12. Thomas J. Sugrue, *Not Even Past: Barack Obama and the Burden of Race* (Princeton, NJ, 2010), 136; Michelle Alexander, *The New Jim Crow: Mass Incarceration in the Age of Colorblindness* (New York, 2012).

13. Paulson quoted in Larry M. Bartels, *Unequal Democracy: The Political Economy of the New Gilded Age* (Princeton, NJ, 2009), 29.

14. This is the argument of Jacob S. Hacker and Paul Pierson, *Winner-Take-All Politics* (New York, 2010); Bartels, *Unequal Democracy*; Thomas Piketty, *Capital in the Twenty-First Century* (Cambridge, MA, 2014). On how this works with regard to race, see Paul Frymer, *Uneasy Alliances: Race and Party in Competition in America* (Princeton, NJ, 2010).

15. Martin Gilens and Benjamin I. Page, "Testing Theories of American Politics: Elites, Interest Groups, and Average Citizens," *Perspectives on Politics* 12, no. 3 (2014): 576–577; Richard Wilkinson and Kate Picket, *The Spirit Level: Why Greater Equality Makes Societies Stronger* (New York, 2009).

16. Steve Fraser, "The Two Gilded Ages," TomDispatch.com, 22 April 2008, at www.tomdispatch.com/post/174922 (accessed 3 June 2015).

17. Henry Adams, "The Dynamo and the Virgin," in *The Education of Henry Adams* (Boston, 1918), at www.bartleby.com/159/ (accessed 3 June 2015).

18. See Suzanne Mettler, *The Submerged State: How Invisible Government Policies Undermine American Democracy* (Chicago, 2011).

19. Mettler, *Submerged State*.

20. Barrington Moore, *Injustice: The Social Bases of Obedience and Revolt* (New York, 1979), 376.

21. On the relevance of pre–New Deal tactics, see Dorothy Sue Cobble, "Pure and Simple Radicalism: Putting the Progressive Era AFL in Its Time," *Labor* 10: 4 (Winter 2013), 61–87; Clayton Sinyai, "Change to Win: A Gomperism for the Twenty-First Century?" *New Labor Forum* 16 (Spring 2007): 73; Dorothy Sue Cobble, "Lost Ways of Organizing: Reviving the AFL's Direct Affiliate Strategy," *Industrial Relations* 36 (July 1997): 278–301. On unions' future as coalition partners, see Rebecca Kolins Givan, "Side by Side We Battle Onward? Representing Workers in Contemporary America," *British Journal of Industrial Relations* 45 (December 2007): 829–854.

22. Nelson Lichtenstein, "Two Roads Forward for Labor: The AFL-CIO's New Agenda," *Dissent* (Winter 2014).

23. Hofstadter, *Age of Reform*, 328.

24. Hofstadter, *Age of Reform*, 328.

25. Ulrich Beck, *Democracy without Enemies* (Cambridge, MA, 1998).

INDEX

Adams, Henry, 50–51, 223
ADC (Aid to Dependent Children), 72
Adkins v. Children's Hospital, 71
Affordable Care Act, 216–17
AFL-CIO, 199–200. *See also* American Federation of Labor (AFL)
African Americans. *See* racial ideologies
agrarian populists, 50, 59
Agricultural Adjustment Act, 103, 127
Aid to Dependent Children (ADC), 72
air traffic controllers, strike consequences, 203–4
Alter, Jonathan, 104
alt labor movement, 225
Amalgamated Steel Workers, 55
American exceptionalism, 30, 237n22
American Federation of Labor (AFL): during incorporation age, 56–57, 58–59; during New Deal era, 105–6, 113; during post-1960s period, 199–200; during postwar period, 163; during Progressive Era, 70, 72–73, 76–77. *See also* unions
Americanism theme, New Deal era, 131–32
American Railway Union (ARU), 56, 57–58
American Sugar Refining Company, 53
anti-lynching legislation, 78, 126
anti-trust legislation, 53, 67
Archibald, Katherine, 146
artisan work, disappearance, 35–36
ARU (American Railway Union), 56, 57–58
Atlantic, 40–41
auto workers, 90, 113, 130, 145, 152,

157–58. *See also* labor *entries*; unions

Badger, Anthony, 105
bakers' hours case, 69
banking system, 98, 102–3, 104, 205
Beck, Glenn, 218
Beck, Ulrich, 229
Beckert, Sven, 60
Berlin, Isiah, 97
Bernstein, Barton J., 14
Bituminous Coal Mine Strike, 55
Black, Hugo, 37
Bourne, Randolph, 141
Boyer, Paul, 64
"Bread and Roses" strike, 8
Brinkley, Alan, 19–20, 137, 143–44
Brody, David, 26, 86, 161–62
Brown, Scott, 260n4
Bryan, William Jennings, 59, 63, 83–84
Buchanan, Pat, 166, 180–81
Buckley, William F., 166
Burgin, Angus, 202–3

Calvary Chapel movement, 258n21
Capital in the Twenty-First Century (Piketty), 220–21
capitalization statistics, 36
Carnegie, Andrew, 36, 55
Carter, Jimmy, 204
Catholicism: during incorporation era, 47–49, 50; during New Deal era, 138–40; during Progressive Era, 79. *See also* religious identity
Chamberlain, John, 81
Chicago, civil rights movement, 174
child labor legislation, 109

Children's Hospital, Adkins v., 71
Chinese immigrants, 198
Chrysler Strike (1937), 90
CIO. *See* Congress of Industrial Organizations (CIO)
Citizens United decision, 214
Civilian Conservation Corps, 103
Civil Rights Act, 172, 184, 188
civil rights movement, 145–46, 172–76, 196–97
Civil War pensions, 69–70
class conflict: and FDR's forgotten man speech, 93; government's role summarized, 17; incorporation age, 52, 54–55; New Deal shift, 115–16, 120; Progressive Era, 72–74. *See also* immigration tensions; income inequality; working-class identity
Clayton Anti-Trust Act, 67
Cleveland, Grover, 58
Clinton, Bill, 204–5
coal industry, 55, 72
Cohen, Lizabeth, 244n29
Cold War ideology, 162–63
collective bargaining rights: as democratic countervailing power, 220–21; during incorporation age, 37–38, 55–58; New Deal era, 106–7, 111–12; during post-1960s period, 203–4, 215–16; postwar period, 159–60; during Progressive Era, 68–69; transformation of, 225–26
collective social movements, post-1960s period, 189–91, 200–201
Commercial and Financial Chronicle, 35–36
Committee for Industrial Organization (CIO). *See* Congress of Industrial Organizations (CIO)
Commons, John R., 51–52
Commonwealth speech, FDR's, 94–95, 150–51, 251n39
communism, 131–32, 139–40, 163
Congress, postwar stalemate, 167–68
Congress of Industrial Organizations (CIO): during New Deal era, 112–13, 115, 117, 127, 129–30; during

post-1960s period, 145, 199–200; during postwar period, 145, 163
conservative coalitions, 132–33, 163–64. *See also* Republican Party; Southern Democrats
conspiracy doctrine, 68
constitutional amendments, Progressive Era, 67–68
corporate liberalism argument, New Deal scholarship, 14
corporate power. *See specific topics,* e.g., Great Recession; incorporation age; labor *entries;* Supreme Court
Costigan, Edward P., 102
Coughlin, Father, 137
Croly, Herbert, 18–19, 74
cultural conflicts, overviews: during incorporation era, 50; post-1960s period, 179–81, 193–96, 210–11. *See also* immigration tensions; racial ideologies; religious identity
Czolgosz, Leon, 63

Dallek, Robert, 169
Darrow, Clarence S., 84
Debs, Eugene, 50, 57–59, 75
de Leon, Cedric, 44
Democratic Party: and civil rights movement, 172–75; FDR's first campaign, 93–94; during incorporation age, 43–44, 47–49, 51–53, 59–60; membership groups, 47–48, 51; during New Deal era, 4–7, 114–15, 117–20, 128–29, 132–34; during post-1960s period, 180–82, 186–87, 196–97, 205–6, 212–14, 260n4; postwar era, 161, 167; Progressive Era, 74–75, 77; World War II impact, 141–42
Depression years, 97–100, 211–12. *See also* New Deal *entries;* Roosevelt, Franklin D.
Dewey, John, 84, 88, 147–48
Dixiecrats, 133–34
Dochuk, Darren, 165
Douglass, Frederick, 128
Drift or Mastery (Lippman), 75–76

Dubofsky, Melvyn, 107, 116, 215
Dubois, W.E.B., 45, 129

Earned Income Tax Credit, 223
economic legislation: and Great Society perspectives, 170–71; during New Deal, 101–7, 127, 151; during Progressive Era, 67–68, 69, 71; World War II impact, 141–44
"economic royalists" rhetoric, FDR's, 2–5, 114
economic security theme: and civil rights movement, 173–74; in FDR's rhetoric, 93, 94–95, 114–15, 150–51, 251n39; during Great Recession, 212–13; and moralism, 134–35; threats summarized, 123–24; in union perspective shift, 120, 155–56
Economy Bill, 103
efficiency perspective, progressive activists, 65
Eighteenth Amendment, 103
Eisenhower, Dwight D., 162–63, 166
elections: during incorporation age, 59; during New Deal era, 108, 113–15, 118, 212; during post-1960s period, 181–82, 196–97, 213–14, 260n4; during Progressive Era, 63, 74–75, 76
Emergency Banking Act, 103
Employee Free Choice Act (EFCA), 214–15
employment statistics, 36, 98
enlightened capitalism, as reform focus, 85–86
environmental movement, 190–91
Equal Pay Act (1963), 190
equal protection argument, corporations, 37–38, 68
Equal Rights Amendment, 190
Estlund, Cynthia, 188
ethnic identities, post-1960s re-emergence, 185. See also immigration tensions
ethno-racial tensions. See immigration tensions; racial ideologies

evangelical conservatism, 193–96, 258n21. See also religious identity
Evans, M. Stanton, 193
evolution, Bryan's opposition, 83
Executive Order 8802, FDR's, 144
executive power request, FDR's, 96, 245n7

Fair Employment Practices Committee, 144–46
Fair Labor Standards Act, 108, 109, 116, 190
Falwell, Jerry, 195
Farewell to Reform (Chamberlain), 81
Federal Deposit Insurance Corporation (FDIC), 104
federal troops, labor conflicts, 8, 37, 55, 58
Fink, Leon, 44
"first" New Deal, 96, 101–8
Foner, Eric, 31
Forbath, William, 57
forgotten Americans theme, post-1960s period, 179–81, 185, 193, 217–18
"The Forgotten Man" speech, FDR's, 91–93
forgotten man theme: African Americans as, 124–30; during civil rights movement, 174; in culture wars, 193, 217–18; FDR's rhetoric, 91–93, 217; Nixon's invocation, 179–81, 185; during Obama years, 217–18. See also working-class identity
Fortune magazine, 144, 162
Fourteenth Amendment, 36–37, 68
"fourth" New Deal phase, 97, 141–44
Franken, Al, 260n4
Frankfurter, Felix, 77
Franklin, Benjamin, 20
Fraser, Steve, 120, 222
freed slaves, 45–46
free labor ideology, 42–46
free market ideology, 15, 95–96, 219–20. See also income inequality
free silver politics, 59
"free soil" and racial ideology, 42–43

Frick, Henry Clay, 55
Frymer, Paul, 145–46
fundamentalism, 83–84, 135–37, 164–65. *See also* religious identity

Galbraith, John Kenneth, 220–21
garment workers, 73, 198
Garner, John "Cactus Jack," 5–6
Gellhorn, Martha, 140
gender equality movement, 184–86, 189–90
General Managers Association, 58
Geoghegan, Thomas, 189
Gerstle, Gary, 79, 243n18
GI Bill, 529 savings accounts compared, 224
Gilded Age, label limitations, 38–39. *See also* incorporation age
Gilens, Martin, 221
Glass-Steagall Banking Act, 104
global capitalism argument, New Deal scholarship, 15–16
globalization of economies, 182–83, 202–3, 220, 222–23
Golden, Claudia, 143
gold standard, 104
Goldwater, Barry, 167, 174
Gompers, Samuel, 56–57, 58–59
Gordon, Linda, 72
Gore, Al, 205–6
Gould, Jay, 54
government failure argument, New Deal scholarship, 14–15
government's role, overview of transformation, 17–20, 223–24. *See also* *specific topics, e.g.,* New Deal *entries;* labor *entries;* Supreme Court
Graham, Billy, 164
Grant, Madison, 79, 199
Great Depression, 97–98, 135–36, 211–12
great exception argument, overview, 9–13, 15–17, 224–29. *See also* *specific topics, e.g.,* immigration tensions; individualism ideology; New Deal *entries;* unions
Great Recession, 208–9, 212–13, 217

Great Religious Truce, 22
Great Society Programs, 168–72, 253n25
Great Steel Strike (1919), 62
Greenspan, Alan, 203, 220

Hacker, Jacob S., 217
Hapgood, Powers, 109
Hardman, J.B.S., 157
Harrington, Michael, 194
Hart, Gary, 204
Hartz, Louis, 17
Harvard Law Review, 68–69
hate strikes, 45–46, 145
health care policy, 110, 111, 171–72, 216–17
Hellfire Nation (Morone), 21–22, 134
Hendrickson, Mark, 85
Herron, George, 40
Hickok, Lorena, 99
Hillman, Sidney, 113, 120
Hobby Lobby decision, 214
Hodgson, Godfrey, 162
Hofstadter, Richard, 30, 49–50, 66, 167, 217, 227–28
Hoover, Herbert, 87, 98, 103
Hopkins, Harry, 18, 98, 99, 108
Howe, Irving, 132

Ickes, Harold, 126
identity politics, post-1960s period, 183–88
Immigration and Nationality Act, 175–76, 198
immigration tensions: as American tradition, 20–21; during incorporation age, 45–50; during New Deal era, 130–31; post-1960s period, 175–76, 178, 198–202; during Progressive Era, 53–54, 78–81. *See also* racial ideologies
Inaugural Address, FDR's, 95–96
income inequality: framework challenge, 224–26; graphical representation, 12*f*; as political problem, 219–24; rise in late 1900s, 181, 182–83, 189

income tax, 67–68, 142–43
incorporation age: cartoon about, 34*f*; class conflict indicators, 54–55; as democracy threat, 35–36, 38–42; free labor idea, 42–44; immigration's impact, 45–50; individualism question, 39–42; overview of economic centralization, 35–39; political activity levels, 50–54; racial conflict, 45–46; religion's role, 48–50; role of judiciary, 36–37
individualism ideology: and American political achievements, 30–31; in citizen responses to Great Depression, 100–102; as Democratic Party tradition, 95; in FDR's rhetoric, 3–5, 92–93; in government failure argument, 15; as great exception theme, 26–28; in Great Society perspectives, 170–71; during incorporation age, 39–42, 49–50, 60–61; in neo-progressivism, 225–26; as new liberalism constraint, 147–51; in populist movements, 137–38; in post-1960s liberalism, 183–88; power of, 227–28; during Progressive Era, 68–69, 74–76, 81–82, 87–88; in radical conservatism, 164; in Reagan revolution, 206–7; and religious identities, 137, 139, 164–65; union perspectives, 189, 215
Individualism Old and New (Dewey), 147–48
industrial democracy idea, 77, 86
industrial work, increase pattern, 35–36
inequality patterns. *See* income inequality
injunctions, during strikes, 37–38, 58, 68
Isetti, Ronald, 140

Jacobs, Lawrence R., 216
Jacobsen, Matthew Frye, 20
Jacoby, Sanford, 192
Johnson, Lyndon Baines, 167, 168–70, 172

Johnson-Reed Immigration Act, 79–80, 84
Jones, William P., 145
Jones & Laughlin Steel, NLRB v., 118
judicial actions. *See* Supreme Court
Justice for Janitors, 200–201

kaleidoscope description, Kloppenberg's, 65
Katznelson, Ira, 18
Kazin, Michael, 61, 158
Kelley, Florence, 42
Kennedy, David M., 251n39
Kennedy, John F., 152
Kennedy, Ted, 176, 260n4
Keynesian economics, 202–3
Keyserling, Leon, 109
King, Martin Luther, Jr., 172–73, 174, 216
Kipling, Rudyard, 53
Kirkendall, Richard, 13
Klein, Jennifer, 171–72
Kloppenberg, James, 65
Knights of Labor, 41–42
Krock, Arthur, 250n38
Krugman, Paul, 10

labor force: in enlightened capitalism vision, 85–87; globalization's impact, 182–83, 202–3; and individual rights movements, 183–86; marginalization summarized, 220–22; post-1960s immigration impact, 198–201; Southern Democratic perspective, 125–26, 133; World War II impact, 141–42. *See also* strikes; unions; working-class identity
labor force, during incorporation age: ethnicity's role, 47–49; and free labor idea, 42–43; identity changes, 39–42, 60–61; judicial treatment, 37–38; in political rhetoric, 43–44; protests/strikes about industrialization, 54–55; racial conflict, 45–46. *See also* unions

labor law and legislation: during New Deal era, 104–9, 111–13; during post-1960s period, 184, 188–90, 214–15; during Progressive Era, 67–69, 71
La Follette, Robert M., 102
Lange, Dorothea, 132
Lawrence, Massachusetts, 8
Lears, Jackson, 75, 195–96
lend-lease aid, 141
Leo XIII, 50
Leuchtenberg, William, 141
Levine, Cornelia, 151
Levine, Lawrence, 151
Lewis, John L., 106, 109, 113–14, 131
liberalism, evolution of meaning, 148–50, 250n38. See also new liberalism, instability factors
liberalism's arrival argument, New Deal scholarship, 13–14
The Liberal Tradition in America (Hartz), 17
Liberty League, 5
liberty of contract, 68–69, 71, 118
liberty theme, in FDR's rhetoric, 3–4. See also individualism ideology
Lichtenstein, Nelson, 116, 159
Lincoln, Abraham, 43
Lippman, Walter, 75–76, 135
"Little Steel" strike, 116–17
Lochner v. New York, 69
Long, Huey, 137
Lopez, Nativo, 201

Margo, Robert, 143
maternalist welfare state, 70–72, 187
Maverick, Maury, 119, 127
May Day demonstration, 178, 201
McCarthy, Eugene, 181
McConnell, Grant, 82
McElvaine, Robert, 100, 149
McGerr, Michael, 65
McGovern, George, 180, 204
McKinley, William, 59, 63
meatpacking industry, immigrant labor, 198–99
Medicaid/Medicare, 171

Meier, August, 130
The Menace, 79
Mencken, H. L., 84
Mettler, Suzanne, 223
Metzgar, Jack, 156–57
Meyerson, Harold, 214–15
Michigan, right-to-work law, 215–16
middle class progressives. See Progressive Era
miner strikes, 55
minimum wage, 109, 118
Mitchell, John, 215
modern liberalism, origins summarized, 91–92, 97. See also liberalism entries
Moley, Raymond, 4–5, 92–93, 95, 102, 250n38
Montgomery, David, 61
Moody, D. L., 49–50
Moore, Barrington, 31, 225
moralism, Progressive Era types, 79, 82–84. See also religious identity
Moral Majority, 195
Morgan, J. P., 36
Morone, James A., 21–22, 134
Mothers' Pensions, 71–72
Moynihan, Daniel Patrick, 170–71
Muller v. Oregon, 71
Mumford, Lewis, 151

National Association for the Advancement of Colored People (NAACP), 78, 127
National Industrial Recovery Act (NIRA), 104–7, 112
National Labor Relations Act. See Wagner Act
National Labor Relations Board, 111–12, 119
National Recovery Administration (NRA), 105, 127
National Review, 166
National Urban League, 127
National War Labor Board (NWLB), 77
National Youth Administration (NYA), 109

nativism. *See* immigration tensions
Nelson, Bruce, 130
neo-progressivism, emergence, 225–26
New Deal coalition, collapse factors:
    collective social movements, 190–
    91; individual rights ideologies,
    183–88; labor's diminished power,
    188–90, 192; overview, 179–83;
    structural economic problems, 182–
    83, 191–92. *See also* new liberalism,
    instability factors
New Deal era, overview: four phases
    of, 96–97; great exception argu-
    ment, 9–13, 15–17, 224–29; role of
    Great Depression, 97–98, 211–12;
    traditional scholarly interpretations,
    13–15; and Triangle Shirtwaist Fac-
    tory fire, 73; as unstable experi-
    ment, 15–17, 28–32, 92
New Deal legislation: first phase, 101–
    8; Obama administration compari-
    son, 212–13; second phase, 108–14;
    third phase, 119
New Deal vision: and anti-monopoly
    tradition, 95; in Clinton's speech,
    204–5; experimental spirit, 94–95,
    102; urgency in, 97–100
New Democrats, 204–6
New Freedom, Wilson's, 76, 81–82
new Gilded Age. *See* post-1960s
    period
new liberalism, instability factors:
    conservative coalition power, 132–
    34, 166–67; immigrant identities,
    130–31, 175–76; individualism tra-
    dition, 147–51; overview, 123–24,
    176–77; policy complacency, 180–
    82; populist discontent, 137–38,
    248n21; racial perspectives, 124–
    32, 144–46, 155–56, 172–76; reli-
    gious identities, 134–40, 163–66;
    structural assumptions, 170–72. *See
    also* New Deal coalition, collapse
    factors
New Majority coalition, Nixon's,
    179–81, 185
New Republic, 76, 103

Newsweek magazine, 195
New York, Triangle Shirtwaist Factory
    fire, 73
New York State Bakeshop Act, 69
New York Times, 214
Ngai, Mae, 80
NIRA (National Industrial Recovery
    Act), 104–7, 112
Nixon, Richard M., 174, 175, 179–82
NLRB v. Jones & Laughlin Steel, 118
No Place of Grace (Lears), 195–96
Northern Pacific Railroad, 37–38
Novak, Michael, 185
NRA (National Recovery Administra-
    tion), 105, 127
NWLB (National War Labor Board),
    77
NYA (National Youth Administra-
    tion), 109

Obama, Barack (and administration):
    health care reform, 216–17; as lost
    opportunity, 210–11; New Deal era
    contrasted, 208–10, 211–14, 216,
    217–19
Obamacare, 216–17
Occupy movement, 225
oil embargo, economic impact, 182
oil industry, capitalization statistics,
    36
old-age support, 69–70, 71–72,
    109–11
Operation Dixie, 133–34
overtime compensation, 109

Packer, George, 218
Page, Benjamin I., 221
Painter, Nell Irvin, 39
Parrington, Vernon, 39
The Passing of the Great Race
    (Grant), 79, 199
PATCO (Professional Air Traffic Con-
    trollers Organization), 203–4
Patten, Simon, 53–54
Patterson, James T., 133
Paulson, Henry, 219–20
pensions, 69–70, 71–72, 109–11

Perkins, Frances, 73, 110–11
Phillips, Kevin, 174
Pierson, Paul, 217
Piketty, Thomas, 16, 143, 221
political activity levels, incorporation age, 50–54, 57–59. *See also* Democratic Party; Republican Party
political polarization, graphical representation, 12*f*. *See also* Democratic Party; Republican Party
populist movements, during New Deal years, 137–38, 248n21
Port Huron Statement, 167
post-1960s period: collective social movements, 189–91, 200–201; forgotten Americans theme, 179–81, 185, 193, 217–18; immigration tensions, 175–76, 178, 198–202; labor's disempowerment, 189, 192, 199–201, 214–16; racial ideologies, 184–86, 196–98, 218–19; religion's role, 193–96, 258n21. *See also* Obama, Barack (and administration)
postal service and Pullman Strike, 58
Postel, Charles, 59
postwar period, worker gains: liberation perspective, 156–58; overview, 153–56; as realistic achievement, 159–63; scholarship debate, 158–59
Powderly, Terrence, 41–42
Professional Air Traffic Controllers Organization (PATCO), 203–4
Progressive Era: class conflict indicators, 72–74; complexities of, 88–89; explanatory challenge, 66–67; failure argument, 81–82; immigration resistance, 78–81; legislative achievements, 67–72; presidential campaigns, 74–75; racial tensions, 78; reform visions, 64–67, 85–87; religious/moralism themes, 82–84; welfare capitalism schemes, 85–87; World War I impact, 76–77
The Promise of American Life (Croly), 74
Protestantism: Depression era trends,

135; during incorporation era, 48–49; postwar era, 164–65; during Progressive Era, 78–79, 83–84. *See also* religious identity
Pullman Strike (1894), 57–58
Purnell, Fred S., 80

quota system, immigration, 80, 198. *See also* immigration tensions

racial ideologies: conservative coalition, 132–34; during incorporation age, 42–43, 45–46, 48, 51–52; during New Deal era, 6–7, 110, 111, 115, 122; in new liberalism, 124–32; overview, 22–24; in post-1960s period, 184–86, 196–98, 218–19; postwar era, 172–76; during Progressive Era, 53–54, 78, 84; in states' rights theme, 196–97; World War II impact, 144. *See also* immigration tensions
radical conservatism, 163–67
railroad industry, 36–38, 54–55, 57–58
Randolph, Phillip, 122, 144
ransomed individualism idea, 40
Reagan, Ronald, 167, 174, 175, 196–97, 202, 203
Reagan revolution/restoration, 29, 206–7
Red Scare, labor impact, 77
Reich, Robert, 205
religious identity: Great Depression era impact, 134–37; during incorporation era, 47–50, 52; New Deal era, 21–22, 138–40; post-1960s period, 193–96, 258n21; postwar era, 163–67; Progressive Era, 65, 82–84
Republican Party: and civil rights movement, 174–75; during incorporation age, 42, 43–44, 47–49, 51–53, 60; membership groups, 47–48, 51; during Obama administration, 213–14, 260n4; during post-1960s period, 186–87, 193–94,

196–98; postwar period, 160–63, 166–67, 179–82; Progressive Era, 74–75, 77
Reston, James, 168
Reuther, Walter, 162, 175, 216
revivalism, religious, 49–50. *See also* religious identity
Rice, Charles, 138
Rich, Frank, 218–19
Richardson, Heather Cox, 46
right to manage, in strike demands, 157–58
right-to-work laws, 215–16
Riley, William B., 83
The Rise of the Unmeltable Ethnics (Novak), 185
Rockefeller, John D., 36
Rodgers, Daniel, 30, 237n22
Roof, Tracy, 159
Roosevelt, Franklin D.: banking system actions, 102–3; cartoon about, x*f*; as civic evangelist, 140; coalition elements, 4–7, 114–15, 155; Commonwealth speech, 150–51, 251n39; disposition, 7; forgotten man speech, 91–93; as hope beacon, 100–101; inaugural address, 95–96; nomination speech, x, 1–4, 93–94; Obama comparisons, 208–9; and populist discontent, 137–38, 248n21; retrenchment period, 118–19; union relationships, 113–14, 116–17. *See also* New Deal *entries*
Roosevelt, Theodore, 63–64, 72, 74–75
Rudwick, Elliott, 130
"Rugged Individualism" speech, Hoover's, 87
Ryan, John, 139

Saez, Emmanuel, 143
Salvatore, Nick, 59
Santa Clara County v. Southern Pacific Railroad, 36–37
Schecter Poultry Corporation v. United States, 107

Schlesinger, Arthur, 18, 101–2
Scopes "Monkey" Trial, 83–84
Scott, James, 192
SEC (Securities and Exchange Commission), 104
"second" New Deal, 96–97, 108–14
Section 7a, NIRA legislation, 105–7
Securities and Exchange Commission (SEC), 104
Sevareid, Eric, 99
sharecropping system, 45
Sherman Anti-Trust Act, 53
shipyard workers, social cohesion study, 146
Shlaes, Amity, 15
Shriver, Sargent, 169
Silent Majority, Nixon's, 179–81, 185
Sixteenth Amendment, 67–68
Skocpol, Theda, 70, 216
slavery, 42–44
Smith, Al, 5, 93–94, 245n7
Smith, Chuck, 258n21
Smith, Ed "Cotton Ed," 6–7
social democratic tradition, absence in United States, 29–30
social gospelism, 50, 65, 134–35
social insurance programs: New Deal Era, 109–11; post-1960s period, 216–17; postwar period, 168–72, 253n25; Progressive Era, 69–72, 86–87; in submerged state, 223–24
Social Security Act, 72, 109–11, 126
Southern Democrats: and civil rights movement, 174–75, 196–97; FDR relationships, 5–7, 94, 115, 117; during incorporation age, 51; postwar power, 168, 172; power of, 124–27; during Progressive Era, 77. *See also* Democratic Party
Southern Pacific Railroad, Santa Clara County v., 36–37
Specter, Arlen, 260n4
spending statistics, wartime, 141–42
Standard Oil, 36
states' rights theme, 196–97

states' role, overview of transformation, 17–20, 223–24. *See also specific topics, e.g.,* labor *entries;* New
Deal *entries;* social insurance
programs
steel industry, 36, 55, 62, 156, 200
Steinbeck, John, 132
Stockman, David, 206
Stone, Katherine, 184
strikes: during incorporation age, 54–
55, 57–58; during New Deal era,
90, 106–7; during post-1960s period, 203–4; during postwar period, 144, 157–58; Progressive Era,
62, 72–74, 77–78; Reagan administration impact, 203–4; during
World War II, 145. *See also* labor
entries; unions; working-class
identity
submerged state, 223–24
Sugrue, Thomas, 181
Sumner, William Graham, 92, 179–80
Supreme Court: during incorporation
age, 36–38; during New Deal era,
107, 112, 113, 117, 118; during
post-1960s period, 214; during the
Progressive Era, 68–69, 71
sweatshop system, re-emergence, 198

Taft, Philip, 160
Taft, William Howard, 74–75
Taft-Hartley Act, 160–61
tariffs, 52–53
taxes, 26, 67–68, 109, 110–11, 142–
43, 154
Taylor, Frederick Winslow, 65
Tea Party movement, 219
Tennessee Valley Authority, 103
textile industry, 73, 198
"third" New Deal, 97, 118–20
Thurmond, Strom, 133, 174, 196–97
Townsend, Francis, 137
Trachtenberg, Alan, 39
Triangle Shirtwaist Factory fire, 73
Trilling, Lionel, 14
Truman, Harry, 25, 133

Tugwell, Rexford, 26–27, 95, 102,
148–49, 150
Twain, Mark, 38

underconsumption thesis, Tugwell's,
95
unemployment, Depression years,
98–99
unemployment insurance, 110, 111
Unfair Labor Practices, 188
unions: ethno-racial tensions, 52, 127,
145–46, 173–74; during incorporation era, 52, 55–58; membership
statistics, 11*f*, 77, 113, 154; during
New Deal era, 105–6, 112–14, 116–
17; post-1960s period, 189, 192,
199–201, 214–16; postwar period,
141–42, 166; during Progressive
Era, 67, 68–69, 70, 72–73; Reagan
administration impact, 203–4;
Southern region resistance, 133–34;
and women's rights movement, 190;
World War I impact, 76–78. *See
also* labor *entries;* strikes; working-
class identity
United Auto Workers, 145, 152,
157–58
United Mine Workers, 55, 106
United States Steel Trust, 36
Uprising of the Twenty Thousand, 73
U.S. Commission on Industrial Relations (USCIR), 76–77

Van, Robert L., 128
Van Osdel, Oliver W., 135
Vietnam War, 171, 182
Viguerie, Richard, 193
voluntarism, 56–57
Voting Rights Act, 172, 184

Wagner, Robert F., 73, 108–9, 112,
126
Wagner Act: elements of, 111–12; expectations about, 112–13; in great
exception argument, 25–26; postwar curtailments, 160–61, 188; race

accusations about, 127; as rare political opportunity, 108–9; role of Triangle Factory fire, 73; Supreme Court ruling, 118
Waite, Justice, 36–37
Wallace, George, 174
Walley, Christine J., 200
war mobilization comparison, FDR's, 91, 96, 141, 245n7
War on Poverty, 168–71, 253n25
Warren, Dorian, 215
Washington march, 144–45
Watergate scandal, 180–81
Wealth Tax Act, 143
Weber, Max, 229
welfare capitalism, 18, 85–87, 192
welfare state strength, role of labor movements, 70
Which Side Are You On? (Geoghegan), 189
Wickenden, Elizabeth, 163–64
Widows' Pensions, 71–72
Wills, Garry, 22, 164, 166
Wilson, Woodrow (and administration), 74–78

Wirtz, Willard, 170
Wisconsin, right-to-work law, 215–16
Wolfe, Tom, 182, 194
Women's Christian Temperance Union, 48–49
women's movement, 184–86, 189–90
working-class identity: Caucasian theme, 130–32, 197–98; and civil rights movement, 173–75, 197–98; New Deal's impact, 24–26; religious factors, 138–40, 165. *See also* forgotten man theme; labor *entries*
Works Progress Administration (WPA), ii, 109
World's Christian Fundamentals Association, 83
World War I, 76
World War II, 141–42
WPA (Works Progress Administration), ii, 109

Yates, Richard, 43
Young Americans for Freedom, 166

Zieger, Robert, 9–10

POLITICS AND SOCIETY IN TWENTIETH-CENTURY AMERICA

Series Editors
WILLIAM CHAFE, GARY GERSTLE, LINDA GORDON,
AND JULIAN ZELIZER

*For a full list of books in this series see: http://press.princeton.edu
/catalogs/series/pstcaa.html*

Recent titles in the series:

*The Great Exception: The New Deal and the Limits of American
Politics* by Jefferson Cowie

*The Good Immigrants: How the Yellow Peril Became the Model
Minority* by Madeline Y. Hsu

*A Class by Herself: Protective Laws for Women Workers, 1890s–
1990s* by Nancy Woloch

*The Loneliness of the Black Republican: Pragmatic Politics and the
Pursuit of Power* by Leah Wright Rigueur

*Don't Blame Us: Suburban Liberals and the Transformation of the
Democratic Party* by Lily Geismer

*Relentless Reformer: Josephine Roche and Progressivism in
Twentieth-Century America* by Robyn Muncy

Power Lines: Phoenix and the Making of the Modern Southwest by
Andrew Needham

Lobbying America: The Politics of Business from Nixon to NAFTA
by Benjamin C. Waterhouse

*The Color of Success: Asian Americans and the Origins of the
Model Minority* by Ellen D. Wu

The Second Red Scare and the Unmaking of the New Deal Left by
Landon Storrs

Mothers of Conservatism: Women and the Postwar Right by
Michelle M. Nickerson

*Between Citizens and the State: The Politics of American Higher
Education in the 20th Century* by Christopher P. Loss